After the Blessing

After the Blessing

Mexican American Veterans of
WWII Tell Their Own Stories

EDITED BY ESTHER BONILLA READ

Fort Worth, Texas

Library of Congress Cataloging-in-Publication Data

Names: Read, Esther Bonilla, 1937- editor.
Title: After the blessing : Mexican American veterans of WWII tell their
   own stories / edited by Esther Bonilla Read.
Description: Fort Worth, Texas : TCU Press, [2022] | Summary: Many Catholic
   families blessed their children before they left home. After the
   Blessing tells the stories of many young Mexican Americans who left home
   to fight for their country. During the Mexican Revolution (1910-1920),
   many families fled Mexico to prevent their underage sons from being
   forced to fight. Ironically, the offspring of these immigrants often
   ended up across the ocean in a much larger war. Despite the bias and
   mistreatment most Mexican Americans faced in the US, some 500,000 fought
   bravely for their country during World War II. Their stories range from
   hair-raising accounts of the Battle of the Bulge to gut-wrenching
   testimony about cannibalism in the Pacific. In After the Blessing
   Mexican Americans reveal their experiences in combat during WWII-stories
   that have rarely been told. Provided by publisher.
Identifiers: LCCN 2021046810 (print) | LCCN 2021046811 (ebook) | ISBN
   9780875658049 (paperback) | ISBN 9780875658100 (ebook)
Subjects: LCSH: World War, 1939-1945--Participation, Mexican American. |
   World War, 1939-1945--Mexican Americans--Interviews. | World War,
   1939-1945--Personal narratives, American. | World War,
   1939-1945--Veterans--United States--Interviews. | World War,
   1939-1945--Participation, Catholic. | Mexican American
   Catholics--Interviews. | LCGFT: Interviews.
Classification: LCC D769.8.F7 M453 2022 (print) | LCC D769.8.F7 (ebook) |
   DDC 940.54/04--dc23/eng/20211012
LC record available at https://lccn.loc.gov/2021046810
LC ebook record available at https://lccn.loc.gov/2021046811

Fort Worth, Texas

TCU Box 298300
Fort Worth, Texas 76129
To order books: 1.800.826.8911

Design by Bill Brammer

This book is dedicated to those WWII veterans who opened up their hearts and shared their experiences and also to those soldiers who did not return. We are eternally grateful.

CONTENTS

After the Blessing

Mexican Americans in the United States

We are told when doing research that you will find something you were not looking for. Thus it was with me. I discovered an irony: some parents who fled the bloody revolution in Mexico and came to this country ended up with their sons or grandsons going off to fight across the ocean in another war, World War II.

Jesús Mendez fought with Venustiano Carranza during the Mexican Revolution (1910-1920). He fought hard alongside other revolutionaries to defeat the dictator Porfirio Díaz. Under his regime Díaz and his cronies kept getting richer while the poor had little or nothing. By 1925 the revolution was over, and after things calmed down a bit, he migrated to the United States. He and his wife waited until their new baby boy Noé Mendez was forty days old, as this period of time was considered the proper period of convalescence for a new mother. The small family settled in Benavides, Texas, a tiny town in South Texas.

Adolfo Yañez Martinez was fighting on the Federalists' side of the Mexican Revolution when he learned that Pancho Villa was coming through Monterrey and that all Federalists would be hung. Because Pancho Villa traveled not only on horses but also by train, Adolfo immediately sent his wife to *San Nicolas de las Garzas* so that she at least would be safe. While waiting for her husband, a baby boy, Robert Martinez, was born. The date was May 2, 1919, and the revolution in Mexico would not be over for another year. Martinez was still concerned about his family and sent his wife and infant to stay with relatives in Brownsville, Texas.

Enrique Ramirez fought under Carranza's leadership. Once committed to a *partido* (political group), it was hard to leave to visit one's family. On one occasion Enrique covered himself with coal powder so that if caught, instead of admitting that he was leaving Carranza's army to visit his family, he could say he was working with coal.

These parents and many like them who left their homeland so their families could live in a more peaceful environment never suspected that in a few short years these baby boys would be involved in a worldwide conflict, a bloody war that would take them across the ocean to another continent. For the present, however, the revolution in Mexico posed an immediate threat to the safety of their families, and moving to the country north of Mexico would solve the problem.

Even before the war, however, Mexican immigrants usually found that life in the US posed its own problems. In the 1930s a migrant family who made their living sharecropping in central Texas told my mother, Maria Bonilla, the following story in Spanish (my translation):

"We were *quarteros*, meaning we were to get one-fourth of the harvest after we had finished planting the fields, caring for the crops, and then bringing them in for this farmer. Well, when it came time to harvest the crops, the *patrón* [owner] came to our little house and began beating up on my husband with the children watching. I took the hoe to him, and we ran him off. Then we left the farm. We just lost all the time and work we had put in. Later, I heard he did the same thing with all his sharecroppers. That way he could keep all the crops and earnings to himself."

Not all situations for Mexican Americans were so dire, but most Mexican Americans endured their own version of Jim Crow repression.

Education

Many of the Mexican American men who went into the service had not graduated from high school. Dropping out of elementary school to help out the parents because of the Depression was a common practice among young people of all ethnicities. Some students were drafted before being allowed to graduate. Others volunteered as young as fifteen or sixteen years of age. A handful attended universities and, knowing that they would eventually be drafted, either volunteered or waited for the draft letter.

Before WWII not only were Hispanic or Mexican American children forced to attend segregated public schools, they were made to feel less than accepted by the dominant members of society. Alicia Salinas Perez, an educator originally from Raymondville, Texas, related the following:

"In the 1930s when I was a little girl, Mexican American children like me and my siblings attended the school for 'Mexicans.' The school for the white or Anglo students was next door to our school. Only a sidewalk separated the two schools. One day during recess a little Anglo girl and I met on the sidewalk and began playing with one another. After a while her teacher ran up to us and said to me, 'No, no. You cannot play together. You little Mexican children must stay on your playground.' Then she took my new little friend away."

Textbooks, circa 1930s

Textbooks didn't help either. Although it is well-documented that several *Tejanos* (Mexicans who lived in the northern part of Mexico, which is now Texas) signed the Texas Declaration of Independence, fought and died at the Alamo, and helped Sam Houston defeat Santa Anna at San Jacinto, the authors of student textbooks wrote the history of Texas in a manner which implied, if not stated outright, that the war for Texas independence was fought between Anglos in Texas and Mexicans from Mexico.

The war for Texas Independence was fought between two philosophical factions: the Tejanos and Anglos who wanted independence from Mexico for various reasons—e.g. religion, land, and other freedoms not realized under a dictatorship; and Santa Anna and his troops, who sought to keep the northern part of Mexico under his rule. Even in Mexico, Santa Anna had his detractors.

This seemingly innocuous oversight in Texas history books, nonetheless, planted a seed in the minds of impressionable children. If you were an Anglo Texan, you were made to feel proud. If you were a Hispanic Texan, you might feel guilty and ashamed. Domingo Treviño, a WWII veteran from Houston, Texas, said that when the subject of the Battle of the Alamo came up, the students gave him a hard time.

Dr. Patrick J. Carroll in his book, *Felix Longoria's Wake*, said that the Mexican American war "relegated Tejanos to the rank of second-class citizenship . . . while elevating the Anglos to a higher social level."

Schools

In 1935 our small hometown of Calvert, Texas, had three schools. One was for the white students, and it was a two-story red brick building built in 1922. The school also had a basement. There was also a school for the black students located in town. The third school was for the "Mexicans" who were mostly Mexican American and had been born in this country. This facility was a one-room school, and it was located out in the country.

When my oldest brother Albert turned six and the next brother in line, William, was five, Daddy drove them out to the country so they could attend school. (The pursuit of education was a primary mission in my father's life.) The drive out to the country to get the boys to school on time and then Daddy's drive back to town and work interfered with his job.

My father, an immigrant from Mexico, was smart, hardworking, dependable, and trustworthy. (His coworkers informed me of his traits years ago.) When Monroe Miller, Daddy's employer, heard of the situation and the loss of time driving back and forth, he spoke to the school board and for the first time the school allowed Mexican American children to attend the school in town. My brothers could then walk to school.

This became a momentous occasion because the integration meant that now the Mexican American children received an excellent education. Unfortunately, not all Mexican Americans in the 1930s were as fortunate as their counterparts in Calvert, Texas.

This fact became apparent when I interviewed the veterans, and most of them realized they had not received equal opportunities in schools in Texas. It is a sad fact.

World War II
Terms, Places, and
Some Important Events

The following terms, names of places, locales, and background information are given as references for those not familiar with some of the facts and lore of World War II.

The European Theater

On D-day, when the Allies landed on the Normandy beaches they were met with many obstacles in addition to the Germans in pillboxes, who awaited the soldiers with plenty of guns and ammunition. Tetrahedra and hedgehogs (metal rods welded together in the form of Xs) and mines on the beaches were some of the obstacles meant to kill or cause great damage to whoever planned to invade France.

After the Allies were successful in taking the beaches, there were more obstacles in their way. Hedgerows, established by the Romans over a thousand years before, formed boundaries around farmland with hedges and small trees growing on embankments with four- to eight-feet drops, with only one opening into the field. At the bases of the embankments were roads. These infamous hedgerows caused much consternation and frustration to our troops after they crossed the beaches. The Germans, already situated among the hedgerows, knew exactly how to deal with the Allied troops. An American suggested welding metal bars to the front of the tanks in order to shear through the hedgerows. His ingenious idea worked, and the Allies proceeded with the invasion of France.

The Pacific Theater

While their friends and brothers fought against the Nazis in Europe, American soldiers fought vicious battles against the Japanese in the Pacific. It was an altogether different scenario. In addition to the enemy, the men variously had to deal with deadly typhoons; cannibalism; malaria; ticks; caves; underground tunnels filled with enemy soldiers; banzai attacks; kamikaze pilots; booby traps of all kinds; monsoon rainfall; and wild animals in various camps. Most men who were captured in the Pacific, if they survived the prisoner of war (POW) camps, chose not to speak of their experiences.

Construction Battalions (Seabees)

For those of us who wonder how the Army, Navy, and Air Force were able to accomplish things in other countries, the answer is the Seabees, or the Construction Battalions. These ingenious crews knew how to build airfields, roads, housing, warehouses, pontoon causeways, piers, pipelines, oil depots, ferries, and just about anything needed by an army or navy. They were issued arms and were often combatants: in the Pacific theater alone they suffered two hundred combat deaths and earned two thousand Purple Hearts.

Mexico's Aztec Eagles

In May 1942 German U-boats sank two Mexican oil tankers in the Gulf of Mexico as they sailed toward the United States. Although Mexico had been neutral, they immediately declared war on the Axis powers. The Lend Lease Program, in which the US lent our neighbor to the south material for their services, resulted in a historical contribution Mexico made to the Allies' effort in WWII.

Over three hundred airmen representing Mexico came to train in the USA. The group became known as *Escuadrón Aéreo de Pelea 201*, or Mexican Fighter Squadron 201. Their nickname was *Águilas Aztecas* (Aztec Eagles).

The Geneva Conventions

The Geneva Convention first met in 1864. At that time European countries, the United States, and some Asian and South American countries signed the agreement, which established guidelines in the treatment of prisoners of war. Countries met several times after that and added more rules, all dealing with the welfare and humane behavior toward prisoners of war in any future conflicts among any of these countries. It becomes apparent when reading first person accounts by American POWs which countries followed the Geneva Conventions and which did not. Many Japanese POW camps in the Pacific theater were particularly horrific.

When I was young, my parents drove from Calvert, Texas, our hometown, to visit my aunt who lived in Maysfield, Texas, a farming community. We traveled on Highway 485 and passed through Hearne, a small town in central Texas, on our way to my aunt's home. On one of these trips my mother pointed to a compound of buildings visible from the highway and said, "That's where they keep the German prisoners." I shivered at the idea because I knew we were at war with them. Later, my mother told me that dances were held at the POW camp for the prisoners. She did not seem too perturbed at the thought of living a few miles from a camp filled with enemy soldiers. While the United States escaped the ravages suffered by western Europe during the war, every citizen was impacted—most grievously, of course, by the deaths of fathers, sons, and husbands killed overseas.

Adapting to Postwar Life

A poignant element in many stories the soldiers related was how they would fight beside a friend or buddy, and then suddenly that man would disappear. The veteran telling me usually commented, "And I never saw him again. I don't know what happened to him. We had to keep moving." Even now, so many years later, they still wonder. One veteran swore he would never make good friends again.

In Europe and in the Pacific these veterans had fought and defeated the enemy and left a devastated landscape behind them. They had witnessed people without homes and near starvation. And now, back home, everything was peaceful as though the war on the other side of the world had never occurred.

The United States government gave each veteran approximately $300 to help him get settled in his new life: $100 down and the balance paid in the following two months. If a veteran did not find a job right away, he was allotted twenty dollars a week for fifty-two weeks until he could find a job.

The Hispanics who returned from WWII were changed, as were all survivors. They knew they were the lucky ones. Some struggled until they found a way to make a living. Others decided that in order to make a difference, they had to work to achieve full civil rights for their compatriots.

Prelude to War

In the early 1940s before WWII broke out, Mexican American families in Texas were living in difficult times. Some of the young people were children of recent immigrants from Mexico. Others were from families who had been in Texas for a century or longer. Their social status as a group, however, was for the most part identical: many attended separate schools, which were established for Mexican American children, then known as Mexicans. Not only were Mexican Americans segregated in schools, they were also separated by neighborhoods. In some towns, the young men couldn't get a haircut in the towns in which they lived. Certain restaurants wouldn't serve them, and many businesses wouldn't hire them.

The Mexican American families were known to be close. Brothers and sisters cared deeply for each other and would go to great lengths to protect one another. That devotion and trust later transferred to their buddies in battle.

Most of the boys were Catholic, and almost all of them received *la bendición*. The religious rite consisted of the person being blessed while kneeling in front of parents or relatives. The person giving the blessing forms a cross with the hand over the person kneeling while saying, "In the name of the Father, Son, and the Holy Ghost. Amen." Words and prayers may be added. Some boys were given medallions, which represented a favorite saint. Other sons were given *tarjetas de oración* (prayer cards) previously blessed (by a Catholic priest), each of which had a picture of a saint on one side and a special prayer on the other. One Mexican American veteran, now quite elderly, still carries his prayer card, which is now a thin worn card with a faint image on one side and undecipherable words on the other side. He says the prayer card his mother gave him in 1944 carried him through rain, sleet, snow, and through three major battles in Europe! Other boys had mothers who made *promesas* (religious promises).

Many promises entailed making a pilgrimage to a favorite church when the son came back safely.

Because money was scarce, these young men had rarely traveled outside their hometowns. Their exposure to the outside world was nil. One soldier said, "When I saw the windmills in Holland, I couldn't believe I was seeing things I'd only read about in my schoolbooks."

Some books state that 500,000 Mexican American soldiers fought in WWII. That may be a low estimate. Several veterans said, "My unit had lots of Mexican Americans." One veteran estimated that his unit had at least 30 percent Mexican Americans.

WWII, for the Mexican American, was the great equalizer. Once enlisted or drafted, the soldier was not asked where he came from or where he lived. No one cared who his family was. "You're in the army now!" meant "You're like everybody else!"

After the war these same brave men came home expecting the same fair treatment they received as soldiers during the war. It was not to be. The soldiers fought again alongside civil rights groups, but this time it was for equality in their homeland. As a result the veterans became agents for positive change in their lives and in the lives of others.

Not only had most of them left their homes for the first time in their lives when they went to war, but they had also acquired new feelings about themselves. They knew they could get along with other men from other parts of the country. They also knew they could do any job they had to do. They could follow leadership, and they could also exercise authority. A veteran who came home and later called for the investigation of an organization received a threat. His response was, "After what I've been through [war], nothing scares me."

And so the men changed because of the war, and the world changed because of them.

Introduction

Joining Up

It was November 3, 1942, and the temperature had turned chilly in the small town of Goliad, Texas. It was deer-hunting season in South Texas, that time of year when you had to wear a jacket. Julian Flores and Raul Martinez sat wedged in the back of a truck on its way from Goliad to Victoria, Texas, amid rattling ten-gallon milk cans full of fresh milk. The sun was just rising, and they were going through with their promise. Pearl Harbor in Hawaii had been bombed, Germany and Italy had declared war on the USA, and with a fever of patriotism in the air, the two best friends vowed to join the service together. A few days prior to this trip Julian had leaned over in history class in Goliad High School and whispered to Raul, "You and I are joining up, right?" He offered his hand to Raul who was at least a head taller—six feet five inches to Julian's five feet six inches.

"It's a deal," answered Raul, and he shook Julian's hand.

All over the country young men were learning about a place called Pearl Harbor, where over two thousand men had died from the Japanese bombing raid. And they wanted to fight back, to get even, to protect their country.

At first, the driver of the milk truck had refused the hitchhikers' request for a ride to Victoria, claiming insurance liability, but then Julian said, "We want to ride so that we can join up."

The driver said, "Well, hop on."

The two boys, looking like Mutt and Jeff from the Sunday comics, opened their brown paper bags and looked at their tacos as the truck drove them closer to Victoria. Then they looked at each other's tacos. Some tacos had a combination of potatoes and eggs in a rolled-up flour tortilla; others were just filled with plain mashed pinto beans. They could share the food their mothers made them and eat in peace. At school when they took out their tacos at lunchtime, the Anglo students made fun of them, as they took sandwiches made with real sliced white bread filled with whatever food was left over from the day before or made with baloney and cheese.

The only three Mexican American boys in Goliad High School who took food different from the majority hid daily behind the nearby water tower. There, feeling like outcasts in their own country, they ate their tacos before returning to class.

But for now, Julian and Raul were embarking on a new adventure, and it began with being sworn into the armed services at the United States Post Office in Victoria, a mid-sized town in South Texas. Raul's three brothers would also join the service.

All over the country young men were changing their lives and leaving their homes and families in a rush to defend their country from its enemies. Before December 1941 a few had joined the service with the promise that after one year they could go home. Others had also been drafted with the thought that the commitment would be brief. December 7, 1941, "A day of Infamy" as President Franklin D. Roosevelt would label it, altered the lives of all Americans.

In a documentary featured a few years ago on public television a commentator asked an older Japanese man why Japan had attacked the United States in 1941. "What were they thinking?"

The elderly Asian answered, "Because yours is such a diverse nation, we thought your country could never bring everyone together to fight us."

How wrong he was! Young men in droves from all parts of the country volunteered. Men born in Mexico whose parents had fled the Mexican Revolution of 1910-1920 and were now living in the United States offered their services. If they were rejected, they didn't quit but tried to volunteer again until they became soldiers in the service of their new country.

PART I

The European/Atlantic Theater

Saragosa A. García

197th Battalion, Triple A, Automatic Weapons
T 5

His Companion: a Bible

Saragosa came from a religious family, and his experiences at the D-day landing on June 6, 1944, proved to him that his beliefs, his Bible, and prayers from the church he attended surely saved him from the horrible devastation he witnessed.

I was drafted in November 1942. I had a brother in the Korean War; then another brother went into the army. I went through the third grade. I helped by selling papers, and picking cotton. I went three to four years to school. They kept us in one room where they kept the Spanish-speaking people (Mexican American students). That teacher was about seventy years old. She kept me there two or three years. After third grade you had to go to school with the whites. She didn't want me in with the whites. By 1935 my daddy moved us to Houston, Texas.

My dad was a carpenter. He stuck a nail in his hand and couldn't work for a while, and I had to go to work. I was going to Jones School over here by the freeway. At the same time in the afternoon I'd go sell papers. My mother made candies and hot tamales, and I'd sell them. I did all kinds of stuff. My dad was sick. He was all wrapped up. That nail passed all the way through his hand. He couldn't work. We were paying rent. It was $1.50 or $2.00 a week. I made enough money to pay the rent. My daddy had a Model T Ford; he also bought scrap iron.

When we was in Rosenberg and I got drafted, my mother took me down to church; she was a Pentecostal, and they all prayed for me as I went into battle not to get hit.

First stop was Ft. Sam Houston in San Antonio. From there I went to Camp Wallace close to Hitchcock, Texas. I had basic training there and truck-driving school. We went to Ft. Bliss, Texas. A rattlesnake liked to kill me.

We went to maneuvers in Las Cruces, New Mexico, at night. It was cold. All white sand. So the guys were up there on the half-track. Middle of the night and I was all zipped up [in a sleeping bag]. All of a sudden I heard an sssssssss sound. It started digging through there and I just held my breath like this. It came out rattling and just went on. He crawled under and went on. I called the guys and they said, "I didn't see a snake." I said, "You were sleeping." From then on I slept on the fender of the half-track.

I went by train to Camp Pickett, Virginia. Then to Camp Kilmer, New Jersey. From there to Newport, Virginia, for amphibious training with the Navy. One day it was cold. Our colonel McHenry was a thirty-year veteran and we were at the beach. He said, "Take all your clothes off." It was snowing a little. It was freezing. He's in there in the water. When we went in there swimming, all of a sudden a jeep was coming with a white flag. We got out and dried. A general came up and said, "Where's the boss?" They told him, "He's over swimming." "Get him over here." He chewed him out, "You're going to kill all these men. Take them back up to the camp and give them coffee."

We went back to Camp Kilmer and prepared clothes and vehicles to go. They gave us a pass to New York City. For three days. At Christmas they told us to get ready. We went by a ferry to New York City. They were loading the ship. We got in there and pretty soon that thing started getting hot or something. They told us to unload and get out of there. It was a French ship. It had trouble with the boiler. We came back to Camp Kilmer at New Year's Eve and had a hot meal. On the second day we had to go back.

We went back to New York and loaded on the world's largest ship, the *Queen Elizabeth*. There were three thousand troops. We went into the ocean. Right in the middle of the Atlantic they told us that we were going to have training, go up and down. I was on the second floor. We had drills. When you have a drill, you'd better get out. Because the ship had big doors, and if a shell hits there, the doors lock and the water will stay there. Pretty soon they told us to be on the alert, because there were fifteen U-boats. So most of us went to the top of the deck. The ship zig-zagged. The colonel said, "We're going to be eight days late," so we had to go around.

We landed in Scotland two miles off the coast. The Red Cross was giving doughnuts and little sandwiches. Bing Crosby was singing on a radio. They loaded us on a train and we went to England. We spent three to four days in camp. They took us close to Bristol to Weston Super Mare. We started working on our vehicles, waterproofing. We were attached to the Sixteenth Infantry Division, First Army, to protect the beach. We loaded up the landing crafts and went down the channel. The infantry was going in on the front. They carried the half-tracks on the LCI [landing craft infantry]. It was at night. After we loaded up a storm came up. Bad weather. Eisenhower told everybody to get back. So we came back to England and stayed till the fifth [June, 1944]. On June fifth in the afternoon, we went all night long. We landed at 7:30 or 8:00 a.m. on Omaha Beach on June 6, 1944. The infantry had already gone in. We lost fifteen half-tracks from our battalion.

We didn't shoot. We didn't get a chance. The Germans had a big gun on railroad tracks. When we got up the hill, they had a big tunnel. The Americans came in B47s and fired. The Navy got destroyers and got the big gun. A piper cub gave the coordinates to the Navy.

I was carrying my Bible. In 1935, a Mrs. Smith at our church gave me the Bible. It went underwater at Omaha, it went through the Netherlands, France, Belgium, and Germany. It went through the snow.

At the landing Captain Peterson got killed and he was close to me. I didn't get shot. We went on the side of the beach where everybody was firing; my sergeant and I went down there. The LCI was full with half-tracks. We went up to unload it. The soldiers ran away. They were scared. We went up to unload. You take the pin out like that. Half a pin. You get the ramp down. And a German (fired) whoosh. The bullet went right by me. So I took off and started digging. That guy shot at us and one of the 88s blew the thing away. My half-track was on the side of the beach. It was way off. The captain was trying to get the guys to fire half-track guns—20mm cannon. The captain, gunner, corporal, and a Pfc. were killed. A new captain came on.

I was in the second wave attached to the Sixteenth Infantry Division, antiaircraft going in at Omaha. By 4:00 p.m. we made it up the hill. The infantry was still fighting. We had to wait for the engineers to make roads.

We went to Cherbourg. They were still fighting there. We stopped two to three blocks from the town. They have like a canal. We got near the canal and aimed our guns. Germans came up from all over the place and surrendered to different companies. Fifteen hundred Germans and officers surrendered.

The half-track can climb, and the sergeant would guide me. Sometimes we go to the front lines. We have to leave them alone. Sometimes the Americans fired at us because at night they couldn't see. At night we protected the mobile quartermaster.

We went to Tours, France. We were attached to the British to protect them. The British went out at daytime and returned at night. The Germans fired at us. A friend and I were in a foxhole and a tank rolled over our foxhole. So I left the foxhole.

They took us to protect the airport. In Paris we protected the Lindberg Airport.

We went to Fayl-Billot, France, and then Liege, Belgium. The French treated us well. We already had wine, and when we stopped at a farm we also had apple cider.

We had .50-caliber guns on our half-tracks. The Americans knocked down ten airplanes. While close to Liege we were up a hill. The Germans surrounded a hospital but released the nurses.

I returned to the 393rd Infantry. We crossed the Siegfried Line. We went to Aachen, Germany. I had to get off my half-track to go through the woods. We were looking for snipers and found an abandoned pillbox. I slept in one. Then I got back on my half-track.

On December 16, I went back to Belgium and dug in. It was raining and my half-track got stuck in the mud. Meanwhile the Germans were coming.

In Germany we went to Brandenburg and to Eisenach. They were training Germans there. We were then attached to Patton's Army. We had to guard the Rhine River and the road to Cologne. Cologne was flattened out. Four of us guarded a three-way road near Cologne. We were told to fire at anyone. I had a Tommy gun with fifty rounds. We guarded for two to three hours.

Some German civilians were coming. I yelled, "Halt!" The Germans stopped. They were men and women and were carrying Bibles. I told them to move to the side.

In Weimar we guarded the Germans against the Russians. Five or six Russians had escaped and they were drinking schnapps. It was made with flying bomb fuel.

One day we heard over a two-way radio, "FLASH! FLASH! FLASH! The war is over!" That's how I heard the news.

We were told to assemble in Frankenthal, Germany. I parked my half-track there and then went to France in a boxcar on a train. Some soldiers sold their duffle bags for francs. A liberty ship took me to Newport, Virginia. There was a storm in the ocean. I was discharged at Camp Hood, Texas.

For a while I had a dump truck business. I lived in Rosenberg. Then I worked at Port Houston Iron Works in the city of Houston. Finally, I worked for twenty-five years for the post office.

Saragosa García still has the Bible that Mrs. Smith gave him before he went to war. He also has a letter, which is actually a prayer that a stranger in Belgium gave him as he was going through that country. The prayer promises safety to all who possess it.

Ernest Eguía
1st Army, 981st Battalion, 7th Corps

A Quiet Man with a Bronze Star
Ernest was born to María Lara and Narciso Eguía on November 7, 1919, in Lockhart, Texas. His parents moved to Houston, Texas, the year of his birth. His father worked for Southern Pacific Railroad. Ernest worked from the time he was a young boy until he was a senior citizen, with a break in between. He was drafted in WWII and, as was his habit, worked hard at his job in the service, which earned him a Bronze Star.

At eight or nine years of age I began selling papers and shining shoes. I also became acquainted with the owner of Buck's Dry Goods. They hired me after school to do cleaning and sweeping. My mother passed away when I was fifteen years old. My father became ill, so I dropped out of high school to go to work. This was during the Depression. I was the oldest, and there were six of us. It was a catastrophe, really. I was the breadwinner for a good while. The store gave me a job right there. I did the same thing but now did it six days a week. I started learning the merchandise. Then I started selling a little bit, learning the entire store.

I was working at the store when I was drafted on October 7, 1941. In fact, the draft office was right across the street. It was supposed to be a

Reconnaissance soldier Ernest Eguía of Houston, Texas. He was awarded a Bronze Star for reconnaissance work in the European theater. Property of author, bequeathed to her by estate of Ernest Eguía.

one-year commitment. My dad was better by then, and he was working. I was sent to Ft. Sam Houston in San Antonio. In San Antonio they give you tests and try to channel you in the area you are best suited for. My IQ was high enough that they encouraged me to go to OCS (Officer Candidate School), but that would place me in infantry, and I didn't want the infantry. We stayed there about three days. Then we went to Camp Roberts, California. My brother, Leon Eguía, also went into the service two years after me.

In Camp Roberts I took my basic training. From there I went to Ft. Lewis, Washington, and I was there when war was declared. It was

Sunday, and I was relaxing when they told us. Everything was shut down. We couldn't go out and no one could come in. When war was declared we were in for the duration.

They decided that our unit should go to the West Coast of California to establish what they called "Coastal Artillery." We were to guard the coast with artillery, because at that time, after Pearl Harbor, there was a fear that the Japanese might attempt to invade the California coast. They had issued us "Long Toms," which are 155-caliber guns, [which fire] missiles six inches in diameter, fifteen-sixteen inches long and weigh 100 pounds. First we went to Redondo Beach, then Hermosa Beach, and then Santa Barbara Beach. We dug in and made holes big as this room to live in that went out to the ocean. Our guns were next to us pointed out—we had four guns. We were C Battery, 144th Field Artillery Battalion. We spent six-eight months there. We had to be alert. Eventually they sent us back to Ft. Lewis, Washington, where we stayed until the summer. We went through maneuvers, practicing and learning skills. I was a forward observer.

In the summertime they shipped us to the Mojave Desert. It looked like they wanted to send us to the Pacific. We stayed there until the fall. In 1942 they sent us to Ft. Leonard Wood, Missouri. We stayed there practicing and doing some more work.

From there they shipped us to Massachusetts. We shipped out from there to England. I crossed over on a Liberty ship. My cot was in the nose of the ship. We ran into a storm. On top of that we had to zigzag because the Germans had submarines out there, and I got very, very sick. But we made it safely in to England and stayed there until the invasion.

We had to be prepared. All the time we were in England we tried to prepare ourselves. You couldn't believe the rumors. You had to rely on people like your captain, because I had been promoted to forward observer and I was next to the captain. He confided in me. He didn't give me any secrets. We had four guns in our battalion and each one is a battery, A, B, C, and D. We were in C battery.

Two days before [the Normandy Invasion] they started moving us at night closer and closer to the channel. By the time we got there [the beaches], the invasion had already started. The infantry had already gone in.

I had seen the paratroopers because while we were there we traveled around—two or three days here, two-three days there. I got to go to London and several historical places. I saw the paratroopers at a distance. I didn't get to talk to them. I did get to go to an air force base, because I knew a friend of mine from Houston was there. And I went to visit him. They were kind of an elite group. They wouldn't associate with us. They were in touch with the upper echelon.

The infantry did not embark at the same time we did. I imagine they moved at night. It was a landing craft that carried our equipment, our vehicles. I was one day ahead of my unit, because I was a forward observer, to establish emplacement for my guns and to look for some places where I could do some observing, high places, maybe steeples of churches wherever I could get a good view.

I went with my crew, the driver who was also the radio operator and a machine gunner, me, and one man to help with maps and instruments and equipment. I had a lot of books that I had to carry because when you have to match something, you have to get coordinates for where the targets are. So I had all this equipment with me. A lieutenant in another vehicle went with me.

We went in the early morning of June 10, called D-day plus five. So before artillery arrived, they [infantry] had the navy. The navy was already in the channel. The air force, not only ours, but the British. The Canadians were there. We went in through Utah Beach.

I saw big ships, little ships, all kinds of boats toppled over that had been hit by the Germans out in the water. When we get to the beach, since we left at night really, the beach was covered with dead soldiers. Waves of people kept coming in. They hadn't had time to pick up the bodies. They had to come in to get a foothold. I found out later that a friend of mine I had gone to school with was right down the beach at Omaha, and he had gotten killed there.

Artillery was firing toward us. They were trying to shoot into the channel, maybe the beach. There must have been scattered pockets of soldiers that were still firing.

Water was chest deep. Our vehicle was floating, and we managed to get it up on the beach. The vehicles [weapons carriers] were protected from the water. We had them waxed in. We drove on in and tried to get a foothold and an emplacement for the guns.

We had to try to do something to get a good place for the guns. Our map showed us that we were in a certain place. We had to get close enough for our guns because the capacity and length would be thirteen miles. And we had to get as close as possible. We had to try to find out where the enemy lines were. And me being the forward observer, I had to go where the infantry was so I could establish my OP, which was observation post. My lieutenant was with me. And I had to find an emplacement for my guns. I was with C battery, and there were other batteries. All the captains came in. And the others came in behind us the next day. And, of course, the contingency of officers that comes in behind you. The majors—the lieutenant colonels who know more than we do—they're in touch with the front lines and we keep in touch, and we establish where we are going to put the guns. A, B, C, and D Batteries—we coordinate everything in and we put everything in. The guns come in later and get set in. We establish the observation post and we start finding out if we can find targets of any kind, maybe railroad yards or maybe ammunition dumps.

The hedgerows were miserable. You couldn't advance too fast for one thing. It didn't last too long. Even if you figured out a way with the tanks, it still wasn't easy. I didn't see many cattle. Hedgerows were like fences. The tanks tried to get through the hedgerows, but they couldn't. Why they [the Allies] didn't reconnoiter, I don't know.

We're doing what we are trained to do. Look for targets. We even fired at targets we knew they might use as intersections. They might be coming through. Or a bridge. Things like that. We fired at different targets. We would look for the targets. The higher-ups, they would get the information where there might be one of their big guns camouflaged. They might know that. We would try to get the coordinates and fire on that.

We went into Belgium, then back into France and then into Germany. Near Aachen, Germany, my driver was also my radio operator. We were on a hill [at the observation post] observing. Pretty good-size hill, just the two of us. I had my equipment with me. We noticed that there was a village. We were there for four days. The Germans knew we were up on that hill, and they were firing mortars at us. After the first barrage of those mortars, we started digging foxholes, four or five because our equipment was facing the sun. The sun would hit our equipment and they could tell we were up there. They would get a pretty good bead on where we were. We would look down and then move to a foxhole after two or three minutes and then to another one and we kept on going like that all morning until the sun went down. We had different kinds of equipment in one hole from the other to observe. We noticed that there was a lot of movement at the bottom of the hill in the village. What happened is that on the fourth day I noticed that there was quite a bit of equipment coming down. And I radioed back that there was a lot of movement down there. They said, "Can you fire on them?" I said, "I'll try." What happened is that I told them [artillery], "Fire with one gun," and I gave the coordinates of a church that was six hundred yards to the left of the village. They fired one round. With one round I [the artillery] hit the bottom of the church. I told them "six hundred yards to the left, bring in the battery," which is the four guns. And they fired the four guns, and I was right on target at that village. I radioed back to bring in the battalion—twelve guns to come in on that village. So they fired about twenty-thirty minutes, all different kinds of ammunition. When I called a cease fire, I waited a while and the radio man and I went down and looked. There was nothing but broken bodies, vehicles. We had destroyed a village. They decided to give me that, the Bronze Star.

We kept on going. The next major incident was the Battle of the Bulge. We were getting ready to have Christmas and come home. It was December 16, 1944. I was on the border of Belgium and Germany. Our captain said, "We're not going to have time to go back and set the guns. You'll have to take your machine gun and go to the intersection here and set up to fight them if they come in." They [Germans] came but not that close. We had a bazooka; there were three of us there and a .50-caliber machine gun and each one of us had guns. Two corporals and myself. I had a .45-caliber gun and a carbine. The others had carbines.

The radio man had the instrument. The wire ran back to headquarters. At this time the radio man was not with us. The machine gunman was going to help me with the machine gun because the bullets are .50 caliber, and you have to feed the machine. We were going to man the machine gun and then the bazooka. There was no radio. We were sent there. Everybody that was available had to do something. They put you here; they put you there. The Germans were all around us. They came but not that close to us. We kept moving until we got to the Elbe River.

I was in the Occupational Army in a German village getting food and water. We encountered some Russians, and they told us the war was "kaput," meaning that the war was over.

We went through a concentration camp in Nordausen. There were dead bodies everywhere. I have the picture to prove it.

On October 7, 1945, I was discharged after having been drafted on October 7, 1941. At that time I had been promised only one year of duty. It turned out to be four.

Álvaro P. Álvarez
3rd Armored Division
84th Infantry Division

Fighting Under an Assumed Name
Álvaro's younger brother was so eager to join the big adventure known as the war that he took his older brother's birth certificate and passed himself off as Álvaro. This action caused Álvaro to have to go by the younger brother's name, the wrong name throughout the war. Álvaro's parents died by the time he was five years old. His sister Celia took on the role of their mother. At an early age Álvaro was in the CCC—the Civilian Conservation Corps, a program under the Roosevelt administration that employed young men on conservation projects. The boys dressed as soldiers and worked on various community improvement projects, which included building parks.

By 1942 the CCC had begun closing their camps and sending the boys home. I was sent home and shortly thereafter was drafted.

Because of Pearl Harbor most of the young men in the country wanted to join up and go fight. My brother Alfredo, who was only sixteen years of age, was also eager to go fight for his country. So anxious was Alfredo to join up that he took my birth certificate and passed himself off as being me, who was eighteen years of age. After his basic training, my brother was sent to Africa where he became ill with yellow fever and had to be sent home.

When I went to the draft board with my draft notice I took Alfredo's birth certificate and explained about the rashness of my younger brother. The man in charge at the draft board said that he would take care of it and straighten everything out. Then he took my brother's birth certificate and merely changed the year of birth from 1925 to 1923 so the birth certificate would indicate that I was eligible to serve although it was with my brother Alfredo's birth certificate.

When it came time for me to leave, my sister gave me *la bendición* and a *tarjeta de oración*, a prayer card that I could carry with me.

I went to war with Alfredo, my brother's name, and that is what everyone called me. Basic training occurred in Cheyenne, Wyoming, a state that I had worked in under the CCC. The next training site was Fort Jackson, South Carolina.

When I arrived in New York, it was learned that the *Queen Elizabeth* ship was too full of men, so other soldiers and I crossed over on the Lexington. I was taken to Liverpool, and after that I spent a year in Cambridge, England. It was there that I met an Irish girl who was working for the English government. We met in the Catholic Church, dated, and finally decided to get married. My best man was Juan Ramirez from San Antonio, Texas.

Although I thought I would be in the First Infantry Division, I was to be a replacement in the Third Armored Division. Finally, I was sent to Plymouth, England, on the East Coast for maneuvers for three weeks. We were also taught to read maps and how to use compasses. During that time I couldn't write, use the telephone, or talk to anyone.

On June 3, 1944, I returned to Cambridge to see my wife. She asked why I hadn't written or called, and I explained that I hadn't been allowed to by my superiors. I insisted that my wife return to Ireland and stay with her folks until I returned.

On June 6, 1944, at about 5:00 a.m., we were placed on a boat and told that we were going across the English Channel to France. I prayed that I would return safely. We landed on Omaha Beach. When I got out of the boat and began running, I was scratched on some wire that had been scattered along the beach. The water was up to my waist. I was hit under the chin and behind the ear, but I kept on running. A medic stopped to patch me up with bandages and I kept on moving until finally some of us made it up the cliff.

I was very scared. We were just shooting at the Germans and they kept shooting at us. I never again saw my friends. I never ever saw the guys who had been on the boat with me.

For two or three days we stayed in a cave. The powdered eggs we tasted were better than the K rations. We walked at night and we rested in the daytime. Sometimes we would rest in trucks.

Sometime after the landing they moved me again, this time to the Eighty-Fourth Infantry. As we moved along, it seems there were dead Germans everywhere. And we could hear the bullets day and night.

In Belgium the people were so happy to see the American soldiers. They hugged us when they saw us. In December 1944, it was difficult to dig foxholes because of the ice on the ground. The captain asked us to stop shooting on Christmas Day. We finally had a quiet time in which to sleep. On December 26 the shooting began again.

I had a buddy from Kentucky, a red-headed guy. We spent Christmas together in the foxhole. Then suddenly I couldn't get up. My feet were numb. He carried me to a truck. They gave me clean socks and a stone that was heated up. After two days, I was given some new boots and clean socks and sent on my way to the front again.

Adam, a good friend of mine from Edinburg, Texas, and I were sent out as scouts to see what we could see. A jeep dropped us off, and we went into the next town looking for Germans. There were Germans there, but our company for some reason or another went in a different direction. Meanwhile we found a service station with a basement. A man and a woman who owned it let us stay in the basement. They gave us cooked potatoes and bread. From time to time we could hear the Germans talking outside. Finally, the Germans left. The man and woman told us that a wagon would be coming through and that we could ride on it. We found our company and asked, "Why did you leave us?" They answered by telling us that they thought we were dead!

We fought from town to town all the way to Germany. I jumped a fence and was cut up on barbed wire. Again, I was patched up, and I continued the tour.

I was involved in three battles: the Rhine River, the Rohr River, and the Battle of the Bulge.

It was not only physically exhausting but also mentally exhausting to some of the soldiers. Some of the soldiers cried. Our platoon sergeant who was from Chicago was a good soldier, but at one point he became angry and agitated. He saw some German civilians and he wanted to shoot and kill all of them. Another soldier did shoot and kill some German citizens. Then the platoon sergeant threatened to begin killing the American soldiers. A soldier took the gun and rifle away from the sergeant and placed him on a truck. The medics came and took the sergeant to a hospital.

A chaplain arrived on the front lines. Adam was suddenly hit and fell to the ground. He did not want to stay down, and he asked me to move him. I was afraid that if I tried to pick him up, they would just shoot at both of us. So I told him to wait until the medic arrived. Someone sent the chaplain to talk to Adam. Adam asked me to tell his wife that we had fought together. Shortly after that Adam died.

As we traveled along, the Germans got the upper hand in one situation and captured me and twenty other men in my squad. They treated us roughly by pushing and kicking us. Then they took our rifles and talked on the radio to some other Germans. After about thirty minutes American troops began firing in our direction. Then the American troops arrived, and the Germans gave up.

About eighteen kilometers outside of Berlin we saw Russian tanks appear. Some of our men said that Russian women were operating the tanks. I wasn't sure. We were told that we were not to go any further, that there were no more Germans to fight. The company commander said that one of our tanks had a message, that the war had ended. As we looked around that night the towns and villages had turned on their lights. Everyone was happy. We saw some barrels of wine and we shot a hole through them and filled our canteens with wine!

We liberated two concentration camps. At one of them, there was a Jewish professor who was considered to be very important. The army sent four men to guard him after he was taken home in a jeep. We had orders not to let anyone kill him or hurt him. I was one of the guards who watched over him for over four weeks, but I never did find out who he was.

I was able to get a pass to Dublin, where my wife was staying. I took a truck ride, then a cattle car to Paris, an airplane to London, and finally a boat to Ireland. I was one of the first American soldiers to get to Dublin. Since Dublin had been neutral during the war, I was not allowed to wear my uniform and had to dress in civilian clothes. Even so, reporters interviewed me. The ambassador called Berlin for me and requested an extension so that I could stay longer with my wife.

After returning from my visit to Dublin I stayed in the army and was discharged in December 1945.

Álvaro P. Álvarez finally regained his own name.

Robert H. Martinez

101st Airborne Division
501st Parachute Infantry Regiment
506th Parachute Infantry Regiment

Excitement: A Special Kind of Soldier

Robert, an individual with dual citizenship, chose to fight for this country. His father had fought in the revolution in Mexico, and Robert would follow in his footsteps. And he would do it as a member of a new group of fighters, the Paratroopers. Robert H. Martinez was born in Monterrey, Mexico, on May 2, 1919. His father, Adolfo Yañez Martinez, had been fighting on the Federalists' side during the Mexican Revolution. He told his wife to go to San Nicolás de los Garza, because he had heard a rumor that the Villistas were coming and that all the Federalists would be hung! (This area became part of Monterrey.)

Eventually I volunteered for the service in 1936 but was rejected because I had been born in Mexico. Then in December 1941, the Selective Service called me. Because my father was a deacon and a lay preacher, my family was accustomed to a daily Bible reading or family altar time. [The family prayed for Robert as he left for the service.]

When I presented myself in San Antonio, an officer came to the group to give a talk. There was to be a special group of soldiers who would wear special parachute suits. These men would not spend time in foxholes, but would serve only on special missions! They would jump behind enemy lines! And they would even get extra pay! Then he asked for all interested boys to "step to the front." Out of 250 men, only twenty moved forward. I was one of the twenty.

We were sent to Camp Toccoa in Georgia for parachute training. It was a terrible time. Often it rained. We were made to get up at 3:00 a.m. and run for fifteen miles loaded down with our .30-caliber machine guns and a full pack on our backs. The trainers yelled and cursed at us all of the time. Another demand was for us to march thirty-five miles to Ft. Benning, Georgia. Then we had to run up and down hills. So many men were lost in this last exercise that the practice was stopped.

Ft. Benning, Georgia, housed the jump school. Out of eleven thousand potential paratroopers, only two thousand were left to make up the 501 regiment. Finally, we won our jump wings.

The next stop was Tennessee, where maneuvers were to take place. There were to be two practice jumps. We were supposed to jump, read maps that had been given to us, march to a designated place, and place markers indicating we understood the coordinates, etc. If we ended up in the right place, our food would be dropped from an airplane. After the maneuvers were completed, I was given a furlough to visit my family.

This time everyone knew I was going to go fight, but I couldn't tell them anything, not now nor later in letters. After my wife, two sisters, and my mother went to the train station to see me off, I left for my mission overseas. It was December 1942. My ship ended up in Glasgow, Scotland, and then it took me to England. Because of the war, everything outside was black.

In England we were stationed in Newberry, and our homes were tents. We were able to visit London several times in between the required training. We paratroopers trained close to our British counterparts and participated in maneuvers and further training.

In the spring of 1944, we were moved closer to the airport. We continued exercising, but now we were invited to a special place. The tents known as War Tents were distinguishable from the others because they had concertina wire all around them, and dogs guarded the tents at all times. In addition, jeeps with guards drove around the war tents keeping watch at all times.

We were taken into the War Tents. Inside the tents were large tables with aerial photographs of the places where we would jump. We were told where we were to be dropped and the directions to follow. After we had visited the War Tents, we were no longer allowed to visit or converse with any other servicemen. We were "incommunicado." Even when going to the mess tent, we were ushered in, watched over, and ushered out by guards. Things had changed!

And now I knew what I was supposed to do. We sharpened our bayonets and made certain that everything was in good working order and in its proper place. We were given metal "crickets" so that when anyone of them heard movement at night, he could click once. That was a challenge, which required another paratrooper to click twice. Then the first paratrooper would know that someone from his group was near.

On June 5, 1944, at 11:00 p.m. with charcoal on our faces we were marched to the airplanes. Sixteen thousand of us were supposed to jump. We were anxious and tense. I just wanted to get it over with. The airplanes circled around to assemble in order. I could see so many lights through the airplane windows. It looked like Christmas!

We flew over the English Channel, then over Cherbourg. Because of the moonlight I could see land. Otherwise everything was quiet and dark.

Suddenly the ground seemed to explode with machine guns. Tracers lit up the sky. Sky lights also shone on our airplanes. We could hear the bullets hitting our airplane. And when the 105-caliber cannons flew by, even if the plane wasn't hit, the airplane bounced. Everything was happening at once. We just wanted to get out of the airplane.

Right before getting to the drop zone, we had to stand and hook up. In nine seconds twenty men jumped out. I jumped between Carenton and St. Come du Mont and landed near a tree. The parachute was caught in a tree, but I was on the ground. While removing my harness I heard the click of a cricket, but I couldn't find my cricket. So realizing that it was a paratrooper I said, "Can't you see my parachute is caught in the tree?"

"Oh, it's you Martinez," a voice answered. Now here was a friend.

We had been told to walk in the direction of the plane that had dropped us, but there were so many airplanes dropping troops that it was hard to tell which plane had dropped us. So we decided to wait until early the next morning.

Early on June 6, we got together with the other paratroopers we found. We began to march on the road toward St. Come du Mont. Because Rangers had been dropped early, now they were working as forward observers and were radioing back to the ships as to the location of the enemy.

We saw lots of dead Germans out in the fields. The stench was unbearable. Lt. Poses and Captain Grimm, West Point men, were leading the way and we were following quite a few yards behind in a column. Suddenly we didn't see them and realized they had been quietly captured. We were walking into a trap. We turned around and walked back.

We regrouped and attacked. There was no front line, just Germans all around us. Out of the sixty men in our platoon who had jumped, only eighteen had survived. I was one of the lucky ones. After fighting and moving on we were sent back to England in August.

On September 16, 1944, we jumped in Eindhoven, Holland, with the intent of cutting off the Germans. The British paratroopers had jumped north of the upper Rhine River. We protected the roads to keep the Germans from blocking the tanks.

Then we went to Nienhagen on the Rhine River to protect the bridge. We used reflector lights and guarded the river so that our troops could use the bridge.

Back to Mourmelon, France [and the Battle of the Bulge].

We were told to hold Bastogne at all costs, because it was a railway center. That winter was so cold and the weather was so severe that we had to break the ice on the ground in order to dig our foxholes. We lived on K rations until the weather cleared up enough for the airplanes to drop supplies for us.

Then the Germans offered us the opportunity to surrender, but General McCauliffe said, "Nuts."

We knew we were going to be safe when we saw US tanks moving in and fighter planes flying above us firing at the German tanks and troops. Many German tanks sat idle because they had run out of gas. The fighter planes would fire at the tanks from different angles until the tanks would fall apart. Later as we left Bastogne we saw miles and miles of pieces of German tanks. Later we learned that the Germans were trying to get to Antwerp where the US had Liberty ships full of supplies for our troops.

We were being driven to Strasbourg when we heard that the war in Europe was over.

My next assignment involved learning how to ski. After the unconditional surrender document had been signed, many Germans were trying to escape through mountain passes in Austria and Switzerland. So the 101st was told to watch the borders and mountain passes.

I had been through battles and had not gotten hurt, but I got hurt on the skis while on duty. I was flown to Nancy, France, to recuperate. By the time I was flown to Austria to meet with my unit, the 101st had been disassembled. So when I was dismissed I was dismissed from the 506th in Selassie, Austria.

I came home to become a preacher, a calling I had experienced from the time I was nine years old!

Pablo Valverde
101st Airborne Division

More Than Nine Lives
Pablo Valverde was born on February 12, 1920, in Brady, Texas. Pablo started training to be a paratrooper, his dream job, but he didn't think he was going to make it. An officer, however, was impressed with the young man and made certain Pablo would get his wish. Pablo Valverde's parents, Juan and Josefa Martinez Valverde, were originally from Mexico.

[My parents] picked cotton—they were laborers. They went to West Texas, to Amarillo. They went up and down because they were migrants. They traveled from Corpus to West Texas. I used to go to school, and they took me out. I didn't like that. I liked school. I enjoyed it. They would drop out and then come back. The students were ahead of me, but I used to catch up. One time they passed me twice, because I knew too much. I went through fifth grade.

I volunteered in '42, in August. I was twenty-two. Right after Pearl Harbor. I went to Camp Toombs, Georgia. [Camp Toombs later became Camp Toccoa.] I saw people jumping and this is what I wanted. Coming down, I knew they were going to shoot at me. I was training to be a paratrooper. I flunked. They put me out. I was not qualified . . . because they give you a test. I was copying the other guy next to me. My grade was very, very low. They gave me an interview and said, "Sorry, I'm going to send you out and you have to wait." And I waited.

Since I was a waiter, I worked in the officer's mess hall. When I was working there I was good. I was fast. I used to get a bunch of plates and did things like that. . . . One officer said, "Are you with us?"

I said, "No, I'm going to be kicked out. They don't want me here."

He said, "You will stay here. I'll see that you stay with us."

So I went to Ft. Benning and made my three jumps and I qualified. They put me as a captain's orderly, the one who takes care of the captain. In combat you are his bodyguard, messenger, valet. You are supposed to be the orderly for the battalion commander.

You had to make three jumps to qualify. We used to get fifty dollars extra for jumping. It is not easy to jump. You never get used to it. When you are in a plane, when you are out, you are free. You are not scared. When you go out, that is when it is scary. Once you're out, you're okay. You're just dropping.

It's automatic. Just a cable. If you jump out and it doesn't open, then you pull the other. You have one reserve. You have a small parachute in front of you.

In Fort Benning I got my wings. You get your wings when you make three jumps. You automatically get the boots. We trained until we went to England. I was there a year and a half before I went to combat.

We knew we had to jump. We didn't know when. I was a battalion commander's orderly. His name was William Turner. When they were shooting at him, he didn't move, and I had to stay guarding him right in the middle when we're fighting.

On June 5 they kept us on shore. They took us to a place. We were supposed to jump on the fifth but we jumped on the sixth. It was raining. They gave us a big meal. We went to a priest that night. In the morning they gave us the clickers, you know click, click, click. The *chicharras*, that's what saved my life.

We knew we were going to jump. They didn't give us a lecture. They put us there and we were waiting to board the plane. We were in the barracks. They said we will not go until June 6th.

It was misty and that little *chicharra* that I had is very important because . . . I put it in my pocket. I closed my pocket. When I put it in my pocket, I knew it was there, and I knew I needed it. When we boarded the plane, they gave me a sort of radio, a very heavy thing about forty pounds. I tied it to my leg. It was heavy . . . the plane took off . . . It was about five hundred feet. It was pretty low. The speed of the plane was supposed to be ninety [mph]. It was about two hundred miles per hour. I was second behind a captain. The captain was not my battalion commander. The battalion commander was in another plane.

I was the second one to jump, and I was caught by air pockets. We were supposed to go down, and I was going up. Three machine guns were firing up when I was going up. I was not going down. I could see the tracers. It was at night.

The captain was gone. Everybody was running. I was watching down. The moon was shining. I saw a lot of bullets coming at me. I was trying to climb up [the parachute]. I had no place to go. I saw the men down and running, disappearing.

So they follow me, the Germans with the guns, shooting at me. I almost hit a tree. I landed down and they kept on shooting at the trunk of the tree. There was a little wind. I knew I was going to miss the tree. I landed down on one side. They began shooting. As soon as they started firing, I went to the road. I landed at Ste. Marie du-Mont. There were hedgerows like this, a lot of brush. I was underneath. I went in there and there was a lot of poison ivy about this high. I lay down in it all over my face. I lay there from 1:30 a.m. when I jumped until 10:00 a.m.

What happened—I was laying down. I heard a lot of people running back and forth in the dark. I thought, I'll get my clicker and call them. I couldn't find it. If I had had it, they would have killed me. How can you click on the Germans? There were about one hundred or seventy-five Germans. I thought they were Americans. This happened in the dark.

I heard the noise. Everybody is running back and forth and shooting above my head. The machine gun was cutting some of the leaves above my head. If I had called them, they would have killed me.

Later on, they keep on running back and forth. Within two hours I was so scared that I wanted to kill myself. I thought, but how can I kill myself with a Thompson machine gun? I can't do that. I wanted to die, because if you see bullets come around your head . . . an inch. I just wanted to die. I don't want to wait. I just closed my eyes and waited for the bullet.

Then in the morning there was a cow trying to eat grass and I tried to shoo it away. I didn't want the cow around there. The cow left. Right in front of me a few feet away I could see a machine gun—two German soldiers with machine guns firing that way and I was watching them. I could not get them, because there was a bunch behind me. I couldn't do nothing.

They looked at me [in his direction] but couldn't see me. The sun was shining. I took my gun and pointed it at them. I was waiting. If I had fired, they would have killed me. I couldn't move, because if I moved the brush, they would know I was there.

They killed somebody. I saw a few shots. Then they turned to me again. The bayonet was dripping blood in front of me. I looked at them like that and put my machine gun toward them. I saw the blood dripping this far [gestures] from my face.

I couldn't turn around. I couldn't move. The blood was about two feet away from me. They moved that way. . . . A tank came by. It was shooting branches off the top of my head. Could have been American. Then they moved that way. Then I heard, "Here's one there . . . There's that. . . ."

I want to get out, but I don't want them to shoot me. I had a smoke grenade with red smoke. If you see that, that's an American. I throw it out, and one guy was trying to kill me. A fellow said, "See that smoke over there. That's an American." I put my head out and the guy had a rifle aiming at me. The sergeant stopped him. I joined up with them. We were there early in the morning. They [soldiers] went in about eight.

There was a sergeant, he had sprained his ankle. I knew him. He said, "I have to go because those are my men. I trained them, and I have to go with them." They had told him not to go [because of the sprained ankle], but he said, "I am going because those are my men." So he was there and I saw him. He was dead. They burned him.

The one that landed behind a dead cow—There was a sergeant, watching everything—what they were doing. The German was burning the sergeant. The one that landed behind the dead cow was watching. He said, "I saw what they did to him."

When we landed—what happened we were fighting. Some company was lagging behind, and our First Battalion commander said, "What happened to that company? Why isn't he advancing?"

I went with him. I was always with him. First Battalion commander, a lieutenant colonel. There was this guy with no helmet. So he got angry and said, "Kill him."

So he turned around. He was an American. He said, "Put your helmet on." From then . . . there's a bunch of men there, and the grass was about three feet high. He said, "Bring me five men, and we'll go forward." And I asked five of the guys. So they went behind me. We went crawling. And if anyone was in front of me, he had to get up and they'd shoot at him, and he'd come down.

That man [battalion commander], he had no business in being there. He is supposed to be in the back, but he was there, way ahead of his company, way ahead of the whole battalion. And then he came back and said, "Are the guys behind?" And I said, "Yes, they're behind." They were way in the back.

They didn't want to follow me, because the machine gun was coming this way. I couldn't see them. They were way back. So then we went back. He went to the road. And he said, "You stay right there. There a lot of trees there [hedgerows?]."

So what happened—there was a tank coming back. They didn't want to go, because the man that used to order them . . . in charge, was killed. So they were coming. My battalion commander said, "Where are you going? You go back."

"No." "You want to go? You come back and I'll take you." The driver of the tank said that.

He [battalion commander] said, "You stay right there."

I said, "No. I am going to go with you. I cannot leave you."

So he went in there and got shot in the head. He got killed, right in the head. For a year and a half I used to talk to him about his wife and all of that. He was directing the tank.

I was in a ditch. He was in front, and they said, "The colonel was killed." And then they told me. I saw a bunch of my men shot in the head. I saw one the vein was running out. He was still alive.

What happened to me . . . I went further. We went in and then we went back. We advanced about half a mile. At night I went into a hole . . . There were two men, I thought they were Americans. And after I slept there . . . In the morning they were laughing, because I thought they were Americans. They were two dead Germans.

There was a big gun there the Germans used to use. In the morning when I got up, everyone was eating. I was sitting here—there was one man over there eating. There was a big gun there, abandoned. They moved each other or something because whenever they tried to hide, the whole gun exploded. Someone tried to fire the gun. [The gun shattered, killing the other man. Pablo was twenty feet away.]

Why didn't I die? I was there. I had so many close calls.

I was in Carentan when my arm . . . I was running and trying to climb over the hedgerows and I couldn't make it. Bullets were going over my head and I couldn't move my arm. Poison ivy probably. Something was wrong. I couldn't use my arm.

I had to cross over [the channel]. I said, "I can't move my arm. There is something wrong." I couldn't continue running because I could hear the bullets going over my head.

They sent me back to England. On account of the poison ivy probably. They stayed a week—I don't know how many days. Fighting. Then I went over there. I was about a week and a half in England.

The 101st went back to England . . . after we jumped. We stayed there a month.

The second jump was in September in Belgium. Before that we got together and they gave us another battalion commander, Lieutenant Colonel Lefebvre. I was with him [his orderly].

He was mean to his company. We were in Reims. If the bus was late, he punished the men: "Dig a hole and fill it up. Six by six." That's bad.

They [the men] said, "We are going to kill him," and I heard them. When we jumped that day they told me, "Don't be close to him."

We jumped from two different planes. Then we got together in the sky. There were bullets from behind us. They missed us both. The battalion commander told them, "I know what happened. I'm sorry. I'm going to admit it. I learned my lesson." He was a good battalion commander. He knew it was his own men because the bullets came from behind.

We spent seventy-three days in Belgium trying to keep the road. It's in the movie *A Bridge Too Far*. We went to a small town, Bussum in Holland. It was beyond the Remagen Bridge, close to the Rhine River. We went to this little town there . . . There were lots of guns on the other side of the Rhine. We got there . . . we lost about 250 men there. We got two hundred back. I've got the picture of the little town.

We stayed there and then we went to, I think it was France. We stayed in this . . . we stayed about a few days because there was a breakthrough [the Battle of the Bulge]. We had just got through from fighting . . . seventy-three days.

We were getting ready to go to Paris, because we are going there and celebrate. Then all of a sudden they said, "Get everything ready, because we are going to go back again." We're moving trucks to Bastogne. We didn't jump; we went in trucks. As soon as we're moving we saw a lot of cannon, a lot of fire.

We're moving and then they surrounded us. When we were there, they said there's no way out. The Germans were shooting from the back and all over the place.

Our Lt. Colonel Lefebvre in Bastogne . . . we were going to a place like from here to Gregory [eight or so miles]. A little town we were supposed to move to that place. I was with the Lt. Colonel and we were in this jeep, and this driver was going fast. And the Lt. Colonel said, "Wait. Don't go so fast. Go slow. Not too fast."

The sergeant said, "This road is zeroing in. You cannot go slow because . . ."

The Lt. Colonel said, "I said go slow." All of a sudden they opened up . . . you see these shells coming all over the jeep. Then he [the Lt. Colonel] said, "Go ahead. Let's get out of here." So we went to this town, this place. In the morning you could see the big tanks coming over the mountains. Big tanks. That day was clear.

In that town . . . they were just shooting. What happened . . . The Lt. Colonel said, "Go and make some coffee." So when I went to make some coffee . . . and while I was gone, they blew the building up. I was in the other side of the building. It was blown up on this side.

They said, "Let's go back to Bastogne . . . everybody will go back any way you want . . . walking . . . " The number one officer said that. It's about fifteen miles from there. Then we moved back to Bastogne. We were surrounded, but that little town was near Bastogne about eight miles from Bastogne.

We went over there, everybody was trying to go to that little town. I got in a half-track to go back to Bastogne. There were two half-tracks. I got in one of them.

As we were going back . . . there was a house right here. As we were going back to Bastogne, I was here. We were about seven in the half-track. There were two driving. There was another half-track behind us [three half-tracks in all]. I am in the back. I was going this way, and there was a man here. They opened fire here from the house. From here to the post [a few feet]. They were firing this way.

So I tried to get out, and go around here [gesturing]. As I went over here, I got hooked by my scabbard here. And he was moving here and almost missed me. So I had to go here. And over here was a German surrendering. So I said, "Get out. I want the hole." There's one here. So what I did; I went around. So I went down. They threw a hand grenade here. That thing exploded on the side of me and it didn't do nothing. But it was not a grenade. It was a smoke grenade.

So then I went behind there and as I was coming down I got the German. They had three men. We were four soldiers here. He [the German] didn't want to fight. He wanted to give up . . . he was dead right there.

So I brought him here and as soon as I brought him here the guy was surrendering. These three guys with M1s trying to kill this German. I got in front of the German and said, "You ain't going to kill him. He's unarmed." A gun misfired. I heard the click. You ought to see the German's face. That guy was almost crying. I looked at him and he looked at me. I still have his . . . [image] . . . It happened in Bastogne.

They said, "Okay. We ain't gonna kill him." They were pointing the M1s at me because I was standing in front of him and they were trying to kill him. One of the guns misfired. Finally, we put him in the half-track and took him to Bastogne. I still see that man . . . the way he was . . . he was thanking me for saving him. You're not supposed to kill someone who is unarmed. If they've got a gun, shoot him. Even if he is walking with his hands down, I don't think you can . . . I didn't kill many of those. I used to shoot them when they were way, way in the back . . . not unarmed.

During the siege of Bastogne in December of 1944, the 101st held the crucial town of Bastogne despite the fact that they were greatly outnumbered by the Germans and were running low on both ammunition and food. The 101st encircled the town and the troops moved from one position to another as the Germans attempted to penetrate their lines at different places.

One thing we did . . . they used to move us from one place to another. They attacked us from here . . . we moved that way. They attacked us . . . we had to move to the other side. If they had attacked at one time, they would have taken us. They kept on shooting.

After that, Patton came in. We were almost ready to give up, because we kept moving and moving. We were running out of ammunition. From then on, all of a sudden Patton came in. I can see the tanks that were coming in. They didn't take us out. We kept on fighting. And they kept on pushing. They were coming in and we were moving forward. As soon as they came in, we fought about half a day and then we moved back to France and we stayed there. We went to Austria until the war ended. A friend of mine had to use skis and broke his arms and legs. The mountain gave way. He was gone about a month and a half.

We stayed in this palace where Herman Goering was captured. He had beautiful horses. We used to go up there and ride them. We used to go out there and I think the horses knew about the time, because at 3:00 the horses used to come by themselves. They used to jump all over the place. They used to come . . . you had to come early because if you don't they'd jump all over and they'd throw you. They probably know what time it is. They jumped big fences and all that.

Goering killed himself with cyanide [during the Nuremburg trials]. They had a silo—from here to there—full of cognac. We cut a hole and we could take buckets out of there. They told me, "You'd better stop or I'll put you out someplace."

When I moved into this big, beautiful place (the palace) the lieutenant colonel said, "We want you to have the best room you want." I said, "The best place for me is in the entrance." In the entrance, there was this big beautiful room on each side. Because if I am inside, I cannot go outside. I could go in or out. After the war.

I did two combat jumps, in France and in Belgium. When you are in the plane it is scary. Once you're out, it's okay. When you jump down you bend your knees and roll. If you fall in water you can float. To me Normandy was more difficult than the Battle of the Bulge.

I was walking with eight men in Holland. A shell came and killed all of them but me. It threw me on the side.

I was twenty-four. I was discharged in August 1945.

John Prezas

101st Airborne Division
3rd Battalion, 506th Regiment
HQ Company

A Fifty-Dollar Raise

John Prezas from Beeville, Texas, joined the First Division and was sent to Ft. Bliss. As with many other families, hard times meant that John Prezas's family had little money. When he heard a soldier could earn fifty dollars more if he joined a new group known as paratroopers, he jumped at the chance. He sent his mother the extra money.

On November 11, 1940, I went into the National Guard and had a year of training in cavalry and infantry. By 1941 I was patrolling the border between Brownsville, Texas, and Mexico on horseback. I covered Boca Raton Island, which had one hotel and one restaurant. I was also assigned to cover the bridge that connected Texas with Mexico at Brownsville.

With rumors of war in the air in 1941, Headquarters Company became mechanized, and I then drove a motorcycle. Already there were rumors that German submarines were visiting the Gulf coast, but the public was not aware of this. When we were alerted that a submarine had been sighted, we would block the highway to bring the traffic to a standstill. On one occasion a German submarine became trapped, and the Navy immediately took over to deal with the problem.

Sometimes, when German drums full of oil would wash up on the beaches, that would indicate to the Americans that Germans were nearby. Also, we were to stop draft dodgers from crossing over into Mexico; however, if any Mexicans came to the US side and wanted to join the service, that was allowed.

When I joined the service I was making $21.00 a month; then as a sergeant I earned $54.00 a month. That is until some friends and I crossed the border to go buy drinks. When a colonel spotted us, I was brought back down to private. Later I became a sergeant again.

In 1943 a call went out for a new group of soldiers who would jump out of airplanes and be known as "Paratroopers." The offer, which was hard to resist, meant that the men who qualified would be paid $50.00 a month more! Why the way I was going, I would be able to bring in one hundred dollars a month! I decided to send $50 of my monthly income back home to my family.

We were sent to parachute school in Fort Benning, Georgia, and since I already knew how to handle weapons, I became an instructor. One day some other men and I decided to go into Atlanta without permission. I was caught. My punishment—so I was told—was to be sent overseas.

I arrived in England where the men could buy a pair of shoes for $2.00. Why some men had as many as three pairs of shoes! I was now with the 101st Airborne Division, the 506th regiment.

And now for the jumping. In September 17, 1944, we prepared to jump in Eindhoven, Holland. Before I jumped, I always said a short prayer, "*En el nombre sea de Dios.*" [In God's name.] Another Mexican American said, "*En el nombre de la Virgen de Guadalupe.*" [In the name of the Virgin of Guadalupe.] The Virgin of Guadalupe was the patron saint of Mexico and hence the preferred saint of many Mexican American Catholics. When some of the others heard, "*En el nombre de la Virgen de Guadalupe,*" some would say, "and me, too, Lupe." [Lupe is the shortened version of Guadalupe.]

It was General Montgomery's plan to have the American paratroopers jump in Arnhem behind the river. He figured that his English paratroopers would join the Americans in twenty-four hours. By Monty's calculations, the war would be over by Christmas. The Americans cleared five miles on either side of the highway, and Montgomery took three days to get there. After the British arrived, the 101st left them there in Arnhem.

All of us men went to Paris on furlough. Shortly thereafter we were told of the new German push [the Battle of the Bulge]. Hitler had broken through. We were taken in trucks to Bastogne immediately. Not long after our return to the 101st, the Germans surrounded Bastogne, an area with seven roads leading to it. We didn't get to eat for three days, and we were running short on ammunition. The skies were full of clouds, which made it impossible for the US planes to drop us supplies.

One strategy we used was to fight the Germans on the North side on one day and then fight them from another direction on the following day. The word was that nine Liberty ships full of supplies and ammunition were waiting for the US. Since the Germans were running out of gas and ammunition, they were interested in getting the supplies we had waiting for us in Antwerp.

Another plan was to be careful with what little ammunition we had left. So when we saw the German tanks passing through, we held back and didn't attempt to attack them. We figured the tanks were on their way to the port to intercept the supplies we had waiting for us. Also, the Germans didn't know exactly how many men were trapped in Bastogne. Finally, the skies cleared and American airplanes dropped supplies for us, the hungry 101st.

Meanwhile, the American generals were meeting to try to figure out a way to save the 101st. The Germans had already asked the American troops to surrender, and General McCauliff had answered, "Nuts!" The Germans couldn't understand the answer at first and finally understood that the Americans would not surrender.

General Patton took the responsibility to save the 101st. We heard the noisy tanks coming. When we saw them, we knew! We would be saved!

[After the Germans surrendered] We were walking along with some Free French soldiers by the Blue Danube River in Austria. It was very cold and the wide river had ice in it. The Germans had blown up bridges to try to keep us from entering Germany. So we followed the river. We saw three men dressed in black walking toward us. The Americans let the men go by. A soldier from the Free French recognized them as German SS men and forced them to stop. The Germans had torn off their insignias and placed them in their pockets. The Free Frenchman then had one German drown another German. Then he had one of the two survivors drown a second German. Then he told the remaining German, "You are going to have a chance to live. If you can swim across the river and make it to the other side, you will be free." The surviving German soldier began swimming across the Blue Danube and before long sank in the freezing water.

When we asked the Free French soldier why he had done such a thing, he told us that the SS men had raped his mother and sister and then he raised his shirt and showed us long, deep one-inch scars on his chest and stomach.

We arrived in Munich at night. There was a terrible smell in the air. We found out that it was because humans had been burned up in the ovens. The next morning the Americans went to open the camps to let the people who were still alive go free. Local citizens began accusing each other and then shooting one another. The incinerators were an ugly sight. (General Eisenhower made the soldiers go look at the camps so that they could see and understand what had occurred.)

Finally, the war ended and I was discharged on November 30, 1945.

Leonel Mejía
29th Infantry, 4th Division

From a Ranch to Omaha Beach
Leonel Mejía was born on February 12, 1922, in a ranch called San Manuel located near Edinburg, Texas, in an area known as "the valley." Like many other folks at that time, Leonel led a quiet, spartan life on a farm with his family. His draft letter from the Selective Service arrived at the local general store. Two other brothers would also serve in WWII.

There were good times, although there was no candy or ice cream and no money with which to buy them if they were available. There was plenty of food, which was raised on the ranch. From time to time my family would meet with the neighbors, and that meant walking to each other's homes, for we didn't own cars. It was about two miles to school, and I walked there for a few years until the school district began running a bus near the ranch.

From time to time our family would stop at a country store and check and see if any mail had arrived. Finally, a friend and I moved to Edinburg seeking a better life. I washed cars and then became a waiter. One weekend I went home to visit my family out on the ranch. They told me that a letter for me had been picked up at the country store. I opened it up to discover that I had been drafted. That was September 10, 1942.

My mother gave me *la bendición* and begged me to be careful. Little did she realize at that time that she would have three sons in this horrible war, and later two sons in the Korean War.

I went to San Antonio for an examination and was then given a ten-day pass to visit my family. After that I reported to Sam Houston and then to Georgia. It was there that I received my basic training. Because of the hard work I had done on the ranch, I did well. Others who were training beside me, however, became ill or fainted in the hot sun.

In Iceland the training occurred in weather which was the opposite of Georgia. I walked in icy waters, hiked over large and small mountains, and followed that with walking in hot valleys. The temperatures covered a wide range.

I sailed on the *Imperial of Russia* on my way to England. While there in 1943 I helped as troops were trained. Finally on June 7, 1944, the day after D-day, we left New Hampton and landed at Utah Beach.

The fighting had calmed down, and the troops from June 6, 1944, were up ahead of us. We saw and fought a German or two along the way, and we saw lots of German prisoners. We traveled and scouted and tried to sleep.

We spent a month in Paris. The people were so happy to see us. They made lots of hand motions trying to tell us how mean the Germans had been. Some Frenchmen even kneeled in front of us to show us how grateful they were.

I was then assigned to be a guard on the trucks that had landed and were to take food up to the troops on the front lines in Belgium. It was very sad. We were supposed to guard the trucks and not let anyone get near the supplies. They were very important things for the guys at the front. Well, some Frenchmen would climb on the overpasses and wait for the trucks to pass. If they jumped and made it, they would then get some stuff from the trucks and throw them down to someone who was waiting. Sometimes they missed the trucks and died as they fell. Others jumped on trains headed for the front and some of the Frenchmen were hurt that way.

The C rations had a box with cheese and crackers and two pieces of chocolate and four cigarettes, but no matches. The K rations had two cans of beef hash, candy, gum, and cigarettes, but no matches. The chocolate candy was considered a front line dinner. If at all possible the cooks who traveled with their kitchens behind the troops would try to take a plate of food to the soldiers at the front, but that was hard to do.

When the Germans broke through Belgium in what became the Battle of the Bulge, I was sent to the front lines. I was in a foxhole day and night for about thirty-six hours.

On February of 1945 I was fighting near the Moselle River. It was night time and I was not even aware I had been injured. Some of the men in front of me were hurt, and the Red Cross came around to check on all of us. The snow was a foot deep and it was so cold and I was numb and very scared; that's one reason I didn't know I had been hurt. Another reason was that a bullet, which had hit my left hand, had cut a nerve and kept me from having any feeling in it. The Red Cross discovered my injury and took me to a field hospital. They patched me up and sent me to a hospital in England.

I ended up having three operations, one in England and two in the United States. It was a doctor from India who connected the nerves in my hand and gave me feeling in two fingers. I spent one and a half months in Colorado getting healed. While there I saw German prisoners working on the yards.

Near the end of the war the Germans were using wooden bullets. They could hurt you, too.

When I arrived home, my mother was thrilled to see me. At first I felt lost. As time passed, I began to feel more at home.

After the war I married and we had four children. I worked for the HEB Grocery Stores and then at a slaughterhouse.

Leonel has seven grandchildren, most of whom are either attending or have graduated from college.

Leon Eguía
13th Division
82nd Airborne Division

A Tailor Goes to War
Leon Eguía, brother to Ernest Eguía, was born on November 13, 1921, almost two years after his brother Ernest was born. Their parents were María Lara and Narciso Eguía. Leon graduated from high school at the end of the eleventh grade, which was the standard established in Texas many years before. Leon was quietly working as a tailor when he was drafted. He went from making alterations to clothes to being a paratrooper and became adept at demolition work in the war. It was a drastic change of pace for a tailor.

I worked as a tailor doing mostly alterations when the Draft Board called me into the service in 1942. After the military processing in San Antonio was over, I shipped out to California for basic training. Then I underwent training in the Mojave Desert. Many thought that the exercises in the desert were in preparation for fighting in North Africa. In Tennessee I was trained in the use of dynamite.

While stationed at Medford, Oregon, a Japanese submarine bombarded a forest on the coast and started a forest fire. Our unit went over there to put out the fire.

When they began recruiting for paratroopers, I signed up. They sent us to Ft. Benning, Georgia. I received my wings. In North Carolina we trained some more. Then, in Tennessee I became attached to the Eighty-Second Airborne Division.

From Boston, Massachusetts, we shipped out on the SS *Washington*, a troop transport ship. It was very cold. We arrived in England. We flew from England to France. From there we rode in trucks to the Belgian battle site. I was a combat soldier for three weeks. Then we regrouped. I jumped from a glider because the English wanted the Americans to join them.

On December 24, 1944, we jumped out of a glider into Düsseldorf, which was across the Rhine River. This was the Battle of the Bulge. I was an infantryman and worked with the combat engineers blowing up bridges. We blew up bunkers. We also blew up these eight-by-twelve columns of concrete, the Siegfried Line. We had to blow them up so the tanks could go through. The way we did that was to drill holes in the columns; then we put the dynamite in the cross-sections.

Then we had to look for gravel to make roads, because the roads were being destroyed. I was on a reconnaissance in a jeep looking for gravel. A lieutenant said, "I need three men." There was a mine field. A soldier from St. Louis named Joseph said, "Let Eguía go." Joseph went instead, and they were blown up. The fragments hit Joseph in his butt and testicles. Later he blamed me.

At this point the army wanted foot soldiers because the Germans had infiltrated the American army. We began looking for Germans that had infiltrated our lines. The ground was covered in sheets of snow. The Germans gave up easily.

We were in the Ruhr Valley in July or August. I was attached to the

First Army, Eighty-Second Division. They held us back. We were blowing up stuff. They stopped Patton before he got to Berlin.

After being attached to the Eighty-Second and the 101st Divisions in France, I became part of the occupation force in Berlin. I went by a concentration camp and saw live people who looked like skeletons. I threw some candy to people going by in trucks.

I left Germany on November 13, 1945. I arrived in Houston, Texas, and worked as a tailor. The Mexican Americans were treated like dirt. I worked in Corpus Christi, Texas, at S&Q Clothiers. Then I went back to Houston and did tailoring.

I was the ninth Hispanic to be hired as a fireman in Houston, Texas, and I did that for twenty years. I married and had two girls and two boys. We are a close-knit family.

Noé Mendez
1st Infantry Division
The Big Red One

The Soldier from the Texas Town That Gave So Many

Noé Mendez was born in Tampico, Mexico, on April 27, 1925. His father, a former Mexican revolutionary with Carranza, moved his wife and new forty-day-old baby to Benavides, a tiny town in South Texas. This small community was to give up sixteen boys who died in World War II, a significant number of casualties for a town this small. Noé, a slight man who weighed 112 pounds, learned to carry the soldier's sixty-pound backpack. He also observed soldiers with famous names—Joe Louis, Mickey Rooney—and he saw they were expected to perform the same duties as any other soldier. Noé revealed his war experiences for the first time in this interview.

I dropped out of Benavides High School and began attending the Navy Aircraft Mechanic School in nearby Corpus Christi, Texas. Also, I began doing work for the Civil Air Patrol routinely inspecting airplanes after three hundred hours of flying.

In 1944 I went to San Antonio to enlist in the Air Force. I was told that everyone had to go to basic training. And so it was that I, who weighed 112 pounds, found myself in basic training carrying a sixty-pound backpack.

Since it was already 1944, and the war was not yet over, our country was getting desperate, and almost all males were being drafted. There were lawyers, doctors, and other professional men from all over the country going through basic training in Camp Fannin, east of Dallas and close to Tyler, Texas. The ages ranged from very young to older men in their forties. Training was demanding and occurred in the daytime and at night; marching consisted of covering twelve to fifteen miles a day with the sixty-pound backpacks. I remember running through acres of rose bushes and being scratched all over by the thorns on the rose bushes. [Tyler, Texas, is known as the Rose Capital of the World.] Three of the older men died during this training.

After fourteen weeks of training we were given a three-day pass to visit our families. After visiting with my mother and father, I left by train for New York. On the train the meals were plain, sandwiches with an apple or an orange.

We reported to Camp Shanks in New York. While in the supply room where the soldiers were issued the supplies they would need, who should be in the same room with me but Joe Louis. The supply soldiers were having a hard time fitting Joe Louis because he was such a big guy! We were to leave on the *Queen Mary*, a British ship, which had been converted to a troop transport ship. But before we left, our company was assigned to man the guns. I had four to five days' training so that I could operate one of the 40mm guns on the ship. At that particular time half of our company was composed of Mexican American boys from South Texas.

The *Queen Mary* sailed from New York City to Liverpool, England. It was October and the weather was atrocious. While manning the 40mm gun I had to be strapped down so that the waves, which reached far above over my head, didn't pull me off the ship. I covered myself with smelly old British overcoats and ponchos to keep the wind and water off. Mickey Rooney was also on the *Queen Mary* and was being harassed by some soldiers until he just found a corner and attempted to hide from them.

Upon arriving in Liverpool, England, we were placed on a train. We traveled across the English Channel on a Liberty boat. The boat took us out further and dropped us down into an LST. We were allowed to drop down into the LST by going down a rope. The lieutenant who was to lead us slipped from the rope and fell in such a way that he died instantly.

Since D-day had occurred in June and this was October, we were to be taken by the LST to the same beaches. The LST which was in front of our LST hit a live mine, which resulted in the deaths of several men. Because of that unfortunate accident our company was dropped off some distance from the beach. This was difficult for the men because the water was deep. We spent the night on the beach.

No time was lost. In two days our company moved across France to the front lines to be replacement troops for the First Infantry Division. I was assigned to a rifle company. The front lines were losing many men. I was moved to a machine gun squad. While the move might seem more interesting, it was a known fact that the average life of a machine gunner was two days!

Although my company was supposed to be going after the Germans, sometimes they [Germans] were actually among us. Sometimes we could hear them talking and moving equipment. We were told to always be on the offensive, to move up and fight, and that there was no way out! We dug into our foxholes and reported their movements to Command Post.

We left eastern France and traveled across Belgium on foot and fighting all along the way. The Germans appeared to be well-equipped with better arms and superior tanks. As the US soldiers approached the German homeland, the Germans fought harder and bitterly.

After December 16, 1944, we soldiers were given a break. We were replaced by new soldiers and we were told we would have a ten-day leave. We could spend Christmas in Paris, which was now free or in Liege, Belgium. We couldn't believe our luck!

But after only two days, the Germans broke through the American lines with a new determination. The Battle of the Bulge had begun. All the men in the company were told after only a two-day break that they had to pick up their equipment and return to the front lines.

The men were told to hold on to a particular area. We returned to find that all our replacements had been killed. During a night patrol assignment, a German threw a hand grenade in my direction. My left shoulder was severely injured and the blow on my helmet knocked me out. A fellow soldier, Julian Martinez, picked me up and took me to the Command Post.

Another soldier from Benavides, José Amador Garza, was killed at that time. Because of the fighting, there was no quick way to move me so that I could receive medical attention. So I lay injured for twelve hours. Finally, after twelve hours I was taken to a First Aid Station and later to Totton, England, to a hospital. As the ship carried me to England to a hospital, I awoke to find myself lying on the floor of the ship surrounded by German and British soldiers, all wounded and defenseless.

At the hospital a British nurse stayed by my side for two days and two nights. Finally, when I came to, she told me that they had almost given up on me; they were even considering a body bag.

After two and a half months spent recuperating, I was reassigned to the front lines. Although I was sent back to the same company, the men were not the same I had been fighting with.

Twenty miles from the front lines, my platoon was assigned to recapture some German paratroopers who had jumped behind the American lines during the night. We were to flush them out. Our platoon worked on finding them, traveling through a forest day and night without the soldiers ever sleeping. Finally, we chased them into a small village in Belgium. The German paratroopers surrendered to our American platoon without either side firing a shot.

It turned out that the German commander of the paratroopers had died when they jumped. So the Germans were without leadership and weren't certain of what to do. We were exhausted, hungry, and actually poorly armed. So it had been an easy victory. We called for back-up trucks, loaded up the German prisoners, and sent them off.

Things were pretty desperate. All companies were running at 50 percent strength. At one point while pursuing Germans, some British airplanes strafed some Americans thinking they were Germans. Because of the mud and dirt, it was hard to distinguish between Germans and Americans.

Some Germans killed Americans and then dressed like them and even drove American jeeps so that they could infiltrate the American lines, and they did. At times the Germans did this so successfully that they directed the German artillery to the American troops. Passwords were then used by the Americans.

Surprisingly enough, five Americans were found to be fighting on the side of the Germans. One American knew Corpus Christi, Texas, well enough that he could name the tourist spots, North Beach and the Carnival that always operated on the beach!

While fighting our way into Germany Max Schmeling, the boxer, was captured. He was an officer with the German paratroopers. He had defeated Joe Louis in 1936 and then lost to him in a rematch in 1938.

From time to time K rations and D bars (these were candy bars which were to be cut into three pieces and would be equivalent to three meals) were dropped down to the soldiers from airplanes.

During the fierce fighting at the Battle of the Bulge, the Germans were killing all Americans and not taking any prisoners. The Americans were told to do the same. Just shoot all Germans. Another soldier and I were taking thirty German prisoners back to HQ. On the way, the other American opened fire, killing all the Germans. His reason: he thought the Germans were going to try to "get" us.

A black captain and sergeant arrived in a jeep and approached me and asked for directions to the HQ. At that time the Americans were a hundred yards from the German front lines. I told him that I did not know and pointed to a corporal who was standing with another group of soldiers and said, "They know where it is. Ask them."

The black soldiers operated the Red Line Express. They were the suppliers for the soldiers. They drove trucks with food, ammunition, fuel, and other supplies needed at the front lines. They also carried messages. Their role was crucial to the success of the American army.

When the two men in the jeep drove up to the corporal to ask for directions to the HQ, although I could not hear what the corporal said to the men, it was obvious that he had given them the wrong instructions. In a short while the jeep drove away and much to my horror, they drove right into the direction of the enemy. Immediately, I saw a mortar fired right above the direction in which the jeep was driving and then I saw in the distance the jeep as it blew up.

Finally I caught up with the men I knew in Nuremburg. They were still fighting there. By this time, the Russians were coming in from the other direction [east]. In Nuremberg the Americans and the Russians, both fighting to defeat the Germans, met up and began drinking to celebrate the big victory. Some men either ran into poisoned alcohol or consumed excessive liquor. Sixteen Russians died and a friend of mine I called "Alabama" because he was from there died. When I went to see my sick friend, Alabama said, "I can't even see you." Eight or nine Americans died because of the bad liquor.

I was assigned to the First Infantry Division and my company's job was to guard the German officers and prisoners who would later be tried at the Nuremberg trials. The American soldiers were not guarding as closely as it was believed they should, because too many German officers were able to commit suicide. In fact, it was believed that some American soldiers were assisting the Germans when they requested knives or some other assistance in committing suicide. Therefore, American officers were placed strategically to look after the American soldier guards, two GIs to every American officer.

Following the German surrender, American soldiers were given a variety of jobs. After guarding for a week, I was reassigned to a detached service in Frankfurt, Germany, to help the occupational army do its job. Because of my background in automotive repairs, I was attached to a railhead company and was to operate a transportation company in Frankfurt. There was a *grossmarkthalle*, a big market which had all kinds of goods for the German people to consume. More troops came in with replacements to assist in this endeavor.

I ended up with sixteen men and seven vehicles to work with. My problem was that I didn't know the German language and didn't know the names of the roads, which led from one city to another. But I did have an idea. I found a German who not only spoke perfect English, but who also looked like some of the American soldiers, and I worked out a deal with him. The German soldier would be dressed in the uniform of an American soldier but no one would know about it. I told my captain, who agreed with the strategy.

Because some of the soldiers were taking advantage of the German women, the young soldier wanted his wife and children removed to another part of Germany. A rural area was found for the German soldier's family. With that taken care of, he would be free to do whatever I requested. Other officers were amazed that I was able to be so successful in my transportation job.

The young German soldier became a loyal and trusted friend. He told me about two young Texan soldiers who resented being under my command. These two Texans were assigned to me. One of them said, "We're not used to taking orders from a Mexican." I gave them the worst assignment, posting guard duty for the company all night in freezing temperatures. One of the men didn't show up, and I reported him to the captain. The captain told the men that they had to take orders when the noncommissioned officer gave them. One of the men threatened to kill me.

I asked for two replacements for these men. My request was honored. I told the men to get their equipment and to climb into the back of a truck. Then I drove the truck 240 miles from Frankfurt to Nuremberg. Needless to say, the men were quite cold by the time we arrived. One of the men said, "When I go back to Texas, I'm going to look you up and I'm going to kill you."

The young German was also resourceful. When asked if he knew how to make whiskey one day, lo and behold, he knew all about it. There was a basement in the building where the men were staying. The mess sergeant and the quartermaster sergeant worked with the German until a still was built in the basement. Few people knew of the existence of the basement, because the trap door was covered up with a piece of carpet.

One day a colonel came in to do his routine inspection. When he asked me how everything was going along, I said that everything was fine. Then behind the colonel's back I saw steam rising through the carpet. I became very nervous until the colonel said he had to leave. When it was finally time for him to leave, I was quite willing, because the still had been operating for three months and I felt that it was a matter of time before it would be discovered.

During my stay in Germany I was able to acquire a German military motorcycle and a jeep. So as not to get into trouble for having an unauthorized jeep, I took the same license number as the captain's and used it on the jeep.

Upon arriving home to Benavides, I felt as though I were in a daze and remained in a back room in my mother's home. I did not want to come out. Instead my brother and I built model airplanes. Finally, my mother insisted I come out of the room and join the world.

I felt that I had simply been in a bad dream. I didn't talk about my experiences for thirty years.

Before Noé left, his mother gave him la bendición and a tarjeta de oración (a prayer card). She, like so many other mothers, prayed nightly for her son. Noé went through France, Belgium, and Germany with the card in his billfold. He fought in the Battle of the Bulge and earned three battle stars. He was injured and almost died. He came back and continued carrying the prayer card. One day he lost his billfold. A few weeks later his billfold was mailed to him from New Mexico. Everything in his billfold was missing except for the prayer card. And now, sixty years later, Noé still carries the card with him. You can no longer read the prayer and the image of the saint has mostly faded away, but the meaning and value remain.

Alfred J. Hernandez

2615th Tech Supervision Regiment
Technical Sergeant

A New Citizen

Alfred J. Hernandez, whose grandfather fought in the Mexican Revolution on the side of the Federalists, would have his own experience with warfare. But his talents in speaking Spanish and being a watch repairman took him a long way.

In 1921 on *El Día de la Raza*—Columbus Day—my family paid a nickel to cross over into the United States of America. I was four years old. My father worked in Houston, Texas, as a jeweler. The whole family worked in the business.

I graduated from high school and worked as a watchmaker and a jeweler. I asked for my wife's hand in marriage five times before her father agreed to let her marry me. In 1943 at the age of twenty-six, although I was married and had a child, I was drafted. Both my wife and my mother gave me *la bendición.*

I was an alien when I was drafted but became a citizen during the war in Castel Del Piano in Italy. I did very little fighting.

First I went to Aberdeen Proving Grounds in Maryland; that's a fire control training there because of my experience with instruments. It was basic training. My watchmaking experience got me there. They had periscopes and range finders, everything that had to do with small things. I didn't use it. I went to Africa as an infantry replacement. Patton was there. He had been fighting Rommel. I was not assigned to a division. I was assigned to a special unit.

I started in North Africa. Then I moved to Sicily, then France and Germany. In North Africa I had taken my jewelry tools and watchmaking tools and replacements. So I repaired watches for the soldiers. And I was in charge of POWs (Prisoners of War). They paid me [for the repairs]. I did that for about six months.

The general was giving a big dinner for the Delta Base Section of the Army [in North Africa]. He wanted to give a Fourth of July dinner for the generals of the Delta Base. So I was called in. I was in a pup tent. I was called in to see the general and I couldn't believe it. I went in and he said, "Pvt., I understand you've been working with some of the POWs." I said, "Yes sir." He asked, "Are you Italian?" I said, "No sir. I am Mexican." "Well, how do you communicate with these people?" I said, "Well, Italian is very similar to Spanish. If you speak Northern Italian, you can understand almost everything that is said. Southern Italian, the Sicilians, speak a mixture. It's not really Italian. I've been able to make out."

The general said, "Well, I tell you what. I want you to talk to the POWs and find out if we have chefs. I want people who have worked for the finest hotels in Italy." I made the request to the POWs and I came up with three or four.

I talked to them and picked those who had been in charge in very prominent restaurants in Italy. It was a big success.

He said [to me], "What do you do here?" I said, "I'm infantry replacement, Sir." "Somebody told me that when the sun goes down"—we eat dinner at 5:00—"after that you're on your own." I work on watches in my pup [tent]. I said, "Yes sir." He then said, "Do you speak any other languages?" "I speak Spanish, Sir; that's my mother language. I am Mexican-born." So he said, "I'm going to show that you are bilingual, at least. That may help you." It sure did. I became the head of this group, this bunch that worked with POWs.

We went to Sicily and stayed for a short while. There was no fighting going on. We went to Italy. I figured I'd be going into combat. It was raining and it was cold and we were all dirty. The sergeant said, "This morning get up early. Put on your ODs." We did and we were called out to a muddy field. A representative from the Naturalization Service talked to us who were not American citizens. Thus, I became an American citizen while fighting for my new country.

I was assigned to a group that worked with POWs from then on, Germans and Italians. They were like Americans. They ran the gamut as far as professionals. People from farmers to men who had jobs in industry. No trouble. One night an Italian tried to escape. They caught him. He couldn't get very far. They were in an area compound. We took over an old plant or factory. A camp. They ate just like the GIs, the same food.

I did the same thing in France. I was sent to the camp of POWs. They needed one [like me]. I understood German. I didn't speak it fluently. I spoke French. They had a lot of POWs. I picked up German from the POWs. We had roll calls and did bed checks. One guy was missing. We decided . . . we'll wait until tomorrow morning. We'll go look for him. We went and couldn't find him. He was German. We were out in the country. He had gone to see a girlfriend.

We had them working in the plant. This was an aviation plant, a refinery. He came back. He couldn't go anywhere. Anywhere he went, he was AWOL (Absent With Out Leave). This was better for him. He was blond and blue-eyed. He couldn't blend in Southern France. Corsica is this island. And they are very dark. They say, "You're the son of a Corsican." Dark.

I went to Balaton in France. That's the place where I spent most of the time. Actually, in Provence. Same thing. From then on that was it. I was taken out of the group there and drafted to go to the Bulge [Battle of the Bulge]. They needed men down there.

The captain wanted me to stay with them, and I was the only bilingual person working with the POWs in France in Balaton. He did everything in the world. He said, "You can hardly see, Al." I said, "Yes sir, I understand but . . ." I was on a train in a cattle car, and we were leaving in a station in Marseille. He [the captain] said, "You wouldn't happen to have your prescription for your glasses?" I said, "I sure have." He said, "Let me have it." So he was gone. We were already on board the train. He finally came back. I don't know what he did, but he finally got me off. I went back to what I was doing before. I was almost blind [without glasses]. I was a technical sergeant and had a captain over me.

We had prisoners coming in and going out. I would choose one of our men to go escort the Italians back to Italy, POWs. We had too many prisoners. They were released because Italy's war was over. Mussolini. Captain Randolph Pierce came in. He came from Boston. He came in and said, "The war is over. There is going to be a declaration. And we are all going to Marseille."

I happened to be with a small group. Very few guys there in the company. We were a very close group. We were taken by the captain to Marseille. Marseille happens to be where I went to celebrate the end of the war.

I came back in the middle of the year—June or July. I was discharged on February 10, 1946. I came back to Houston.

After Alfred Hernandez returned from his duty with the army, he became an attorney and practiced in Houston, Texas. However, he did not limit his activities to practicing law. He became active in an effort to change laws and practices to benefit Mexican Americans. He worked through LULAC (League of United Latin American Citizens), eventually becoming its president.

Dr. Hector P. García
Founder of the American GI Forum

Having to Prove He Was an MD

Books and articles have been written about Dr. Hector García. He learned a great deal in the army during WWII. He utilized this experience and his natural skills to aid returning Hispanic veterans from the war, veterans who wanted the same rights and benefits accorded to other US veterans. He rose to become a national figure as the founder and leader of the American GI Forum, an organization established to fight for these rights for all Hispanic veterans. The following text was taken from an interview with his daughter, Cecilia Garcia Akers.

Like many other immigrants, Hector's family fled the Mexican Revolution of 1910-1920. He and his siblings were raised in Mercedes, Texas. He attended Pan American University in Brownsville, Texas, then transferred to the University of Texas, where he graduated in the top 10 percent of his class.

He attended the University of Texas Medical School, which accepted only one Mexican American student a year. After graduating in 1940, he attempted to get a residency, but was refused time and time again. Finally Creighton University in Omaha, Nebraska, offered him a two-year residency in General Surgery.

One year into his residency Hector was drafted into the army. The draft board allowed him time to finish his residency, however, and he earned his certificate. Because he had participated in ROTC (Reserve Officers' Training Corps) in high school, that credit helped earn him the rank of second lieutenant.

The army, however, did not believe he was a medical doctor. His assignment: the infantry. After his medical school verified the authenticity of his certificate, the army sent him to the Medical Corps in Italy.

After the war, the young doctor met and married Wanda Fusillo, a native of Italy, and they settled in Corpus Christi, Texas. There Dr. García saw the need to assist veterans of the war in which they had all participated. He knew firsthand the hardships and sacrifices the men had made. It was only fair that these men be given every opportunity afforded all veterans. Initially, that was the purpose of the American GI Forum. Eventually, other issues were addressed, with great emphasis on education. The organization has helped many a soldier in meeting his goals.

Raymond Ramirez
705th Bomb Squadron

Determined to Join Up
One does not often hear this, but Raymond begged to join the service. While the army folks were reluctant at first, they finally accepted the young man who was eager to fight for his new country. Raymond Ramirez was born in Mexico to Panchita and Enrique Ramirez. While living in Robstown, Texas, Raymond, known as "Nito" to his family, wanted to join the army in 1942. He had been born in Monterrey, Mexico, and the sergeant to whom he spoke said he would not be allowed because he didn't have citizenship papers.

I wanted to join up desperately. The sergeant made a call to the consulate office. They responded by saying to take me because Mexico would be sending soldiers to join the Allies anyway. Eventually they sent troops in Squadron 201. It became a bombing group from Mexico [The Flying Aztecs].

Training was in San Antonio. I loved the service and placed first among the men in training. I earned my first stripe there.

When I arrived in England I was assigned to a bombing group. I was one of the cooks. Although I was a cook for the group, I also had to know how to handle a gun. At night, all the soldiers had to take turns or shifts guarding the airplanes. We had machine guns and rifles, but could not use them because if we fired, we would give away our positions and the valuable airplanes would be destroyed.

At one point there was word that the Germans were going to invade England, and that Germans were going to be dropped from airplanes. We were given only forty bullets each and were told not to be wasteful with the bullets. "Don't shoot unless you can hit to kill," we were told. Meanwhile, Allied airplanes were sent to shoot any incoming German planes. The invasion never happened.

One time while walking by a POW camp, a prisoner called me over. The prisoner was Italian, and since Italian and Spanish are similar, we were able to communicate. The prisoner wanted a cigarette. I had accumulated three packages. I didn't smoke, but I could use them for trading purposes. The Italian offered to give me a handmade aluminum cigarette holder for a cigarette. I saw it and gave him all three packages. The cigarette holder had inscribed the following words: HARDEST DAYS OF MY LIFE. It was written in Italian, but since I knew Spanish, I could read and understand the inscription.

Although I didn't know how to gamble when I joined the service, I learned how and became good or lucky at it. I often sent money home to my mother, who needed it. I "broke" some gambling games. For many servicemen, it was something to do to pass the time. When I ran out of money, which was rare, a friend, Layton Harris, lent me money to gamble. I was considered a lucky player.

My bombing group flew B-24s. One morning at 1:00 a.m. I heard a loud noise. A bomb was sitting at the base of a tree behind the Quonset hut where I was staying. It was a dud. The hundred-pound bomb didn't go off. The Germans had POWs working in factories where the bombs were being assembled. The POWs were apparently putting bread dough between the firing pin and the mechanism that discharged it. Thus, unknown to the Germans, their airplanes were dropping some bombs that were duds.

I was in a B-24 that was forced to crash-land. Three motors had failed and the one motor it had left wasn't sufficient to keep it from hitting a bomb crater on the runway. The first sergeant was seriously hurt. I hurt my back. I was flown back to the states in a full body cast, front and back. I had been overseas for three years!

I understood that when I recuperated, I was to be sent to the Pacific theater to fight in that war. One day while still recuperating, an announcement came over the radio. JAPAN HAD SURRENDERED. I yelled to my mother to come and listen to the radio. Then we both cried, because we both understood that for me and for everyone, the war was over. We went to church to give thanks to God!

Armando Flores
Army Air Corps

A Medical Problem Interfered
Armando Flores was born in Mission, Texas, on September 17, 1921. He came to Corpus Christi in 1929. Armando, whose family traced their presence in this country two hundred years back, was proud of both his background and this country. He worked hard and looked forward to defending the United States of America. He and his friends joined as quickly as they could.

I am of the original Land Grant people that came here in the 1750s. *Porción*—which we call section now—thirty-eight, thirty-nine, and forty belonged to my great-great-grandfather. His name was José Antonio Flores.

I attended Cheston Heath School, the segregated school. From 1896 to 1919 the school was known as the Ward Four School for Mexican Children. Cheston Heath was not named Cheston Heath until 1919 when we had that storm here.

We came in 1929. I am the only one—me and my sister are the only "city slickers" in my family. All my brothers and sisters were born on the Pinto Ranch. I had a doctor when I was born. Eventually one of my sisters moved to Corpus Christi—Rose, the older sister. She would visit us and say, "Why don't you move to Corpus Christi? Corpus Christi is a big town."

There were thirty-five thousand people when we moved here in Corpus Christi in 1929. Cheston Heath was 99 percent Hispanic. Most of my friends were there, most of my friends I grew up with, most of my friends who went to the army.

No one told us it [Cheston Heath] was a segregated school. We just knew it as a matter of fact. Everybody said, "*Anda a la escuela de los mejicanos-la raza.*" (He/she attends the school for the Mexican [Hispanic] race.) They were indoctrinated. Do you want to go to school? You go to Cheston Heath.

I went to Miller, which is now Roy Miller High School. It was great. I was with all my friends. By that time we had been integrated due to circumstances, so we all went together. All the students were either Hispanics, Lebanese, Syrian, Irish, German—you name it. We got to know everybody. We played football with them and everything like that.

[When asked about playing football] I had to work. I graduated from high school in May 1941.

My last two-and-a-half years of high school I worked for Western Union. But working for Western Union was a big leap in my life. They paid $.30 an hour, twelve hours a week. And if you could sing Happy Birthday, you'd make a quarter extra. So I was a singing [telegram], myself and Gilbert Casares, and a lot of those other fellows. We would fight for those kind of telegrams.

When the war started I was riding a bicycle down Leopard Street on December 7, 1941. Many of the guys who had graduated with me were in front of the "Chat 'n Chew" [restaurant], which is right there where the city hall is. I was loaded down with a bunch of packages, and the guys yelled at me, "Hey, now we can enlist. Let's get ready to go." And three weeks later I was in the service. I enlisted, just like that. In fact, a very good friend of mine and I enlisted together. He is still alive. He's eighty-two already. I'll be eighty-two in September. It was January 15, 1942.

Harry Ogg, a personal friend of mine, was writing letters to me from Pearl Harbor. And he was there when . . . [the Japanese attacked]. He's here in town. He's quite a guy. He is one of the Pearl Harbor survivors. The Guien boy was there. Mike Acuña, my brother-in-law by marriage, was there at Pearl Harbor and Harry Ogg. They were knocked into the sea.

I wanted to go to the air force. We wanted to be machine gunners like James Cagney. We didn't know any better. We thought it was going to be some fun. A big deal.

I ended up in basic training in San Antonio with the US Air Corps, Army Air Corps, which became the Air Force. San Antonio is the Eighth Corps Area for military identification. For anyone who enlisted in that time our serial number would be eighteen. I'm 18102108. My friend who enlisted with me is 18102116. I'm Flores; he is Gonzalez. There were eight guys between us. He says, "Do you remember me?" I tell him, "I even know your serial number." And he knows mine.

Then it was basic training at Sheppard Field, Texas, in Wichita Falls. And that's where I first had that deal when they called me "an American."

Most of the guys who were there [training] were Hispanics from South Texas. They had never been called Americans. Here was this lieutenant on the platform telling us—it was a very, very cold day in February, very cold—and we were there just in our overalls. We had forgotten to get our coats on. We get up there in formation and we had to do calisthenics. So the deal was . . . this lieutenant gets up there and says, "American soldiers don't huddle and put their hands in their pockets on a cold day. They stand at attention." And we stood at attention.

All of a sudden the buzz went up and down the line—"Hey"—this was in Spanish—"Hey, they called us Americans." [Flores laughs joyfully.] Because we never thought about things like that. It's just a shock. It was really something. We felt a little better.

We took exams and all that kind of thing. They want to find out how smart you are. I ended up being sent to an Armament School in Lowery Field in Denver, Colorado.

Load the bombs, take care of the armory and the machines and the machine guns and the bomb bays. It's a school there, and I think the school is still there in Denver, Colorado. [I learned] armament about bombs, how they work and how to fuse them and how to put them together and all that kind of stuff. And, of course, that is when I had a little mishap.

By mishap, I contracted rheumatic fever. I had never been sick a day in my life. I went out there like a dodo and played in the snow, sometimes barefooted, played football and got sore throats and came down with an awful fever. But I thought it was just a cold. And one day I passed out in ranks and I ended up in the hospital.

Believe it or not a few months later they said, "Hey, that's rheumatic fever," after being months in the hospital. I came out with a disability discharge, because the rheumatic fever had affected my heart.

With rheumatic fever the heart gets bigger, expands, and you are supposed to die at the age of thirty-five. And here I am eighty-two right now.

In spite of Armando's eagerness to fight in WWII, illness prevented him from fighting. Armando Flores married and had four children. Three graduated from the University of Texas and one child graduated from the University of Colorado.

Gilbert Oropez
531st Antiaircraft Battalion

Overcoming Bitterness
Gilbert Oropez is a longtime citizen of the state of Texas. As a young boy, Gilbert witnessed some unfair discrimination against his family and especially against his father. What he saw as a boy made him a bitter young man. His experiences in the army cured him of the bitterness, because he saw buddies fight against the enemy and protect each other.

My father was a fisherman while his uncles farmed. I quit school after the third grade and worked at picking cotton and farming. I spoke broken English at this time.

As a young boy I witnessed incidents of discrimination that turned me into an angry and bitter young man. My father was a simple man. He fished to earn money to feed his family. He went to the bay here in Corpus Christi and collected oysters. By 6:00 a.m. he was already collecting oysters. Then he shucked them and placed them in a bucket to sell. When he went downtown to sell his oysters, the so-called inspectors went up to him, took his bucket, and threw the oysters on the sidewalk. They did this because the fish houses were making complaints that the Mexican was taking business away from them. Look what they did to my dad. I saw that happen and it made me very angry! Also, I saw people selling candy and products on Leopard Street, and they closed them down. These folks were doing what they do in New York. But they stopped the people here because they were Mexican.

Then my father and his two brothers owned thirty-eight acres on an island which now has Texas A&M on it. A white man bought a house somewhere and wanted to put it on my father's property. My father said he couldn't, so the man put the house outside our property line. It stayed there for a month. One night the man and others put the house on our property. My father went to the courthouse and they told him, "You've got to hire a lawyer." How could my father hire a lawyer when he barely had money to feed us? After that, the man moved his house on to our property, and he always had a rifle on him. My grandmother used to tell my father, "Get off that land. Do you want that man to kill you? What is your wife going to do with all these children? It is just dirt, so leave it."

When we went out my father tied two mules to the back of the wagon and two mules to pull the wagon. My mother and my sister were on top of the wagon. We were going out of the ranch. My older brother and another brother and I were walking alongside the wagon. My father led horses to the main road. When we hit the main street, then we got on the wagon. We used to call that the ranch. My uncles never left the ranch. That's the way it was. So when I grew up, I was upset.

I was drafted in 1942. Since before the bombing of Pearl Harbor, single men were the first to be drafted. By 1942 I was married and had a child and another one on the way. Even so, I was drafted.

My mother gave me *la bendición* in our home, and she also gave me a medallion, which featured the face of Jesus Christ.

After visiting the induction center at Fort Sam Houston in San Antonio, Texas, I traveled to Camp Callan in California. It was there that I, with my experiences of discrimination, fought some other soldiers more than once. Sixto Aguilar from El Paso, Texas, and I were the only Mexican American men among this group of soldiers, and Sixto stuck with me because I knew how to defend myself. And then all of us became the best of friends.

A troop train took us to the Mojave Desert. I mean it was so hot and we marched and marched. I think they were training us to go to North Africa. We stayed there six to eight months. We dug holes and put the cannons in, pulled them out, dug another hole and did it again. We went on maneuvers. Our trucks would get stuck in the sand. We had to get out and dig trenches and push the trucks. Sometimes a half-track would help us out. At 3:00 a.m. we would still be pushing the truck.

We went to a place in Virginia, not a camp. We were under some pine trees. We were on our way. We pitched our pup tents and during the night it poured and the water began to come in. The next day they brought in cots. When we went to bed, it rained again. I put my blankets and my raincoat over me and the water still got in and I could feel the water on my back. We were soaking wet.

We went to Boston, Massachusetts. We sailed on the *Empress of Australia* to Liverpool, England. At night a train took us to Reading, England.

When the D-day invasion started on June 6, 1945, I was put on a ship at Southampton. Now I was with the Thirtieth Infantry Division. Around 3:00 or 4:00 p.m. they took us across the English Channel to France. That was Omaha Beach. The Germans put a lot of obstacles out there. I feel sorry for the Twenty-Ninth Division. They were in the first wave and that was a suicide mission.

There were still snipers when we got off the boat. I think they were suicide snipers that they left behind. They were used to delay us in moving. At the beginning there was walking. A lot of the Germans pulled back. Then they put us in a truck and took us over there. We were fighting in towns: Cherbourg. So many things happened, I tried to put them behind me.

You could see dead soldiers floating in the water. Before we left they told us, "You will remember today, but I guarantee you will never forget tomorrow." We didn't know what they were talking about. They were talking about the invasion. We were under Omar Bradley. He used to come and talk to us.

The soldiers that climbed up the hill used the bayonets and butts of the rifles to climb up. I thought it was pretty brave of one young man . . . when the fighting was going on, a young soldier climbed on top of a pillbox and threw grenades into the pillbox.

One of the first cities we went to was Paris. We walked under the Eiffel Tower.

Battle of the Bulge. St. Lô. Only one church was left standing in that town. The town was demolished.

We had missiles coming toward us. You hear the whistling sound and you don't know where it is going to hit. The Germans also used the V2, the plane without a pilot. The Germans calculated how much fuel it would take for the plane to reach the target—us—and the plane would go down and explode. I saw a brave act by an American pilot. A V2 airplane would be coming toward us and the Americans found out that if they could get under one of the wings, they could guide it elsewhere away from the American soldiers and then the V2 would explode elsewhere. I saw an American pilot do that.

We were being bombarded by artillery shells. A shell came and hit the tree, so I tried to roll out. The tree came down and hit me on the head, but I never reported it. I got cut but we were on the move. That was in Belgium.

You always have a buddy and you see other soldiers, but you don't know who they are. There was a ditch and a man who was not in the ditch got shot. He was hollering for help. Another buddy was there in the ditch. He jumped out and grabbed the injured man by the feet and dragged him to safety. While he was doing that a machine gun hit both of them. I grabbed the one who was trying to save the first man and I pulled him into the ditch. Another friend helped me. He was shot so bad that he didn't last long. I heard young boys say, "Mother," just before they died. He died trying to help a friend. He was a hero. He didn't have to die. They both died. I wish I knew who they were.

I didn't go into Germany. I went to the Rhine. I didn't fight there. The Americans were afraid of the German tanks. Many German tanks were abandoned because they didn't have parts for them. I felt sorry for the young German soldiers. They didn't want to fight. You could see it in their faces.

They took a group of us soldiers and brought us all the way to Paris. There were still some snipers in Paris. Then it was back to England and then back to the United States.

I came back to C.C. after the war. I got a job doing construction work. I wanted to buy a house. I went to the Veterans Administration. They told me I needed a paid lot. I purchased a lot. Two years later and I went back to the VA. Have to have the prints and the contractor to agree to build the house. We're already building houses for the GIs. Go talk to the man in charge. I went. I selected a house. We went back to the VA. I had three children and one on the way. I told them I had selected a house. How much? I was making $30 a week. They said, "You don't qualify for a loan."

Since I was in the construction business. . . . A friend said, "That's a bunch of bull. Why don't you build it yourself?" "Where's the money?" "A bank will lend you enough money and you can make small payments. We can help you. You can do some of this yourself." They helped me. I had to get lumber on credit. I paid for that. Some people helped me and they left. I knew enough that once I had the frame, I continued doing it. My house is at 1526 South Nineteenth Street.

Celia (hurricane) came and some houses fell and my house is still standing. My family kept growing. I continued working on the house. When I moved into the house, I didn't have sheetrock in. A plumber gave me credit. An electrician helped me. My children began to grow, so that if I said "Hold this, honey," they would help me. I stood on a bench and hammered the ceiling on.

My wife was always working. She was a wonderful wife. She could paint, cut. I had seven children—me and my wife. I never earned more than three dollars an hour. I never was on welfare. I am so against welfare. They can get a job.

Gilbert Oropez, a veteran, a hero, and an independent man, became supportive of the American GI Forum and its leader, Dr. Hector P. García.

Pfc. Alejandro Rivera
70th Division (Replacement)

Not My Time to Go

Alejandro Rivera's parents arrived from Mexico in 1914, at the height of the Mexican Revolution, to earn some money. They returned to Mexico and then came back to Texas to stay. Alejandro was born in Rogers, Texas. By the grace of God, Alejandro lived through the war. His brother did not. Alejandro was on guard duty and was replaced by another young soldier. A few minutes later, the young replacement was shot and killed.

My family picked cotton in Texas, Oklahoma, and Louisiana. In September of 1944, I received my draft notice. I wasn't supposed to be drafted. There was supposed to be just one [in the service] in a family. There were three boys in the family. Then they started calling everyone. Among the Anglos if there were two sons, only one went, and later all the Mexicans [Mexican Americans] were going to go. If there were two [sons], they took the two. If there were three, they took two or three. The Hernandez family had three sons and three went.

They didn't take my father in the service because of all the family he had.

My grandmother Guadalupe Lopez [gave me the blessing]. My mother did also. Every day they gave us the blessing whenever we left the house.

From San Antonio to Camp Claiborne, Louisiana. They needed more battery. They sent me to Camp Maxie in Paris, Texas. Six weeks of infantry training and then overseas.

When my brother died, they wouldn't give me a leave. So the captain asked me if I promised to come back and I said, "Yes." He had been with the camp for just a few days. The captain gave me a pass from Camp Maxie to Dallas and then another from Dallas to here [Cameron, Texas], with the promise that I would be back the next day. I went late in the evening to Dallas. In Dallas I took the bus at 8:00 or 9:00 at night. I returned the next day. They brought him [José's body] later. I came in to see my momma after they notified her that he was killed.

I wanted to go overseas, and I didn't have to go overseas. My captain told me I didn't have to go overseas because there were just two males in our family and he [brother] had gotten killed. So I could serve anywhere besides France in the war.

I knew I couldn't get my brother back, but you don't think. I wanted to go overseas, so I went overseas. I went as a replacement wherever they lacked men.

I shipped out in the spring and arrived in France with a convoy of sixty-five ships, accompanied with two destroyers in front and one destroyer in the rear. Besides soldiers, the ships carried equipment, food, supplies, etc. for the war. The smell at the beaches was still awful. They only had a certain place to land.

We went by trucks in France to the distribution centers. From there we went to Germany by train. I joined the Seventieth Division there. I don't remember his name, but this white boy . . . we used to eat together. He got killed. I was looking to replace someone in the division who had just gotten in from the front for a rest. We were doing guard, guarding bridges, the Rhine River, railroads and different things. The soldier I ate with replaced me. After four or six hours, he got shot through his head. Five minutes' difference! It wasn't too far from where I was staying, the overpass that I was guarding. So he relieved me, and as I got to the house where we were staying, a soldier drove up and said that a guy had been shot. We went right back, and it was him, the one who relieved me. It could have been me, but it wasn't my time. That's the way I see it. That was in Germany. We were away from the Rhine River then.

First, when I joined the Seventieth Division we were guarding the Rhine River. From there on we got relieved. Somebody else came over and took over and we left for different places where we were guarding bridges and everything.

They [Germans] had the eighty-eight rockets. I was back from the front. That division was in the front so long that they pulled the division back and put another division in. And the division they pulled back was doing the guarding and all that.

When I got into Germany there was a convoy getting out. And Basaldua, he was from Corpus Christi, Texas. We took training together. He recognized me as I was coming in and said, "Rivera." When he called me Rivera, I recognized his voice right away. He said, "Wait for me, because we are headed toward the front." Some of the men I trained with went to replace men at the front lines. Depends on luck as to where you are replacing; if you are replacing someone in the back or you have to go all the way to the front lines.

We [Basaldua and I] took training together. I've got a picture of one of those outfits when Cameron was one hundred years old. He was in Fort Hood. He came in to march with the soldiers. We got so drunk, it's the first time I ever passed out. I was pretty loaded. My sister picked me up and dropped me off. My momma, we couldn't, you know we respected her. She [sister] took me over to another street and dropped me off under a big tree and went and got another one of my buddies to stay with me until I was okay.

I was twenty-one [when called] on account of the farm. There was no work, so I went to Houston to work and told the woman to let my uncle know as soon as they had something to do, I would come back. The owner, John Henderson [farmer], turned me in. He said I wasn't working anymore. So I went to Houston on a Saturday, Sunday; Monday I went to apply for a job, and I got a job. I worked Monday, Tuesday, and Wednesday. I got a letter Wednesday to report back to Cameron.

The majority of the Blacks were quartermasters, drivers. They passed themselves off as American Indians. This is when we had a problem. We tried to make love to the German girls, and they were already involved with the colored ones. We told them [German girls] they were colored and they said, "No, they're American Indians." We were fighting for the women. The German girls were pretty. Real nice.

We were living in their houses. They had to move out. They forced the people occupying the homes out. We had our own K rations. Those of us who were in the back, not at the front, had our own kitchen. The company had its own kitchen. Not very good cooks. We'd get one slice of bread a day. We didn't get enough. The coffee grounds, the Germans had picked them up and reboiled them. They had oxen. They didn't have mules or horses. They had cows. We milked the cows.

A lot of people don't believe that officers were at times killed by their own men.

It was a whole lot different with the officers here in the States. They were real strict here in the States. But as soon as we went away—overseas—everybody is the same. One officer got killed by his own people. Only divisions went on with their own officers. With replacements they divided the officers from one place to another outfit.

I had a buddy of mine, Raymond Ramón, from San Antonio. He was fighting and when they captured Germans, prisoners, they wouldn't take them in. He told me that. The Germans were prisoners. They made them run for any reason. They started running and they started shooting them. Because they didn't want to be messing with them. He would tell me. I doubted it. We used to tell him, "If they ever find that out . . . "

If I ever made it to the front I was [to be] the ammunition carrier for the mortar squad—60mm. When I got overseas, first they issued me a rifle. Then they took my rifle away and gave me a .45, because I was the ammunition carrier. Carried on my back. Pretty heavy. I weighed 167 pounds. A full field pack was seventy-five pounds. You set it on the ground.

Germany surrendered in May. As soon as Germany surrendered all "lower" pointers came back to the States. I didn't have but twenty points. All lower pointers came to the States for forty-five days on vacation, I guess before they went to Japan. I refused to go to Japan.

They had a lot of deer. We did kill one, but it was at nighttime. You see, nobody was supposed to have any ammunition. This was after the war. But I had ammunition on my .45 pistol. I used to keep two clips. The lieutenant killed the deer. You see he had ammunition but not us. I left that morning. They had to butcher it that night and throw all the guts and everything away so they wouldn't find out. So the lieutenant said, "Anybody got any ammunition?" Nobody had any. I said, "Yes, I've got some."

He said, "Let me have it." So I gave him a clip. And then he shot it [the deer] with that clip. The next morning he called me in. He wanted to know how come I had ammunition. I said, "I'm protecting my life, Sir." He said, "Do you know what will happen to you if you get caught?" I said, "I know what's going to happen to me. Court martial." The lieutenant said, "What about your other clip?" "I'm going to keep it." He said, "Well, you know what's going to happen."

"You don't know nothing about it," I said. "I can't say that you knew about it."

Japan surrendered and I was here alone [in Cameron, Texas]. I was walking in town when everybody started hollering. I didn't know what it was. Someone told me that Japan had surrendered.

He [Basaldua] came back. He got discharged. He's about my age.

I had letters, you know. That's the reason I say I volunteered to go overseas. I wasn't supposed to go overseas. I just sent my letters to Washington [regarding going to Japan during the war, after Europe].

I had a friend of mine who was a prisoner in Japan. When he got captured he weighed 240. And then he was in prison camp until they sent him back to the States, because he was in bad health. He weighed seventy-five pounds. He is still alive. He is Jack___.

We weren't supposed to [mingle with the Germans]. We did anyway. They [German girls] wanted to marry you right away, because they wanted to come to the States. We traded with them. We used to cook at nighttime. We traded for eggs and bacon. You couldn't do nothing in daytime.

Pfc. Guadalupe Almendarez
9th Infantry Division

Be a Good Soldier! Don't be a Coward!
Guadalupe Almendarez was born in Skidmore, Texas, on June 18, 1918. He finished the eighth grade and terminated his education. As threats of war loomed over this country, the draft began. Guadalupe was drafted before Pearl Harbor was bombed. His father encouraged him to be a good soldier, while his mother couldn't be comforted.

I was drafted and inducted on November 6, 1941. I was in the first group to be drafted from Bee County. Before I left I sat down with my mother and father. My father told me, "Be a good soldier. Don't be a coward!" My mother cried the whole time we said goodbye.

When Pearl Harbor was bombed, I was at Fort Sam Houston. I went through basic training at Camp Wolters located near Dallas, Texas. From there I was sent to Ft. Bragg, North Carolina, for further training.

Finally, we were sent to Staten Island, New York, and we boarded a ship headed for Europe. Because it was in the winter, it was a dreadful trip. A storm in the Atlantic Ocean rocked the ship severely from one end to the other. There was no way a person could even stand on the deck.

The ship docked at Belfast, Ireland, and the soldiers stayed on the ship. From there I saw land I had never seen before. After two or three days we were taken to England. In Manchester, England, American and British forces trained together. The British soldiers attempted to impress the American soldiers by doing such things as jumping down from buildings with full field packs. The American troops were taught how to use hand grenades with their hands and with M1 launcher rifles. We also had to climb ropes that were twelve feet long and we had to run twelve to fourteen miles a day. Some men fell over from exhaustion.

From Manchester we were taken to Algiers in North Africa. And we were not told anything. We arrived at around 5:00 or 6:00 p.m. We spent our first Christmas away from home eating turkey dinners in Algiers. I remember the Arabs as being friendly, but they seemed to fear the Americans. Because I am olive-complexioned, I was often asked, "Are you an Arab?" by the Arabs, but in Arabic. Finally someone told me what they were asking.

Meanwhile the Germans shot flares up into the sky at night to see where we were located. At night we would be in foxholes, which were dug into the sand. Once, a tank ran over my foxhole, but I didn't get hurt because the hole was deep. Also, it was very hot.

I remember the American artillery stopping German tanks and the tanks retreating in the heat of the battle. In Tunisia I ended up with shrapnel in my left arm. I had to undergo surgery in my left hand and wrist.

While in the hospital in Manchester, England, a famous visitor appeared. A rough-talking loud voice asked me, "How are you doing, soldier?"

"Okay," I answered.

General Patton continued visiting with the other soldiers who responded in the same manner. He arrived at the cot of a young boy and asked the same question, "How are you doing soldier?"

The young boy began crying and answered, "I want to go home." At that point General Patton slapped the boy and said, "And you will."

After I healed, I was returned to action. This time it was to Palermo, Sicily. There I didn't see much fighting. We were sent back to London. Something big was brewing.

A lieutenant told us, "We are all soldiers. Keep your eyes open. And take care of your buddy!" There were many divisions stationed there, so that the soldiers were aware that some big activity was about to occur.

We were taken on a big ship and then placed on a smaller landing craft. We were taken to Omaha Beach! During the landing we held on to each other's shoulders because of holes in the sand under our feet.

It was very early in the morning. The Germans shot flares up into the sky so that they could see the Americans better. I was shot in my left leg and was sent to a hospital.

When I returned to the action the men were already on their way to Paris. They found a river but without a bridge. So they built a bridge using fifty-five gallon drums. Then trucks drove right over the makeshift bridge.

Since the action was ahead on us, I was able to ride in a truck into Paris. Some German snipers had remained and had to be taken care of.

As we got closer to the Germans, we went on foot. Outside of a town in France, we ran into a winery. A large barrel was spotted. The captain told us not to try to drink the wine because it might be a trap and the wine could be poisoned.

My best friend during this time was Billy Sunday King from Nashville, Tennessee. We were like brothers. Often Billy would say, "Sing me a song, Amigo."

I would tell him, "But I can't sing."

Then Billy would say, "Well, just sing *El Rancho Grande*."

So I and my best friend Billy Sunday King decided to risk it and drink the wine. We drank the wine and enjoyed it; it wasn't poisoned after all.

One night Billy and I were told to patrol. By now we were in the Ardennes Forest. We came so close to the Germans that we could hear them walking and even talking. When we heard the Germans nearby, we would freeze in our tracks. We went back to headquarters and reported that the Germans were nearby.

Fighting broke out the next day. There was a path in the Ardennes that was about eight to ten feet wide. The path made a sharp right turn. I was walking on the path and when I got to the right turn I realized that a line of German tanks were coming down that trail. I took my grenade launcher and angled it just the way I had been trained in England aiming to hit the first tank. The grenade hit the tank and destroyed the tracks, rendering it useless. The tank began spinning in a circle. The tanks following the lead tank ran into the rear of the tanks in front of them. Since the path was narrow and the forest was thick with trees, the remaining tanks had no choice but to turn back.

A few days later the lieutenant who was in charge was promoted to captain! My actions were never recognized.

We arrived at the famous Siegfried Line. Patton and his tanks were there, as was the infantry. In an effort to get through, Patton ordered a tank to break the gates down. After several failed attempts, General Patton suggested the soldiers climb over the tanks to get past the Siegfried Line. Meanwhile the general stood atop a small hill and said, "I can see the SOBs in there." Bullets whizzed all around him but never hit him.

The tank kept ramming until it broke down the gate. We ran in with our rifles ready for another battle. I was shot in my right foot. This time this injury would not allow me to return to battle. I was sent home.

The young man from the tiny town of Skidmore, Texas, had been in seven campaigns and was injured three times.

Yrineo Peña
756th Tank Battalion

A Fighter in a Tank
Yrineo Peña, a young man from the small town of Falfurrias, Texas, had absolutely no idea where he would end up when he entered the service. He started off as a tank driver and ended up as a tank commander.

I was now twenty-one years old. I was sworn into the service in El Paso and sent to Camp Roberts in California to train for the infantry. For ninety days I drilled in parades, went over a bridge with full field pack, went to the woods for maneuvers, hiked in the rain, waded through water with only one uniform and one pair of shoes.

From Camp Roberts I went to Fort Lewis located near Olympia and Seattle, Washington; there I was selected to be in a tank battalion. In training for tank warfare five men would be assigned one of the following roles: assistant driver, driver, loader, gunner, and tank commander. We trained without tanks at first but used two by fours and sat in positions. The tank commander was to stand in the back and signal the driver with his foot to go either left or right.

Finally, we were able to practice for three months on real tanks at Fort Ord in California.

Virginia was the point of embarkation, with Casablanca in North Africa being the destination. It was November 8, 1942, when we made an amphibious landing. The tanks had shrouds on them to keep the motors from getting wet.

We knew nothing until we were in the boats. After landing on the sand, some tanks were stuck. Because of the violence of the waves in the water, the gun on one of the tanks hit the side of another tank. The recoil on the gun was stuck. With only one machine gun on top, the tank was virtually disabled. My job, along with some buddies, was to help the disabled tanks and put them back into working order.

The first night I was assigned to guard the ammunition and fuel dump. I spent the night at the dump. The next morning an Arab was staring at me and asking me in his limited English, "Cigarettes? Chocolate?"

The next day we went to see about a tank which had a broken track. Airplanes, meanwhile, were flying and shooting at us. We were, quite naturally, frightened as it was the first experience we had of someone trying to kill us. So there we were dodging bullets, and trying to fix the track on the tank when a man with two pearl-handled pistols stops and says to the lieutenant in charge, "Don't you know how to salute?" Then he added as he looked at the new recruits, "Are you scared?"

No one answered General George Patton. Meanwhile the men happened to look toward the water and saw dead bodies floating in the water. Patton said, "They're not afraid anymore." Then he suggested that someone get an apparatus to place under the tank track. The tank was repaired successfully.

Our group fought all the way to Algiers. Then we, who had been trained to invade Italy, fought all the way to Southern France. The 756th Tank Battalion supported the Thirty-Fourth and Forty-Fifth Infantries. My tank was named "Adiós," which means goodbye.

The 756th Tank Battalion fought in Cassino for forty-five days. Because of the Normandy invasion, the 756th experienced some relief as some

Axis soldiers had left to support the Nazis at Normandy.

In Southern France the tank commander was looking out through the hatch of the tank. A sniper immediately shot the tank commander in the head and killed him. I decided to climb up to see who had killed the tank commander when a buddy in the tank grabbed me and pulled me down, thereby saving my life.

The "Adiós" went down the road and up an embankment and turned over. It was pure bad driving on the part of the tank driver. We had to wait for someone to help us upright the tank. It became dark, and we slept on the ground. Since no one had come in the morning when we woke up, the men decided that one of them needed to go into the last town we had passed to see if they could get help.

I took my rifle and went for help. As I went down the road I saw two soldiers sitting on a log. They spotted me at the same time as I saw them. So I wondered what was going to happen since I was outnumbered. The two men were Germans and they immediately surrendered to me. I took them back with me and when an infantry unit came by, they picked up the two German prisoners.

Ironically enough, the driver of the tank ran off and was never seen again!

On another occasion the tank commander asked the driver to back up. There was a drop causing the tank to fall backwards and upside down. We crawled out and started running as we were being fired at by the enemy. A grenade hit nearby and caused me to lose some teeth. I ran to the other side of the road. The commanding general, known as "Iron Mike," sent someone to take me so that I could be taken care of.

I was returned to the front lines. Again, we fought all the way to Germany. In Nuremberg, the "Adiós" tank was fourth in line as the five tanks were parked on a street. Someone fired a bazooka in the area near the track of the tank where the tank was vulnerable. The tank exploded and burned my hands and face. The tank commander died instantly. I opened up the hatch and jumped out. As I looked at my buddy who jumped out after me, I noticed the man's ears were missing. After that I never saw the other members of my tank.

I was sent to a first aid station in Nuremberg where I heard a nurse tell someone, "As soon as a plane comes, put him on it." I felt very sick.

I arrived in France at a hospital that had many wounded soldiers and no mirrors for anyone to look at himself. The men in a tank are always looking dirty, greasy, oily, sweaty, and in my case, very bloody!

When I arrived at the hospital, in addition to feeling very sick, I must have looked awful. There was a young man all dressed up in full uniform and apparently now healed from whatever wounds or injuries he had had. He looked at me and said, "They want to send me to infantry. I don't want to go. If I looked like you, I'd shoot myself." Only my wounds kept me from getting up and hitting the soldier.

I was taken to England where there were rows and rows of wounded soldiers. The man in the bed next to me had been in an airplane fire and had been burned all over his body. His feet had been burned down until they appeared to be the size of the feet of a small child.

All of a sudden music was heard, wonderful music, and girls had come to the hospital to entertain the soldiers. The young man in the bed next to me arose, put on shoes over his bandaged feet, and went to dance with the girls. It was at that very moment that I thought to myself, if he can do that, I know that I, too, can make it! I will be all right! The unknown soldier in that bed gave me hope that I had not experienced before!

My combat suit with its quarter-inch thickness had helped me when fire broke out in the tank. As I was healing, however, I had thick bandages around my head and hands.

After spending time in North Hampton, England, at a burn unit, I was taken to El Paso, Texas, to a burn center hospital.

I started as an assistant driver and ended up as a tank commander. Yet I was a young man who knew I wanted to do my military service in an airplane!

Genovevo "Gene" Villarreal
3rd Army, Armored Division,
Attached to 4th Armored Div., later 10th Armored Div.

A Teenager Goes to War

Barely eight months out of high school Gene Villarreal, of Edinburg, Texas, ended up in a war he only read about in the newspaper. Like many other boys, he was shocked to learn how vicious and unforgiving war was, especially for youngsters.

I graduated from high school in May 1943, and was drafted in January 1944. Many of my friends were drafted at the same time.

On the eve of my departure, my family went to church. The priest invited the family to join him in the rectory. The priest prayed and added, "*Diós va por adelante. Con el favor de Diós regresará Genovevo.*" Then he blessed the family. My mother said she would pray *novenas* [nine days of praying] and make *promesas* so that I would return safely. The following day, my uncles, cousins, and my immediate family all took me to the train station and sent me on my way.

I reported to Fort Sam Houston in San Antonio. There I was given a physical, injections, clothes, shoes, and a trench coat and was sent on my way to Fort Sill.

I trained in Fort Sill in artillery. From there I trained in Camp McCoy, Wisconsin, in an armored division. I learned how to use Howitzers, 150mm, and 155-meter field artillery guns capable of firing twenty miles away, and drove half-tracks, each of which was half-tank and half-truck. They had .50- and .30-caliber machine guns mounted on top and were protected with armor in front.

In January of 1944, the United States called men of all ages. Seventeen weeks of training, which included exercises and running obstacle courses. Marching for twenty miles taxed the older men, some of whom died on the spot. After basic training, then the men were assigned to special units. We were in good condition.

We were sent overseas via *Queen Mary* to Glasgow, Scotland, October 12 to October 17. We landed there because the port is deep and the boat can anchor. We traveled to Southampton, England, and rested for two days.

We crossed the English Channel to France on LSTs—two hundred men. Landed on Omaha beach four days after D-day. Cluttered beaches. We went around obstacles and things from old ships. Still went through water—waist high. We were told, "It's going to be them or you, and some will not come back." That scared the heck out of me, so scared that it makes you brave. The rifles were too big. We had tommy guns, called grease guns because they were small.

The machine guns and bazookas were behind the soldiers to protect the infantry. We had infantry in front of us; we the armored were behind them. If they met resistance, we would go in and take care of it. Then we would come back. Remain to protect the infantry. The infantry would go in and mop up.

We would tear up anything we saw in front of us and then retreat. The infantry would take over the position. We had help from artillery guns behind us. They would hit pretty close to us. Early in the morning the airplanes came ahead of us and bombed five miles in front of us. Sometimes they were too close, too.

November. It was raining hard. Some troops went back to rest. We were hit with artillery. They missed us and hit the people back. You have to go forward. Sometimes we were low on fuel. George Patton didn't want us to stop. They would bring us fuel.

We had two close calls, at Worms when we crossed the Rhine. Lohr, a small town on this side of river Saarbrucken. Scared me. It was near the Battle of the Bulge. We went in and were sitting ducks. The panzer division was there and scared the heck out of us. We had to retreat. And that's hard for me to admit. And they were just too strong for us.

The Germans' tanks were three times better than ours. We turned south and crossed the river to Lohr. Wow, I tell you they were waiting for us there. They pounded us day and night. We arrived in the afternoon. I thought I was going to die right there.

The sad thing about that: there is a river at Lohr. We finally called the Air Force in. They bombarded the place. We went into the town the next day. You should see the number of young SS troops dead. Young kids, fourteen to eighteen years old. My first thought was that we had hit a military school and these were the students. The people firing at us were just kids. I felt bad about it.

We met some resistance after that, but kept going toward Austria. We looked for pillboxes and machine gun nests. I operated an aiming circle which sat inside a motorized vehicle. It was a survey instrument and helped in giving instructions to the men firing. We used degrees in measuring from left to right and used elevation when wanting to fire farther. In Germany we were to search and destroy anything that seemed to be a threat. Then we were to keep on going and mopping up. The philosophy of our West

Point leader, Captain Willis, was, "We're just trying to get out of this alive."

Near Vienna, Austria, we met up with the Russians who had already taken Vienna. There were Germans there, too. When we were about twenty miles away from the Russians, communications received a message telling us that the Russians were already there and not to fire at them. If fired at, we should fire back, however.

The Russians told us that the war was over. They looked awful and wild. They were unshaven, and we were fairly clean shaven, because Patton liked to have his men clean. The Russians had been drinking and had schnapps on them. We had been told that the schnapps were made out of wood alcohol and might be poisonous. The Russians were loud and singing in circles like they do in the movies. We celebrated with them, but they were crazy.

We received orders to retreat to Munich. We left our equipment there and went back on trucks. They drove me to a rehabilitation hospital because of malnutrition. I now weighed one hundred pounds. Many of the men were nervous, shell-shocked, and tired.

I had 108 points and had to remain as part of the Army of Occupation. The men who had less than one hundred points were sent to the US with the understanding that the Pacific theater would be their next war zone. Well the war in the Pacific ended, so they were through. Meanwhile, those of us in Europe continued in the service until 1946.

We supervised the prisoners of war, so that they wouldn't regroup and try to fight us. Some of the POWs didn't want to go back home and face their families and neighbors because they had been defeated. They chose to go to other parts of Germany. Some Germans joined the US Army.

We also supervised the rebuilding of streets. We couldn't socialize with the population until August 1945.

I came home in 1946.

Thomas Ayala Fernandez
3rd Army, 76th Infantry Division

Unable to Say Goodbye
Like many other Mexican citizens, Thomas Fernandez's family fled Mexico

during the Mexican Revolution and settled in the United States. Thomas's father fled one war only to have his sons fight in another war across the ocean. Thomas was born in Eagle Pass, Texas, on March 15, 1923, to Benita Ayala and Manuel Fernandez Méndez. (Méndez is the father's mother's maiden name.) Manuel Fernandez, who was a droma, an itinerant peddler, was a Spaniard. Thomas's sister, Melba Fernandez, said, "Our father had a hacienda. He imported fabrics and items from Europe. He had a factory at the hacienda where they made coats, hats, and pants out of mezclilla [denim]. Pancho Villa, who was Manuel's friend, warned him that the Carranzistas were coming to kill him because he was a Spaniard.

"My father said, 'I left Mexico with dos mochilas de oro y con balas en las suelas de mis zapatos.'" [Translation: "I left Mexico with two bags of gold and bullets in the soles of my shoes." In other words, he was on the run.] The family crossed over into the United States shortly before Thomas was born. They traveled through various small towns before settling in Corpus Christi. Thomas and another son, Willie, served in WWII.

As a young man, I was in the CCC, Civilian Conservation Corps. We were stationed in New Mexico. We helped farmers and put out forest fires. It was a training ground. We used dynamite for building tanks and ponds for cattle. If there was a big storm, the cattle could get out from the ravines through steps we built. We also dammed the water so that it would run into the fields. There were many things to learn. You could learn about being a barber, a cook, or a mechanic. In Silver City, New Mexico, they trained you in baking and how to run a restaurant. Every week we went into town.

I was drafted in 1941. At that time my mother was in California. When she learned I was leaving for the service, she was anxious to come home and see me off. She worked at different jobs to earn enough money to pay for her trip back to Corpus Christi, Texas. She didn't get here in time, so I went to the Greyhound Bus Station to leave for Fort Sam Houston in San Antonio, Texas. At the moment that my bus was taking off, I saw my mother arriving in a bus from California. She saw me, too, and we waved at each other through the windows. That was our goodbye to one another.

After going to Fort Sam Houston in San Antonio, we shipped out to Riverside, California. The airfield was across the street from our training

Army camp. We were also in Death Valley.

I guarded at an airfield near Fort Ord. Also, I was in the infantry and worked with antiaircraft radar. In San Diego there was a marine camp and army guns, antiaircraft. The recruits were trained in two groups. One group was at one end and another group was in another place. We were supposed to see who got someplace first. We trained to survive in the desert.

When we trained in Colorado, we used blanks in our guns. We also learned how to find the foes in the forest. We climbed Pike's Peak in our training.

We shipped out to San Francisco to go overseas. I had some things I had bought and didn't want to take them with me and risk losing them. So I decided to visit my brother in Los Angeles and leave my things with him. I traveled on a bus all the way to Los Angeles, left my things with my brother, and went back to San Francisco. I had to get back on time.

When I arrived, I found out that my unit was gone to the Philippines. They told me, "You were supposed to stay put to be shipped out." I told them that I had thought LA was not too far. A colonel questioned me about what I had done and I told him.

So while my buddies went to the Philippines I shipped out to Fort Meade, Maryland. From there we sailed on the SS *West Point* to England. I crossed the channel in a British ship full of troops.

D-day had already occurred. We went in to replace the dead troops. We went through Belgium and Holland and then crossed the Rhine River into Germany. We arrived at a camp in Germany. We had an American officer with German blood. We opened the gates and freed Spaniards and Poles. They had used them as slave labor.

One time I was at an outpost in Germany in a village. I had dug a hole behind a hedge along the road and I stayed in the trench. I had my M1 rifle and was guarding for the night. Suddenly I heard a twig behind the slope. I popped my head out and said, "Halt." A German answered in German. My second lieutenant asked me, "Got trouble?" I answered, "I got one German right here. Another one is running back down the hill." I took the German to our headquarters, which was in a house. The German had gotten lost from his troops.

Things were slowing down. If they shot at you, you shot back. In Belgium we were there to build.

In Germany we went into a house to search. There was a very pretty girl with her mother on their way out. The American soldier with me called things to the girl. I blew my top. I told him, "Leave the woman and her daughter alone. They're not hurting you." The soldier said, "What are you going to do—take them with you?"

Sometimes when the Germans surrendered, the American soldiers yelled at them. General Patton always talked to his men at night. One time he came by and asked, "You boys hungry?"

Thomas returned to the US and worked at Chrysler for fifty-three years.

Vicente Puente
459th Air Service Group
Air Transportation Technician

Present on a Momentous Occasion
Vicente Puente was born near Laredo, Texas, on April 5, 1917. Vicente did not go beyond the sixth grade in his schooling. He felt the teachers who dealt with him were unfair. Nonetheless, he became a soldier and a witness to one of the most important events in the history of our nation.

I went up to fifth or sixth grade in Bastrop. Moved to Rockdale. "You don't know enough to be in sixth grade . . . back to third grade." Didn't make any difference. Walked four miles through pastures in Milano to go to school. During the winter my soles came undone. My daddy took an ice pick and tied them with baling wire. Rockdale to Rosebud, "We better put you back down to third grade." So then I went up through sixth grade. I can write in English just as well as I can write in Spanish.

Every time I moved from one school to another the teachers placed me in a grade below my level, because they felt that I wasn't ready for my assigned grade. Finally, after the sixth grade, I stopped going to school.

I was drafted on August 15, 1942. I trained first in Camp Wallace, Texas, and then in Camp Kearns, Utah. Right before I left, my mother gave me *la bendición*.

As part of the 459th Air Squadron Group, my title was Air Transportation Technician. For three months my group delivered supplies to the Americans in England. In 1944 my group was assigned to France. On D-day we were still delivering supplies in England.

In France my boss established a pattern for me. From 8:00 a.m. to 4:00 p.m., I cut hair for my squadron. They made me the squadron barber, and they told me "They are going to pay you 50 cents for each haircut." Well, you are not supposed to charge the officers, but I said, "They are coming through the line, and everyone who comes through the line has to pay the same thing. If fifteen officers come through the line, I won't be making nothing." Sometimes I cut thirty or forty heads a day, because I was using hand clippers.

But when I went to England I found electric clippers that took 220 volts. I went into the store and asked about them. The clerk said, "Soldier, I don't think you can buy these electric clippers. We don't have too many of them here. We sell them pretty high." I said, "How much?" He said, "L35 pounds." At $4 a pound [exchange rate] that was about $100 and something. I had a pocket of a roll of pounds and another pocket of pounds. He said, "What do you do?" I said, "I cut hair in the army." I sent my mother back home $500 about three times. I thought I'd have $1,500 when I got back home.

On weekend passes I took a girl to show me around. We ate and danced and paid five pounds for a bottle of whiskey. We sat at a table and there were five or six ladies and men and got another bottle. I paid for the stuff. Sometimes they would put your name on the board, which meant you were going to the front lines. When I saw my name I thought, "What do I need all this money for? Spend the money."

At 4:00 p.m. we went to the mess hall to eat supper. At 5:00 p.m. we went on the plane to deliver supplies. We made three trips from 6:00 to 11:00 p.m. We delivered supplies wherever they told us. At first we delivered supplies on this side of the English Channel. Then we delivered to Germany, France, and Italy.

We had a pilot, electricians, MPs. Four men on the plane were the crew. Five men were on my crew, the loading crew. I was in charge. We were also MPs and carried guns. I carried a .45. We used a billy club. I did guard duty and did whatever they told me. We had guards watching the supplies, because the English might get the supplies and take them home.

They were rationing.

We dropped K supplies. We dropped a small square bag.

They tried to make me a staff sergeant, and I didn't want it because if I made staff sergeant they wouldn't let me cut hair. I had pockets full of money, English money, from cutting hair. I spent the money. They put me to work at different kinds of work. Sometimes it was carpenter work. They would say, "You're going to work in a certain place tomorrow." Sometimes they would say, "You are going to work in a motor pool doing mechanic work." I do whatever they tell me to do.

England was the best place. The army said, "Be careful. You are going to get a pass." Twenty women to each soldier. At that time England didn't have men. They were in Africa. England sent all the men to Africa. The ladies drove the trains and fixed the railroad, transported supplies and worked the telephones. Everything was run by ladies in England. You'd go into a beer joint, a pub, God almighty, women just as pretty. All shapes and all sizes and all ages. You can just imagine.

You've seen the Eiffel Tower? They have a restaurant. I'd go to Paris and I went to the Eiffel Tower.

We got shot one time and half of the plane was cut off. We had problems. We came across the channel and barely made it just topping the trees and found a place to land. I said, "I ain't going back there no more." We were volunteers to go and unload the plane. I told them I wasn't going no more. They said, "You go the next couple of days and I'll try to get someone to take your place." So they found someone and I stayed cutting hair. Sometimes I worked in KP. I hate that work in the kitchen, pans and more pans.

After they pushed the troops back to Germany, they sent me to France. I was on guard duty one night. There were guards all around the building, which was General Eisenhower's headquarters. We were not to let anyone in. Then some American soldiers brought in some Germans. This was in Rheims, France, and it was 2:30 a.m. All the lights in that town turned on. Suddenly people got out [of their homes] and danced, yelled, screamed, and jumped hollering and everything. And I was on guard duty and I thought, "What happened now?" They told me, "The war is over. The Germans signed the papers." The Germans [that were brought in] signed the Unconditional Surrender Document. [General Jodl and Admiral Freideburg signed for the Germans. General Walter Bedell Smith signed for the Americans. Representatives from other countries signed, also.]

They gave me a pass on the same day that my squadron shipped out to the States. I was in France and was supposed to come back to England to reunite with the squadron. They didn't call me. I was in Paris on a three-day pass. When I came back to the base, there was nobody there. My bags were on the bed. I went across the street and asked the first sergeant what had happened. He said, "They told the MPs to look for you, but they couldn't find you in Paris."

My squadron came back to the US and the other part of the squadron was in France. In about two to three weeks they came back. I came back with the engineers to Camp Miles Standish in Massachusetts, the POE. Two or three days later when I was in the bathroom shaving, there is my first sergeant shaving next to me. He said, "Well, I'll be a son of a gun. Where were you at?" I said, "Same place you were at when you went to Paris." We had been going with two sisters in Paris, but he never told the MPs where I was, so I was left behind.

In Paris they would feed you and let you spend the night for 75 cents. They had big buildings with cots.

The first sergeant said, "Tomorrow you come with us, and I'll get your paperwork fixed up." The next day, "Get all your stuff and take it to my squadron. You're coming with us." They sent us to Camp Fannin in Mexia, Texas. That's where we got discharged.

Before I came back I was working in France in Service and Supplies with three Frenchmen and two Italians. So I had to speak French and Italian. When I came back I could speak French and Italian. Italian is like Spanish.

After all the difficulties Vicente had in getting through school, he made certain his children would succeed. In fact, his four children became educators.

Santana Galván
104th Division
3rd Armored

Young Boy Learns to be Tough
Santana Galván was born on the San Luis Ranch in Hidalgo on February 6, 1926. Santana was a farm boy, and because of this he was strong.

After quitting school I worked in the fields. In February of 1944, the army drafted me. In Fort Sam Houston, where I took and passed the physical, I noticed that half the men were Mexican American.

Before I left, my mother and father gave me *la bendición* adding, "*Que Diós y la virgen de Guadalupe protejen a nuestro hijo* [May God and the Virgin of Guadalupe protect our son]."

We ended up at Camp Hood near Waco, Texas, for sixteen weeks for infantry training. Four months later I visited my family. Although it was hot and some of the men collapsed, I weathered the training well.

At Camp Gruber, the next stop, we underwent advanced training and night training. The officers and noncommissioned officers awoke us in the middle of the night to do compass readings. And we trained on dark nights with hard rain falling on us.

An assignment was for two of us to go in the night and follow instructions such as so many steps going south and so many steps going east. Then we were to stop and one of us covered our body with a coat and took out a flashlight to read further instructions. If a ray of light was escaping, the other man had to tell where the light was showing.

We shipped out to Maryland and then to Camp Miles Standish near Boston, Massachusetts. A ship by the name of *West Point* took us to Edinburgh, Scotland, in February, 1945. I spent my birthday on the ship.

From Edinburgh we took a train to Southampton, England. Later on we crossed the English Channel and landed at Le Havre, France. Another train took us to St. Charles, France, and then we transferred to a truck, which took us to a little town in Belgium. And now for the first time, I could hear the sounds of gunfire. At night I could see flares up in the sky. A truck transported us to Cologne, right by the Rhine River. Our men were separated into companies. None of my friends were in my group.

We fought our way across the river. That first battle was known as the Rhineland Battle. The truth of the matter is that that first battle made my hairs stand on end. I was the assistant to the man who carried the BAR [Browning Automatic Rifle], which could be set up on a bipod. One time this guy and I were pinned down. He was from San Diego, Texas, and had been in action for about six months already. He began laughing at me and said, "When do we get to see Edinburg again?" I told him to shut up. (After the war my mother told me that she heard my voice telling her, "Mom, I just went into combat.")

After that battle most of our fighting was city fighting. There were always snipers you had to look out for. If you crossed the street, you had to run. If a buddy was lying on the street wounded or dead, you just had to leave him there and keep on running until you got to the other side. If a soldier dropped a helmet, you kicked it as you ran. If you didn't kick it far enough, the next guy to run across the street would kick it farther. Once I had my helmet knocked off. My buddies kicked it until I got it back.

Our A company was down from three hundred-plus men to over one hundred. The German burp gun was quieter than our American guns. Every time we took a town, our company commander would get us a house to stay in. We took fifteen towns. One time we stayed in a basement that had bottles and jars of food that had been preserved. There were peaches and pears. Some guys ate the food and others were scared and didn't touch it.

After I had fought a while I got to the point that I didn't care. I just wanted to go forward. The Germans were beginning to throw their guns down and giving up. SS troopers never gave up unless you had a gun pointing at them.

When we were staying in a barn in between towns I saw a German standing alone at another building. I got a bead on him and a corporal came up to me and said, "Let me take him." I agreed, and the corporal shot him in the head. We walked over there and the German had already killed an American who lay nearby, and we didn't even know about it. An elderly woman was in that building and she began screaming at us in German.

We left that place and were going down beside the highway, which was built up higher than where we were walking. Suddenly we heard German artillery. We were near some pyramids of potatoes that some farmer had harvested. They placed a layer of potatoes followed by grass and then another layer of potatoes until they had a pyramid about four feet high. I hit the ground when I heard the artillery and I got potatoes all over me. So I told the guys, "Anybody want potatoes? I've got them."

So many new soldiers went in and in a few hours or in a day they were dead or wounded. My buddy who had been carrying the BAR was wounded; now I became the BAR man and got an assistant. He carried the boxes of ammunition. That assistant stayed a week and complained that I had no fear. So I got another assistant.

We had a first lieutenant who always led in front. He was a brave man. He would ask for five volunteers. When nobody answered he would pick five of us. Then, he and the five men would make up the patrol. I volunteered because the lieutenant always went with us. We would crawl on the ground because of the possibilities of land mines. And we went on patrol at night.

One day he got wounded and was replaced by another lieutenant. This leader stayed in back and yelled orders from the safety of the rear of the whole company. As we approached Dessau, Germany, near the Elbe River, the lieutenant yelled his orders as usual from the rear and he told one guy near me, "Tell that SOB to move to the left." The corporal said, "He's calling you."

I turned around with the BAR I carried and pointed it at him and called him an SOB. Then I told him that if he ever called me that again I would shoot him. Slowly he lowered his gun. Meanwhile guys near me were saying, "Kill that SOB."

One week before the war ended the sergeant was wounded, and the lieutenant promoted me to sergeant, but I refused the promotion. Then while at Dessau we heard the war had ended.

I was so relieved. Then I was assigned to the Army of Occupation. We fixed up the towns and helped the German people clean up and rebuild. I drove a three-quarter ton truck and carried supplies to the mess hall.

One day two other soldiers and I were called in by the commander. He offered us a proposition: enlist for another six months and we would be made staff sergeants and up, and he'd throw in a thirty-day furlough.

All the men rejected it. I sailed back with 1,500 men and landed in New York. From New York I took the train to Fort Sam Houston and then a bus to Edinburg.

I felt happy and relieved to be back. My mother and father were so happy to have me back, also. I returned to farming. My wife Librada and I raised seven children. Most are professionals and supervisors.

Reynaldo García
3rd Army,
94th Division, 302nd Infantry

A Burden in His Heart
Reynaldo García, from Laredo, Texas, quit school in the sixth grade to help his father drive a truck, which delivered the produce for their business. Reynaldo was a Catholic and worried about the steps a Catholic must follow. Because he had not made his First Holy Communion, he felt certain God would punish him. Nonetheless, he fought for his country and did his best in his job as a soldier.

Like many other young Catholic children, I attended catechism classes in preparation for my first holy communion. When any of the children misbehaved, the nuns hit us with a ruler, which they carried with them at all times. Finally, I told my mother I could no longer attend catechism classes because the nuns were hitting me often. My mother warned me that without the classes I could not make my first holy communion, and without my first holy communion I could not go to confession and receive communion. Although this didn't bother me at first, it would gnaw away at me later.

In 1943 I was drafted. I reported to the Fort Sam Houston Induction Center in San Antonio, Texas. From there I was sent to Fort Knox, Kentucky, for basic training. I remember it as being tough, and it was very cold. They trained me to drive jeeps, half-tracks, and all armored vehicles.

Because Laredo has always had a large percentage of Spanish-speaking people, I spoke primarily Spanish and didn't know much English. Also, in Laredo I had seen only one Black family, and my mother always made the sign of the Cross when she saw them because she felt they brought us good luck.

So I was a young man who had never left home, knew very little English, and was limited in my knowledge of people and the world. But most soldiers possessed the same limitations.

At Fort Knox when I saw someone who was of a similar skin color as mine I would approach them and say, "*Quiúbole, de donde eres tú?* [Hi, where are you from?]"

The other soldier's reaction was: "What's wrong with this Mexican?" I later learned that I was using Spanish to greet Italians, Jews, and other ethnic-looking boys.

In January of 1944 I was given a furlough to Laredo. My mother insisted we go to church because she had heard that many young men were dying in the war.

I returned to training, but this time it was in Camp McCain, Mississippi. I was now trained specifically as a cannoneer and as a switchboard operator. I was to carry a switchboard on my back, along with my field pack. Another soldier and I were to lay the telephone lines so that communication could be established. In this manner a lieutenant and a soldier would set up an observation post and then relay messages back to headquarters, who would then decide on firing strategies.

I was again given a furlough back home. It was there that I learned that an invasion had occurred in France. I learned later that my unit was involved in the invasion.

In July 1944, my division was sent to Camp Shanks, New York. On August 6, 1944, we left New York and sailed on the ship *Queen Elizabeth* for Glasgow, Scotland. A voice over the loudspeaker announced that German submarines were following us. However, they told us that the *Queen Elizabeth* was faster than the submarines.

We left Glasgow for England. On September 13, 1944, we headed for France and went up the same way that the troops had advanced through Utah Beach. The waters near the beach were filled with many, many things; parts of ships were sticking out of the water. All kinds of things were floating on the water.

Before landing the captain told us to prepare our guns and to fill them with live ammunition. During the excitement of finally getting to the war, a man accidentally fired his gun and injured the bugle man, who had to be sent back to the hospital.

The captain pointed to the steeple of a church and said, "That's where the Germans are." It turned out that there were two pockets of Germans still in the area at Lorient and in St. Nazaire. The infantry handled the situation.

My first night I had guard duty. I stood near a tree and during my duty I kept hearing footsteps but never saw anyone. The next morning I found out that we were in an apple orchard and that the "footsteps" were the sound of apples falling on leaves.

Since I was with the switchboard and was a cannoneer, we traveled behind the infantry, but our cannons were fired way above the heads of our soldiers and the cannons traveled a long way off.

In the Ardennes Forest we found out that some Germans had infiltrated our area. My buddy, Herman Delowe, and I set up our switchboard on the tripod in our shelter. All of a sudden everything went dead. So we knew that our wires had been cut, and there could be no communication. Herman and I took our roll of line with some hooks so that we could hang the line high enough on trees to keep the tanks from running over it. We found the cut and spliced the wire and repaired it.

There was a lake near us. Soon the Germans spotted us and fired at us. The bombs hit the water, and I ran behind a tree. At the tree I prayed. I knew that I might die, but the thing I hated the most was that my mother would get a telegram telling her that I was dead. Herman and I didn't worry about hanging the wire anymore. We just let it extend on the ground by the side of the road and took off in our jeep.

While in the Ardennes Forest a priest came to give mass. We were kneeling on the ground with our helmets in our hands and our rifles by our sides. I wanted to go to take communion, but I remembered what my mother had told me. I decided to go talk to the priest about it. I told him why I hadn't finished my training for my first holy communion and how I really wanted to participate in the Lord's Supper. The priest told me that I could receive communion and that from now on I should participate. That experience there in the forest lifted a burden I had carried in my heart for so many years!

As we neared Germany our captain told us that the Germans would fight hard because they would be defending their homes. Lt. Bowling from our Ninety-Fourth Division went with a soldier to set up an observation post as he usually did. He was captured by the Germans. While the Ninety-Fourth Division was fighting, the Eighty-Fourth was not far away and joined us in the fighting. The Germans were defeated. It turns out that Lt. Bowling's father was a general with the Eighty-Fourth Division.

In Germany we were walking on a road by some woods. There was a highway parallel to us, and we saw some Americans coming down the highway in our direction with German prisoners of war. After a while we saw some airplanes flying above us in the same direction we were going. We yelled at them, "Go get them," and other things of that nature. Suddenly we saw the crooked crosses and realized they were actually German airplanes. We saw them make a U-turn and we scrambled toward some trees and a cliff. The German airplanes also made a mistake. They fired at the German prisoners of war thinking they were Americans.

One night we had a shelter made of metal. The temperature was below freezing, and I had guard duty. The soldiers were inside the shelter sleeping away. They had made some sort of stove and the wood had burned down. I had some lighter fluid, so I took a little bit and threw it into our "stove." It suddenly made an enormous amount of light, something that was prohibited during the war, and then it died down again. No one even woke up. I went to sleep. I could have been court-martialed for that.

The Siegfried Line that bordered Germany was called dinosaur teeth. By the time we reached it, it had already been broken through by American troops. We were crossing the Rhine River over pontoon bridges and had made it to Düsseldorf when we learned that the war was over.

After the war I was assigned to Czechoslovakia for six months with the army of occupation. I had a girlfriend, and when I visited her family I took them sugar and things they could not get. They cooked meals for me and gave dances for us. They were not allowed to write to anyone in the United States, so they used my name as a return address. After the war I received a letter from a wealthy man in Oregon. He was thanking me for being so nice to his family in Czechoslovakia. He said that if I ever needed anything to call on him, but I never did.

We returned to the states on a ship named *Westminster*. Another ship left before us, and those men made fun of us because we were left behind. Well, after two days at sea, that ship had to return, because there was a bad storm in the Atlantic Ocean. We took another route and still ran into part of the storm. The ship moved violently from one end to the other. And I had guard duty. I was sick for twelve days.

There is one thing that I consider the most beautiful sight I have ever seen in my whole life. And that is the sight of the Statue of Liberty as we sailed into the New York Harbor. Ships were blowing their horns. Hundreds of people were out there to greet us, and even Miss America was out there singing and dancing. But the sight of that statue shall always stay with me.

Sam Coppola, a friend of mine, said, "See that place over there? That's Brooklyn. That's where I live." I told him, "I have a long way to go, all the way to Laredo, Texas."

From Camp Kilmer in New York, I was sent to Camp Fannin, which was to be my separation center. They gave me a clean set of clothes and sent me on my way.

Jorge Flores, Tech 5
84th Infantry Division
909th Field Artillery Battalion, (Service Battery)

War and A Special Mission
Jorge Flores was born on February 22, 1921, in Laredo, Texas. He was drafted in 1942. His brother, who was drafted later, was married and was the father of two young daughters. Besides Jorge and his brother, his mother and father had two daughters. Jorge was a devoted son and had a good heart. As a young man he worked and gave his mother his salary. As a soldier, he worried about his brother Ángel, who was captured by the Germans. He even looked for his brother in foxholes and other places.

During the Depression my father, like many other men, had no work. People on the farms weren't so bad off because they could grow food to eat, but many people in town had nothing to eat. We went on a wagon close to Alice, Texas, to pick cotton. We also went to Robstown, Texas, to pick cotton. The wagon was about three feet wide and seven feet long. It took us three days to get there. We put everything in the wagon, and it was crowded. Every now and then we had to stop to let the horse drink water. We would stay in these places for two to three weeks. Then we went back to school.

At night Daddy slept in front of the wagon on a board between the horses. We all drank water from the river. Back then milk was two cents, and you could buy a steak for five cents.

One day we didn't have anything in the house and my mother prayed that something good would happen. At 5:00 a.m. a bricklayer came and asked my father if he had a load of sand. My father gave him the sand and the man paid him $5.00 for it.

My mother came in from church and began watering the plants. She fell backwards on a nail and cut her calf. She got lockjaw, and Daddy had to pay for a shot a day until she got well.

Before I was drafted I was earning $5.00 a day doing construction work. They paid me twenty-five cents for every bundle of shingles I put in. I gave my mother my earnings.

Before I left, my mother gave me *la bendición* in the living room of our home. I knelt as my mother administered the blessing in which she made the sign of the cross over me, "*En el nombre del Padre, y del hijo, y del espíritu santo* [In the name of the Father, the Son and the Holy Ghost]." Then my father, brother, and two sisters went to see me off as I left for my first assignment.

As soon as I was drafted I rode a bus to Fort Sam Houston in San Antonio. I stayed there two days. Then I was taken to Camp Howze, located in Texas near Denton and Gainesville. I was in basic training for twenty-six days. There were twelve to thirteen more weeks spent in pup tents as we practiced crossing rivers and other kinds of maneuvers.

I joined the Eighty-Fourth Infantry Division, which had fought in WWI and had been disbanded. In 1942, it was reactivated. The group of men who ended up in the Field Artillery Battalion Service Battery trained together and stayed together for three years, unlike men in the infantry who fought side by side with friends who were often replaced by new recruits. Therefore, we felt as though we were working beside family members.

Because the boys were from all over the country, all sorts of names were heard. Many names were new to the sergeants, and they didn't know how to pronounce them. All the soldiers had to get up early and line up in formation while the sergeant looked us over. One day at roll call the sergeant kept calling for someone named Solecer. No one answered. "Solecer," he yelled. And again, "Solecer."

Finally, a Mexican American boy from South Texas said, "Do you mean *Salazar*?"

The sergeant yelled at him and said, "To me you are Solecer. So when I say Solecer, you answer!"

"Yes sir," *Salazar* answered.

Salazar was noticed by everyone for several reasons. One day as we were marching the sergeant yelled, "Right!" Everyone turned right except Salazar. He turned left. The sergeant picked up a big rock and placed it in Salazar's right hand. "Now that is your right hand," he yelled at him. "When I say 'turn right,' you turn toward that hand with the big rock. Got that?"

"Yes sir," Salazar answered.

Another time we ran out early in the morning for roll call. The sergeant approached Salazar again. "Solecer, you are out here without a helmet. Don't you realize you are not wearing a helmet?"

"No sir," Salazar answered.

"Well I'll help you remember!" The sergeant took a bunch of rifles and told Salazar to extend his arms. He did. Then the sergeant placed all of the heavy rifles in his arms and said, "Now run and go get your helmet." Salazar ran to his tent and put on his helmet and ran back carrying all the rifles in his arms. "Do you think you can remember to put on your helmet, Solecer?"

"Yes sir," Salazar answered.

We were sent to Camp Claiborne in Alexandria, Louisiana. While there I trained for six more months in preparation to go fight in the European theater.

I made friends with people from all over the country and especially remember two friends, Anthony Lando from New York and Anthony Garliardi from Pennsylvania. Finally, we were put on a train and rode in a Pullman all the way to New Jersey. We attempted to relax by playing cards and games. One young man cried often, for it was his first separation from his new wife. This was my first experience on a train, and I was fascinated with the Pullman cars.

We were given a pass to New York. I spent all my money there. The city with its tall buildings was an impressive sight. Then we were told to go to a large ship, which was to take us overseas, to England. We soldiers were loaded down with our duffel bags, our field packs, rifles, and gas masks.

In September 1944, the ship was moving and there was a heavy fog in which you couldn't even see your hand if you extended it just a few inches away from you. Then suddenly the boat felt like it had jerked back in some way. At that time, we had not been instructed in the use of life preservers. All of us were ordered to the top deck. It turned out that a tanker had hit the ship. All the drinking water had been lost in the collision. At that time ships traveled in convoys and with a dirigible above them sometimes. The only ships that did not travel in convoys were the *Queen Elizabeth* and the *Queen Mary* because they were fast ships and could move quickly if they had to.

The ship had no choice but to return to New York City. While waiting for the ship to be repaired, we were given passes to go into New York City, but I had no money. Both Anthony Lando and Anthony Garliardi invited me to their homes, but I didn't want to go. I was so homesick. The ship was finally repaired and we went back on it. We reached England in five or six days. English trucks with drivers were waiting to pick us up and take us to some large tents. I remember that it was very cold.

A sergeant called four or five boys from each company. The outfit was called the Red Ball outfit. Its mission was to go to France and carry ammunition and rations from the beachhead to the front lines. This was after the D-day landing when a beachhead had already been established. The soldiers were to leave from Portland. The boat, which was an LTC—landing troop carrier—took four days. We were told to be careful. Not only was the water rough, but it was believed that German submarines were in the English Channel. Only that one trip was made at that time.

When the LTC arrived on the beach, it threw an anchor. Then when the tide receded, the boat was stuck in the sand. The ramp was lowered so that the men could get out. A bulldozer had to come clear the sand. Then when the high tide came, the boat was able to leave and go back to England.

We landed on Omaha Beach on November 1944, five months after D-day, June 6, 1944. We spent the first night in tents in an apple orchard. The weather was severe and so we were very cold. Sergeant Gunn, however, visited each tent to check on us. I'll never forget that.

US Army T/5 Jorge Flores. He searched for his only brother José Ángel, also serving in the European theater, who was missing in action after being captured and detained at Stalag 12A. Property of author, bequeathed to her by estate of Jorge Flores.

By November 6 we began the march by truck to the front. The artillery section of the army traveled a few miles behind the infantry. We also carried the supplies for the infantry: gasoline, rations, and medical supplies. I worked with firing the howitzer rockets. Many times I drove a truck and sometimes a jeep for an officer. We arrived at an abandoned train station. Some of the soldiers were playing cards. Others decided to sleep. Everyone was apprehensive. One of the soldiers said, "Don't be afraid," since the town appeared to be void of people. Some took off their clothes to be more comfortable. I went upstairs and wrapped myself up in my blanket to sleep. After a while I heard a bomb go off. Everyone was surprised and ran every which way. The guy who had suggested that no one be afraid had run and jumped into a "swamp hole" which was where the cooks threw all the leftover food, scraps, and waste in general. I quickly looked around for my rifle and found it semi-buried in some dirt.

Meanwhile, my brother and I were writing to each other. By now he was already fighting in Germany. One day my letters to my brother were returned with the message that he was MIA—missing in action. It was a very sad time for me.

Then Germany began their next big front, which became known as the Battle of the Bulge. Orders came in for us to head for Belgium. We spent all day traveling. Many vehicles were moving bumper-to-bumper. We really didn't know what was happening at this point. We arrived at night. Captain Edwards left and returned. He told us to head for the woods and to hide there. The men used nets up above them to hide everything from airplanes above us. Before going to sleep, all of the trucks were checked out and serviced. The motor sergeant made sure that it was all done. One of our men was using the cutting torch on a metal box and somehow accidentally died doing it.

While out in the woods we had to take turns standing guard for two hours. Instead of using two men, however, we used four. At 2:00 a.m. someone woke me up so that I could go on duty. A different password was used each night; it usually had something to do with a baseball team. The concern was that Germans who knew English were infiltrating the American army. Someone told us that the Germans were even imitating the way the soldiers tapped their cigarettes on their fingernails before lighting up. It appears that some Germans had captured a warehouse and had taken everything including uniforms. They had even found some German soldiers in American chow lines.

I drove a command car; that was the first vehicle in a convoy. The command car carried a big radio with a radioman. I couldn't sleep in the car because of the radio. So when I had guard duty, I put some tarpaulin on the ground. It rained hard and I got cold and wet and there was nothing I could do. Finally I decided to turn on the vehicle and put my feet by the exhaust to try to dry out my socks.

On one occasion after pulling guard duty, Captain Edwards told me to get the jeep so that I could drive him somewhere. He led me to a house in the woods. There were other jeeps with drivers waiting for their officers. One by one the officers came out and left with their drivers. When I noticed that only our jeep was there and that I was about to be left behind, I decided to go out with the last jeep without the captain. I was afraid to be alone in this strange country not even knowing where I was. In a short while a jeep came in a hurry and the driver said, "Go back and pick up Capt. Edwards."

When I picked him up, the captain asked me why I had left. I didn't know what to say. The captain could have gotten me in trouble, but he was a very decent guy.

On our way back to the group some soldiers stopped us. They said, "Watch out for those haystacks you see in front of you. There are some tanks under some of them. We've gotten two tanks so far."

The captain ordered us to move on to the next town. There had been a mix-up. Instead of us being behind the infantry, somehow or other we had gotten ahead of them. As soon as the infantry arrived, they began digging foxholes for themselves.

We arrived at a little town in Belgium. The people were very nice. Although they had very little, they gave us what they had, which was wine and coffee but without cream or sugar to go with it. When a woman gave Anthony some coffee, he said, "Gracias." She began speaking in Spanish. Since Anthony didn't know how to speak Spanish, he called me over. I found out that she was from Spain and had married a man from Belgium. So we talked to each other for a while.

Four men went to sleep in a small room. I went upstairs and wrapped myself in a blanket and slept on top of some wheat. Then we began hearing the whistling German artillery, and there I was alone in the attic. The US artillery fired back. A barrage occurred and there was no sleep for us that night.

In Christmas 1944, in Belgium some friends and I went to Mass. Although we saw the owner of the house where we were staying at the church, no one recognized him for quite a while because the man usually wore wooden shoes; that day he was all dressed up in church and was wearing regular shoes. As I was leaving the church a woman with her daughter walked near me. The young woman placed her fingers in the blessed water and then extended her hand toward me. I was at a loss as to what to do. I took her hand and shook it and said, "Merry Christmas!"

Anthony Lando commented, "I guess you like her." I was puzzled. When I went back to the group I asked the sergeant what it was all about. The sergeant said that when the girls did that, you were supposed to touch her fingers and then bless yourself. Then you could walk her home.

In Belgium a division had been overrun by Germans. So when I found out that there were Americans present, I asked if anyone knew anything about my brother, José Ángel Flores. No one knew of him. Then I began looking in foxholes thinking that perhaps my brother was there and that by some miracle I might find him. But he was not there.

Meanwhile a German airplane shot down two American planes. Finally, we brought it down but the German pilot jumped out trying to save his life. The parachute didn't open, and the ground was frozen with ice. The German died. When looking through his papers our men found that he was just about nineteen years old and that it was his first flight. The American GIs took his clothes for themselves, because it was so cold. This was one of the first signs that the Germans were using very young people to fight in the war.

Now it was back to Germany. I was firing the howitzers. The Germans had developed robot bombs, which looked like telephone poles. Once one of the robot bombs landed in our mess—kitchen—but it was a dud.

In Germany the men were to cross the Rhine River, but the Germans flooded it to try to keep us from crossing it. We had to wait three or four days for the water to recede. The engineers who traveled with us made a pontoon bridge. That is they lined up small boats and then placed wood over them so that everyone could pass. We crossed the river that way. Close to the river the Americans had big balloons attached with metal cables to protect them from German airplanes.

When we heard an airplane coming we could tell it was a single German plane. We fired at them with antiaircraft fire with a tracer, a red bullet, in every fifth bullet. That way we could tell exactly where the firing was going. At this time, we were using a piper cub to observe and then radio back what they were seeing. Also, I saw my first jet; we were all amazed by the speed of the airplane. And it was a German airplane.

Each battery had forward observers. That included a jeep driver and a radio man. They would go to a building and try to find the enemy. They would call back for fire and give directions. A howitzer shell would be fired as a marker. If it was not hitting in the right location, then the soldiers would radio us and tell us to go right or left of where we had hit.

Meanwhile, I found out that my mother had received a letter from a German officer written in German in which he told her that my brother, José Ángel, was a POW, prisoner of war. When my mother received the letter, she went to someone who could read and write German, a priest named Father Elsing who she knew had been a soldier for Germany in WWI. He translated the letter for her. So there was a little bit of hope there.

When my sergeant found out that my brother was a POW, he told everyone that my brother was alive so that I could be cheered up. The guys were happy for me. The sergeant was that sort of guy.

After the Ruhr Valley Battle, the group was told to wait because the Russians were going to go into Berlin first. The captain told me to go to B Battery and get a jeep because he was taking me somewhere. We also picked up Lt. Keene. The captain asked, "Do you know where we are going?" I didn't.

We were going to the Elbe River because they had heard that American prisoners had been freed and were coming through there. "Maybe we can find your brother," they told me. Again, I was hopeful that I would find my brother.

Sure enough, there were American soldiers who had been set free by the Russians. They told us that when the Russians arrived at the Prisoner of War Camp, they told the Americans, "You're free now. Go on." So they were just walking along in this foreign country of Germany. I looked at all of their faces, but didn't find my brother, but I found another boy from Corpus Christi, an Alberto Cano.

Along with the Americans there were German soldiers who were anxiously wanting to be taken prisoners by the American military because the Russians were looking to get even with the Germans. So the Americans were the preferred army to take in the Germans as prisoners.

Some of American soldiers said they had gone to a concentration camp and had seen awful things. One man said he saw the cadavers of two people who had died embracing one another.

As we traveled on a particular day, the rain had fallen and the mud was deep. I saw a woman walking in the mud with a child. As soldiers often do, one soldier threw some crackers for the child. The crackers fell in the soggy mud; the mother took them, wiped them on her sleeve and gave the dirty crackers to the child. Then I saw two men approach a horse, which had been killed accidentally by some fire. They took a knife, cut into the horse and took some raw meat and began eating it.

Two days later word got around that Germany had surrendered. Now finally we could drive with our headlights on. All through the war we had been driving with blackout lights; they were triangular in shape and were equivalent to the circumference of a pencil. But a scary rumor had gotten started, that we would be sent to the Pacific to finish the war with Japan.

I then became part of the Army of Occupation of Germany. I stayed in Steinsfurt, Germany, for six months and became acquainted with the people.

For some reason or other Heidelberg had been spared from the bombing. I went only to the outskirts on an errand to get gasoline to deliver to the companies. Also, there was a castle across the river, and the castle had not been bombed. Our men went to the castle and placed their insignia, a circle with a hatchet in the middle, up high on the castle. It could be seen a long way off.

From Germany we were taken to France. The division was sent to the POE—point of embarkation. Four to six men of each battery company were left behind in Steinsfurt, Germany, to return equipment to Stuttgart in Germany. Then trucks with men in the back were driven to France. Again, it was very cold.

In Paris, I saw all the sights: the Eiffel Tower, *Arc de Triomphe*, and the Chartres Cathedral. The church was very old. The stone steps leading up to the cathedral were worn down from so many people walking on them throughout the centuries.

On January 1, 1946, the French celebrated the New Year in a big way. They had much to celebrate about. Finally the Germans were gone from their land.

On the way back home, the ship rocked severely. We were scared; people were sliding back and forth. Our food left our hands and slid every which way. Finally we arrived in New York. I had been gone more than two years.

We were taken to Camp Kilmer, New Jersey. From there the soldiers were separated so that they could be sent west, south, or north. I arrived in Camp Fannin, Texas, near Waco. Then I took a bus to Corpus Christi.

I felt strange in civilian clothes. In order to feel comfortable, if I left the house, I would put on my uniform. Then I began to feel better. It took me a while to feel relaxed enough to wear regular clothes.

After the service I became an apprentice carpenter. I joined the union, and I gave my mother my paycheck. When I married in 1949, I didn't own a car. My sisters gave a down payment for us to have a refrigerator.

Servando Lopez
Co. K, 3rd Battalion,
175th Infantry Regiment,
29th Division (Let's Go!)

We Didn't Start the War
Servando Lopez was born on April 8, 1925, in Lara, a community located three miles West of Alice, Texas, a small town in South Texas. His parents were Candida and Daniel Lopez. His father farmed for himself and others. Servando Lopez attended school in Lara and eventually moved to Alice with his family. Servando was always working. His father died early on, and Servando knew he had to contribute. He swept at a bakery in exchange for bread. He also learned to caddy for golfers. Naturally, when he grew up he became a businessman. Meanwhile, there was a war going on and he had to fight.

My dad was a farmer, and my mother stayed home. They owned a piece of land in Lara. He farmed his own land, and then he worked for a man who owned a big ranch. After I was born they moved to Alice, and I went to school here. In 1936 we moved to the ranch. In 1937 I went to school in Lara. He died in January 1938. They said it was a heart attack, but I think it was pneumonia. Then I came back to Alice with my mother. My daddy had $1,000.00 Woodmen of the World insurance.

Hilda Gomez Lopez, Servando's wife, said, "She bought the lot and built a two-room house in the front and a two-room house in the back. She rented the front house to have a little income with her five boys. The youngest was about five months old."

She did a lot of alterations. Then she was hired by Klein's Department Store, and then when I came back from the service, I was hired at C.R. Anthony's. I was at the opening of Robstown's [store], and I was at the opening here.

When I was twelve years old and going to school I'd do odds and ends jobs. I would go sweep. My first job was at a bakery, the Alice Bakery, and I used to go sweep every morning before I went to school. They wouldn't pay me. They'd give me sweet bread.

As I got a little older I started going to the golf course, and I was a caddy. When the NYA, National Youth Association, had the program, by the government, we built the Alice gymnasium. I was very fortunate that I was made a clerk. I worked two weeks, and I had a friend, a neighbor who worked two weeks. They only allowed us to work two weeks. We took turns.

They asked the older boys, "Who has a driver's license?" The ones who raised their hands, they gave them a wheelbarrow for concrete. That was a big laugh. They tried that and those poor guys . . . the older they got, the more responsibility . . . to build the foundation of the gymnasium. We worked there until I got a night clerk job at Queen Alice Courts. It was a motel and it was owned by the people that own the Hotel Alice where the bank is now.

We were married, and we opened a drive-in grocery store when we came back from Raymondville. My uncle had a drive-in grocery. He had been a banker. Then he retired and sold it to me. After I moved back from Raymondville and opened up my own store, they called me from Stickler's Man Shop to go help out for a couple of weeks, and I stayed there until I retired. He sold very good clothes. That's where I met Mr. Cubriel.

My mother was a seamstress, and she went to work for C.R. Anthony Company. She worked for Klein's Department Store, and when I got a job with Anthony's, I brought her to work with me. She was a very good seamstress.

I had to quit school when I was fifteen. I quit school in about 1940 to help out with my mother. My mother would get help from the government, food. I used to carry a little wagon to go get the food.

I was drafted in June 1943. I was a night clerk at the Queen Alice Courts. When I was eighteen, you had to register for the draft. I was eighteen in April and in June I was already in.

Mother gave us *la bendición* every night.

At 101, almost 102, she was still telling people that—people who would come and see her. She only stayed one week in the hospital and one week in the nursing home. She was almost 102. She would go to the bathroom by herself. We were glad and she was glad. I would pray to God that we wouldn't have to put her in a nursing home. In fact, I didn't want to put her in there, my brother either. It was just too much, because she didn't want to eat anything. This way they could take good care of her.

Three brothers are still alive. One is in Michigan. My brother Curly is here. He's on the school board. He is a Korean veteran. I was the only one of age in WWII. Daniel was in the Navy. Curly was in the Army.

I went in San Antonio. From there I went to Camp Wolters near Ft. Worth, near Mineral Wells. We were just getting ready and we had very good training, trying to get us in shape. Lots of walking, started out with five miles, ten miles, and went up to thirty miles. Thirty miles is when we graduated from basic training.

We didn't know if we were going to Europe or the Pacific. We were just in the infantry. I was with the Twenty-Ninth Infantry Division. The Twenty-Ninth and the First Divisions were the first ones to go on Omaha Beach. I was there on June 6th, but we stayed in the boats right there on the beach, and we were being bombed. Fortunately, we didn't get hit. Our mission was to get in and contact the First Division about where the two divisions were going to meet.

When we landed we had to secure the beach. The Twenty-Ninth had three regiments: 116th regiment was the first one that went in. The 115th went in. The 175th was to make contact. We landed at Omaha.

We were too busy. We were being fired on with artillery. But we were missed. When we landed, first thing we did, go into position on the beach. It had been taken by the 116th. From there on we went from hedgerow through hedgerow. We were fighting the Germans all the way through. We hit Isigny and from there we went to St. Lo.

After the beach I did have a little scar but I didn't apply for that. It happened a couple of days later. Just some skin on my leg and the medic was going to put in for a Purple Heart, but said, "No, you're not." He said, "Why?" I told him, "My mother's a widow and I don't want her to have a heart attack when she gets a telegram." After I got out they were getting twenty-five points for each Purple Heart, so I missed out. Anyway, I had enough points to get out and come back home.

The boat landed on early June 7, 1944. It was about two or three o'clock in the morning. We made contact with some of the 116th. A few days later, I went to the 116th Aid Station, and I asked for one of my friends. A medic—Mauricio Cuellar. I asked for him and he didn't make it beyond the beach. He was killed at the beach. Mauricio was in the 116th. He was one of the first that landed.

The only friend I heard about—he was a replacement later—we had basic training together—was Morris Dittlinger. He is supposed to have a filling station there in Houston somewhere. He used to be in Robstown. He joined our outfit in August. He was in a different company.

The Twenty-Ninth Division was called—the nickname was LET'S GO! The logo . . . St. Lo was the big battle we won. We went through the streets. We had M1s. We took St. Lo. Our regiment went through there. I think our division also went through there.

There were very few people, but they had those little white flags. The commanding officer called me in. They were happy that I spoke Spanish. There was this lady from Spain. She gave us a lot of information. We were in the Brittany Peninsula [possibly the Normandy Peninsula]. That's when I was wounded. She told us just about where everything was. She didn't know any English, but she knew Spanish and French. She told us just about where they [Germans] were. She gave us very good information. I went in and talked to the commanding officer. I told them what she said. She told us where they had foxholes and where they were hiding. In Normandy they had the hedgerows. And we didn't want to lead an attack, because anytime they would get a tank through, that was a good target for the Germans. They could see where we were going through. So we jumped the hedgerows. We were in a line going to the next hedgerows to get that land, and we had them on the run. We had a map and the woman told us where they were.

[In Germany] I ran into a lady and she was mad because we had taken her potatoes. That's when I found out potatoes were *kartoffeln*. In Germany they had a cellar in the bottom in this house that we took. They had sacks of potatoes. So we took them to our mess sergeant in the kitchen so they'd make french fries. She was mad because she was looking for the potatoes. Couldn't find any *kartoffeln*. We took everything she had, bags of all the potatoes. I said, "This is not our trouble. We were not asked to come to you. We were not supposed to be here. We're down here on account of your mess." I think that was in Jülich or Suhl in Germany.

That lady was real mad, but we said, "We're here. You started the war." That's how I found our *kartoffeln* were potatoes. We were there at that house and spent the night there. The Germans were on the run. . . .

After the war was over, we didn't have much trouble. The Russians were attacking from one end, they were coming in. We were supposed to meet at the Elbe River. The Germans were giving up to us, because they didn't want to give up to the Russians. We were taking lots of prisoners. They were just standing there with their hands up.

We were supposed to meet the Russians at the Elbe River. The Germans were coming over giving themselves up. The commanding officer said that he had met with the Russian officers, that everything was cleared. That's when they assigned us to the Bremerhaven Peninsula.

The generals had met with the Russian officers. They had had a meeting. Everything was over and taken care of. That's when they announced VE Day.

I was in the Army of Occupation for three or four months in Bremen and Bremerhaven. That's when I got a two-week leave to the French Riviera. It was beautiful. I was supposed to go for one week and I stayed two weeks. I thought they had given me two weeks. Everything was free, we were just guests—food, cigarettes—and I don't smoke, still don't smoke. I gave my cigarettes to my buddies. They could sell them for a lot of money. Everything was given to us there. I served in Bremerhaven, fulfilling my obligation as to the point system, and then I came home in 1945. I was discharged October 21, 1945.

I came into Anthony's to buy me a suit, and they hired me. Everybody was coming to me and asking me about the war and everything. I guess the manager kind of liked me. He put me to work. I went to work on

November 1, 1945.
Camilo Gomez
Army Air Corps
Air and Sea Rescue Unit

From a Tough Neighborhood to Rescuing Soldiers
Camilo Gomez was born in Manclova, Mexico, on July 28, 1924, to Gilbert
and Candelaria Gomez. He was raised in a rough neighborhood in Houston,
Texas. It was known as the "Bloody Fifth." His stint in the service required
Camilo to save soldiers. Eventually, he gave his time to civil rights.

My daddy brought me and my mother (to the USA) when I was two months old.

We grew up in the Fifth Ward. They used to call it the "Bloody Fifth." There was blood floating all over the place. That was the roughest neighborhood. Just fighting. Sometimes, and it's still divided by wards; one ward couldn't go into the other ward and stuff like that. I didn't know until '42 that I was born over there [in Mexico]. I found out because me and my friend went to sign [up] in the Marine Corps and they had to have my birth certificate. I went to tell my mama, "I need my birth certificate." She said, "It's not here, you know." And I said, "Why?" "Because you were born in Mexico." "What?"

I dropped out in the tenth grade. I started working. It's not that I liked the money. When you have to eat . . . A bunch of people in Fifth Ward finished high school. There was quite a few that dropped out. Quite a few that went on to college.

I volunteered in 1942. I wanted to be in the Marines. I was not an American citizen. I went to the draft board and told them I wanted to be called. They said, "You're not a citizen." I said, "I don't care. I want to go." They said, "Will your father sign?" I said, "Yes." Well, they called me in May 1943.

My mother gave me *la bendición* before I left. I was seventeen. I got my older brother—his name is Gilbert, too—and he signed the papers for me. I wanted to go in the Air Force. While we were at Fort Sam they asked, "Do you really want to go?" I said, "Yes." Army Air Corps then.

At first I went from San Antonio to Wichita Falls to take my basic [training]. From there they shipped me to New Orleans to Engineering and Navigation School. Then Uncle Sam shipped me all the way back to Wichita Falls [Sheppard Field] to take basic training all over again, because they don't want you sitting around doing nothing. It is hot as hell in the summer and cold as hell in the winter. I went both times. When I first went in it was summer. Then when I went back it was winter.

They shipped us to Homestead, Florida. I did a lot of KP. Just put on KP. Just work in the kitchen. Handyman. Mess hall. Clean pots. I got tired of doing that. So I went to the mess kitchen office and told them, "I want to go overseas or I'm going to go AWOL."

They shipped me to Iran and I finally ended up in Casablanca, North Africa. That was my home base. I flew some. I got put in navigation. They put me into Air and Sea Rescue Unit. The Air and Rescue was on a ship stationed right up on the waterfront in Casablanca.

When I flew I was a right side gunner. I did that for two-three months, something like that.

If something fell into the water, we'd go get it. Anything. They'd radio to us. The base was about eight miles from the harbor. We'd go out in PT [Patrol Torpedo] boats.

We went to Algiers. We went to the Rock of Gibraltar. We'd go see what the problems were. Uncle Sam tells you what to do. We went out to see if everything was perfect just like the Rock of Gibraltar.

When the war was over, I was on the ship or the rescue boat. We got orders we were coming home. They shipped me back to the base. That's when they made me an MP. I was an MP for four months before I came home.

I came home in April 1946. I was discharged in Camp Chaffee, Arkansas. Uncle Sam brought me to Houston by train. They [his family] knew I was coming, but they didn't know where or when. I didn't know myself. Uncle Sam is secret[ive]. He doesn't tell the left hand what the right hand is doing. Even in peacetime.

At the train station I caught the bus home. I knocked on the door, and my mother answered. She couldn't say a thing. She was just crying.

I was ready to go back after I was out about a year. My momma started crying. She said, "You don't need to go. You already went."

When I left I had started working with the Star Jewelry Company after school. Then [after dropping out] I went full time.

In 1946 that's where I went to work. I stayed there twelve years. Then I worked for Corrigan's. The owner was named Corrigan. Zale's bought him out. I stayed there seventeen years. I opened up my own shop—Camilo's Jewelry. I had it until 1993. From 1976 to 1993.

My wife Olga helped me. Her and myself had it for quite a while. Then I started hiring people.

Gilbert and his family were successful in the jewelry business. The girls went to college and followed professional careers. Gilbert joined LULAC and contributed to the community by working with that group. He has pride in the fact members of his family have served their country.

I was in LULAC. My brother, Gilbert Gomez, was the national president of LULAC. He was the first one to start in the jewelry business. He was in the infantry. None of us were wounded. There were three of us in WWII. Gilbert was in the regular army. My second brother Roy was in the Navy. And I was in the Air Force [Army Air Corps]. My kid brother, Oscar, in the Vietnam War was a Marine. He was the only one who got wounded.

Pfc. Raúl Martinez
73rd Station Hospital

Making History
The late Raúl Martinez of Goliad, Texas, belonged to a family of seven boys and four girls. Of the seven brothers, four served in WWII. Two served in Korea and one served in Vietnam. Raúl was an exceptionally tall Mexican American. As a soldier he drove a truck. When he came home, however, he made history. Unfortunately, Raúl had passed away by the time I started interviewing. His widow Lucy and his sister Estella, however, kindly told me his story. During WWII Raúl drove a light truck 345, serving in Rome and Arno. Polo (Apolonio) Martinez served in the infantry and as an MP in North Africa and Italy. Rubén Martinez was in artillery in New Guinea and in Japan. Elías Martinez served with the Merchant Marines out of San Diego.

Lucy Martinez, Raúl's widow, related the following:

He was in Italy. After the war was almost over, he was with his division and they were all parked along the highway, and that is where he went looking for his brother Paul (Polo). And they met in Italy. They hadn't seen each other in a long time.

The only thing he mentioned was Italy. He used to sing "Oh, Marie, O Marie." The trucks he drove, he was taking merchandise and stuff for the army. Food.

They gave candy to girls they knew. They used to give cigarettes. And the little kids that ran around when they were traveling. They would give them goodies that they had.

He knew a lot of Italian when he came back.

Raúl's claim to fame was that he was the first Hispanic to join the police force in Houston, Texas, a city that has a large Hispanic population.

There were no *Mejicano* policemen then. He met a LULAC lawyer, two lawyers—Herrera and Hernandez [Johnny Herrera and Alfred Hernandez].

They saw him, and he talked to them about getting a job. He wanted to do something. They said, "I'll tell you what, Raúl, let's make a date and we'll go to the police department and talk . . . " Chief Morrison was the one then. They said, "We'll go talk to them and take you."

The first thing they [the police department] said was, "No, they couldn't hire any *Mejicanos* because they weren't tall enough." That was an excuse they gave. When my husband went up there with them [the two attorneys], they spoke for him. Of course, they were lawyers. They had their own way of explaining themselves as to what they wanted. They told him [Morrison] about my husband. They [chief of police] came up first with that deal about not being tall enough. The attorneys said, "Raúl, would you please stand up?" He stood up—six feet, five. The chief didn't know what to say. And of course he was very fair. . . .

[The day before President Kennedy was assassinated] Raúl called and said, "I'm coming home to change because I am guarding him [President Kennedy], and some other policemen are going to be there, too. Richard

After serving in WWII with the US Army, Raúl Martinez
returned to Texas, where he became the first Hispanic
police officer in Houston. Here he stands behind and left of
President John F. Kennedy on November 21, 1963. Martinez
guarded President Kennedy the night before the president's
assassination in Dallas. Property of author, bequeathed to
her by estate of Raúl Martinez.

Delano was there, too." Raúl said, "I'm going to have to take care of him." Later he told me, "If I had been in Dallas, they would have killed me first. They would have had to shoot him and shoot me."

Twenty-three years [Raúl Martinez was on the police force]. He retired from that and went into politics.

Raúl's sister Estella added the following:

They appointed him as a constable, because they didn't have a constable. He was the first Hispanic constable. The commissioners decided it was time they got a first. So he was appointed. It was 1973. After that he had to run. He was elected.

Raúl Martinez came from a long line of Texans. In 1821 his great-great-great-great-great-grandfather Manuel Beccerra accompanied Commissioner Don Esteban [Stephan F. Austin, known as the father of Texas] and his party of ten men as they explored the Goliad territory for a possible future settlement. Thus, this family whose ancestors lived in the Goliad, Texas, area for centuries offered their sons to fight for this country, and they proudly did.

President Kennedy visited a LULAC Convention in Houston before he traveled to Dallas in November 1963. Because of Raúl Martinez's experience as a peace officer and because of his height, he was selected to guard the president during his visit in Houston. Raúl had more than one claim to fame.

Arturo Vasquez
Staff Sergeant, gunner
8th Air Force

An Analytical Soldier
Arturo Vasquez, from Laredo, Texas, graduated from high school, and two weeks later was on his way to basic training at Sheppard Field in Wichita Falls, Texas. Arturo described his service experience with precision, a clue he would later in life work with numbers. He said that most recruits wanted to be pilots, and although he didn't make pilot he was a part of an airplane crew.

While at Sheppard Field during parades when they raised the flag and we marched, if they saw a recruit faint, they just dragged him away. Some bodies couldn't take it.

From there we trained in gunnery school in Harlingen, Texas. Everyone wanted to be a pilot. The Air Force did not draft anyone. You had to volunteer. Those that didn't make pilot became bombardiers, navigators, or copilots. On the B-24s. The B-25 and B-26 required less people.

The class dealt with camouflage, ammunition. We trained by firing from an airplane to a target connected with a long wire behind us. The bullets were colored and we all shot at the same target. We trained with two airplanes, also, using .50-caliber bullets. We used machine guns. The army used .50-caliber machine guns.

The B-51 was the best airplane in the word. The B-47 could fly at a high altitude. The B-38 allowed the enemy to see what the pilot was doing. It had a wheel like an auto; it allowed the pilot to turn the plane in any direction.

We went to England. On D-day I was back home in Laredo attending my mother's funeral. So my crew replaced me. I trained with another crew and began flying with a bomb squad.

On the B-24 I was a nose gunner. They removed the ball turret. The enemy flies right, left, and above you. The Japanese came from the direction of the sun so you couldn't see them.

We were dropping bombs in Germany on military targets, oil places, marshalling yards, ball-bearing factories. The airplane had to gain altitude and then nose dive and glide.

We found out that Germany got one third of its oil from Ploiesti, Romania. The Americans made mistakes. They flew at low levels and broke radio silence. The Germans shot them down. The Americans bombed Ploiesti until everything burned.

If we bombed something in Germany, they built it back up at night. There was a railroad in Salzgitter and a bridge that led to it. The Americans bombed the bridge to that road. The Germans built it back up in two to three days.

We flew over it and saw no bridge. At night the Germans rolled a bridge out, and in the daytime it disappeared.

The bombs weighed 250, 500, 1,000, and 2,000 pounds. We also had incendiary bombs. Fifty sticks, which were long and narrow. A certain altitude triggered a switch and dispersed the sticks in different directions.

We dropped a two-thousand-pound bomb. The Germans rebuilt a factory. The bomb had delayed action juice. So the bomb didn't explode. One and a half hours later as the Germans were rebuilding, the bomb went off.

The incendiary bombs were the sticks, explosive. Then there was the plastic. They could put it around a tree and it blew up the tree and other things.

Before flying they served us fresh eggs and milk. On the next day, when we didn't fly, they served us powdered eggs and powdered milk. They believed that fresh eggs and milk improved our vision.

We saw airplanes going down when they were hit by antiaircraft shells on the wings. We got a direct hit, but the shell didn't explode. We didn't go to our place to land. I was told, "Don't look at the flight deck." They showed us the shell, and I asked if I could keep it as a souvenir. They said I could, but that it could explode at any minute.

The flak suit was made of cloth but had copper in places to protect our bodies from flak.

I was in the nose (nose gunner), and I didn't care. I would go down fighting.

The British flew at night. They didn't have the same sights we had. The US had the best sights. The British had maps and places—anywhere in that particular neighborhood, residential areas or raw land. They damaged churches. The Germans accused the US of bombing churches. The US did make mistakes.

We were awakened at 2:30 a.m. We went to the mess hall and had breakfast. Then we were driven to a building. They showed us a map, how to go in and come out. If we became lost, we were to take a bearing of 270. Getting in and out would be tricky.

The Germans were defending a military target. The land was barren. No antiaircraft was seen.

The leader said to go to the right. One plane went down. Someone said, "That guy is always looking for a medal."

There was an island, Sylt Island. They told us to stay five miles away from it. It was in the North Sea close to Germany. The submarines went there to be serviced. There was a tall cement wall with a number on it. It had antiaircraft guns. One plane didn't have a chance. It fell two or three miles from the coast of the island.

Bullets in machine guns were .50 caliber. We had bullets which were regular, armor piercing, explosive, and tracers. The tracers were slower than the others, because of their weight.

England had everything there for us. In Italy the men didn't have mess halls or barracks, only tents. They ate out in the open. The men flew B-24s. Later they built a mess hall.

They told us that we received more money for flying. And I was a staff sergeant because if we landed in Germany they wouldn't bother you as much with that rank.

The B-24 had four engines. The B-25 had two engines. The B-25 bombed close to front lines. They were supposed to go beyond front lines. The infantry sent flares to tell the fliers: "This is the front line."

I left right before the war was over, because I completed my thirty-five flying missions. I was back on a troop ship. My future son-in-law's father was also on his way back. That was the first time I saw waves that were so high they came up over the ship. There must have been a hurricane because the waves were like that for two days. They told us to stay inside behind locked doors. We opened the doors and saw the size of the waves. The ships have to face the wind.

I was on the ship coming home when the war in Europe ended. The loudspeaker spread the word: "The war is over!" The men who had not finished their thirty-five missions might have to go fight in the Pacific.

The Japanese fight until they are dead.

During WWII I felt patriotic. Every day we heard that Germany rolled over a country. I felt I had to go to war. Hispanics were the same as everybody else. The service tried to get the healthy men.

After the war I went to the University of Texas and graduated in 1949. I went to Laredo and found the political situation pretty bad. So I came to Corpus Christi. I joined LULAC and the GI Forum. I started my accounting firm.

Arturo Vasquez became a respected citizen of Corpus Christi. He served on the CCISD school board for twenty years. He was active in civic organizations throughout the city.

Cesario Reyna

4th Army Company 934
Heavy Automotive

Not a Handicap

Cesario Reyna from Waco, Texas, was two years old when his brother ac-cidentally injured him in his left eye with an ice pick, and Cesario lost sight in that eye. He never allowed that loss to define him, however. Instead, he begged the army, and enough officers, to let him join. Finally they agreed, and Cesario showed everyone he could succeed. Even after the war, Cesario excelled in his work. In his senior years he served as an honor guard at mil-itary funerals.

My mother was sick in bed with fever. My brother was making lem-onade for her. He was picking at the ice on the table. I was pulling his pants and he turned around. They told my Mama that I would be blind the rest of my life. That it would start hemorrhaging and that it would have to be removed.

In 1929 we moved to Houston with my mother and my brothers and sisters. I worked at the Farmer's Market by unloading trailers. I sold vegetables until I was sixteen years of age. My next job was delivering telegrams on a bicycle. Substation on Lyons and Harney. We went from there. We had this territory. Everything I made I gave to my mother. Times were hard.

I didn't even know my father until I got out of the service. I asked my brother what had happened and he said that Mom and Dad were always arguing. I believe that my father liked to drink a lot. She wanted him to save a little money so they could buy a place of their own.

I finished the sixth grade and at age seventeen I went to work at the Houston Ship Yard. Graveyard shift. I was eighteen in February. In March 1944 they called me up.

When I got called I went to my examination and they didn't want to pass me because of my one eye. I argued with that guy (a first lieu-tenant) because I already had three brothers in the service. Two in the Army Air Corp and one in the Navy. [A younger brother went to Ko-rea.] The lieutenant said, "Son, you can't go because you can't see out of one eye." I said, "You don't need but one eye to shoot." So he went up there to talk to a major or colonel. They motioned me over there so I went. By that time we were all naked because they were examining us. He said, "We just can't pass you." I said, "Why?" "On account of your eye." "Well," I said, "I'm sure I wouldn't have no trouble shooting." He said, "No."

I argued with them so long they finally said, "OK. We're going to take you but you won't be going overseas." I said, "Well, okay. That's all right." That's how I got into the service.

But you know once you get in there—we went overseas.

My mother said, "Son, did they examine your left eye?" I answered, "Yes ma'am." "Well, what did they say about that?" "They didn't want to take me on account of my left eye, but I told them that you need only one eye to shoot." She just laughed.

By that time I was married and my wife was expecting. My mother gave me *la bendición*. We got married on March 11, 1944. On March they called me for the examination and in April I left for San Antonio.

My mother told me to be careful and to do whatever I was told. I didn't have any problems, because I always respected my mother. What she said went. That's the reason I didn't have any trouble in the service. Every time that sergeant hollered my name I said, "Yes sir."

From San Antonio we went to Camp McCain in Mississippi. Basic Training. And from there we went to North Carolina for more training. They put me in Heavy Automotive, Company 934th. What we did we repaired any kind of vehicle from the largest to the size of a jeep. Fourth Army, Co. 934, Heavy Automotive. We came to South Camp Hood in San Antonio. More mechanic training. Then to North Camp Hood. Shipped out to New York.

Arrived in Le Havre, France. When we got to Le Havre, there was a big bunch of sunken ships out there. From there we went to France. We had a certain place to stop to do repair work. Anytime we moved there was a need somewhere else. We went through France and Germany. Belgium on our return trip. They stopped us at Munich, because the war was just about over. That was the last place we worked.

We soldiers don't ask questions. We heard rumors about the Russians. We stayed in Munich doing nothing. No spare parts for tanks. We could do electrical work. We saw huge German tanks just sitting there.

In Munich there were mostly elderly people—from forty or fifty to older. They respected us. You could tell by their faces. They looked sorry about the war. We had our own provisions.

The only thing we got from them was liquor: beer, wine, or schnapps. Anytime you have a bunch of GIs that's the first thing they want to locate. They said the schnapps was made out of potato peelings. It was strong.

In Munich was the first time I had seen a plastic canteen. Me and this other fellow were sharing the same room. It was a big house where some of us were staying. The plastic canteen belonged to one of our men. We went and got some schnapps in it. My canteen and his. Next morning I woke up and had one heck of a headache. I looked at my canteen and wanted to get a little drink. It tasted awful bad. So I spilled a little bit and you could see a porridge. I looked at his [roommate's plastic] canteen and his canteen was flat. I had to get rid of the canteen. I got up with a big head.

Mostly we were in the rear. At one time we were with the Fourth Army and they transferred us to Third Army, which was Patton. He was moving pretty fast. We were always behind them. We weren't actually in combat, but you could hear all that bombing. Those vehicles had to be fixed so we'd sleep inside a truck or on top of the truck because we were so tired. We lay down anywhere.

In Munich when we were stationed there and the war ended, there were some people who went to Dachau. They wouldn't let us go. Infantry went to the camp and saw all that in the camp. I had some pictures showing piles of skeletons of Jews. I got them from a Russian. I had ten to fifteen, but the last time I looked I have about three, but I don't know where in the world I got them. They were piled up just like lumber. It was pitiful. I traded the pictures for a pack of cigarettes. I had pistols and stuff that I sent home. It disappeared.

In the pictures you could see the bodies hanging out of boxcars. Flies, bugs, and everything on top of those people. It was terrible. I don't have to tell you about the smell. They didn't let us out because they knew that if they did, we'd go down there and look for ourselves.

A little before this, the second or third week after we got to Munich, Sgt. Long, the mail clerk, he had to go into town and he asked me if I wanted to go. We left that morning. We stopped at a little town and got us a bushel of wine bottles. Got the mail and came back. We were coming back on this lonely road and saw lots of GIs hollering, dancing, and shooting their rifles. I said, "Man they must have one hell of a party. Let's stop." We got there and asked, "Hey, fellows, you got a party?"

They said, "Don't you know? Don't you know? The war's over." That's how we found out it was over. We looked at each other and couldn't say nothing.

We got in our trucks and were going to Belgium. Got to Belgium and stayed there. After the second or third week, we are getting mad. Waiting on a ship to take us back home. One day they called us in the morning. The captain told us, "There is a freighter here that is willing to take us. But the only problem is they don't have any supplies to feed us. We would only get one meal. Shoot, we didn't care if we didn't get no meals. So we went ahead and said that we wanted to go home. The whole company. We slept on top of the deck, anywhere you could. That's how we got back home to Newport, Virginia.

The first thing they assigned us to was barracks so we could clean up. By that time it must have been noon. They told us we could go eat at a particular camp. They had German prisoners serving. I remember lots of those guys were talking trying to tell the Germans, "Put some more on that tray." It was the first American meal. The Germans kept saying, "Nein, nein." We said, "Put more meat on it fella." They did. You've never seen a GI who's hungry and hasn't had a good meal in a long time. I had been eating C rations, potatoes in a little can. Egg and ham in cans. Green beans. We ate that when we could get it. If not we did without or caught a rabbit. One time we stopped on the way to Belgium after the war. We had German cooks. There was a big pond. They were preparing a meal and I heard a German say something about a big snake. They were jabbering and pointing to the water. A couple of them took off their clothes and ran to the water. Whatever they caught they sort of wrestled with it. Three or four of them went in and when they came out they brought a snake with them that was about six inches thick. They cooked the snake. I didn't taste it. A lot of the GIs ate the food.

When shooting a rifle you always close one eye. That's what I told that colonel. When we took training with rifles, we had Springfield 03s. That thing was as tall as me [five foot two]. Three inches above my head. We went to the rifle range for training. Them guys used to laugh at me because I was the skinniest and shortest guy in the company and weighed a hundred to a hundred and twelve pounds.

We shoot from the prone positions—different positions. They laughed at me because every time I shot, that thing would almost knock me down. Some of them were used in the First World War. You had to hold it against your shoulder because when you fire, it is going to hit you hard. After you took all that training it came out of the bulletin board what was your grade. They had: experts, sharpshooter, and marksman, different categories. And right by my name Cesario Reyna was expert. All those guys who had laughed at me—I just pointed to my name. I had already seen where they were.

I got along fine with them. There was one Italian, Balsimo, who was just a couple of inches taller than me. He always liked to kid me and we were always wrestling. We would go to the PX and him and I would dance. When we got overseas him and I used to fight one another. That day that Long and I went to pick up the mail, when we got back, we had German prisoners there; they would cook for us and do whatever chores. They didn't want to escape. They were eating there. When we came back, everybody was so sad. I said, "What the hell is wrong?"

They said Balsimo had died. I said, "What do you mean? How in the hell did he die?" There was this machine the size of a jeep but it was like a half-track. It's open—no top. He had been playing with the Germans chasing them with the half-track. He had cut it too short and the thing fell over; he fell out and it crushed him. That was the only fellow we lost. Trying to think of his name, Balsimo. We were always kidding around and boxing. We went through training together.

Back to San Antonio. One hundred dollars to get back home. Then they sent you $100 every other month until you had $300. It was a lot of good experiences that I had knowing those guys that came from different parts of the country.

I tell everybody that these kids coming out of high school; they ought to make it mandatory for them to go [into the service] for two years.

Came back on a bus. My wife was glad to see me. The first thing I wanted when I got back was to get a job. There were no jobs. 1946. After trying so many places. Before I went into the service, I used to help my brother;

he was a jack of all trades. I learned a lot from him. Anytime I ran into someone building a fence, I used to stop and ask them if I could help them. I know how to hang paper. Little jobs like that before I went into the service.

After I came out I went everywhere. Finally, I met a friend of mine. He said, "Shorty, you working?" I told him, "I've been looking and looking." He said, "That's what happened to me. I'm going to the University of Houston. I'm studying to be a mechanic. You ought to try it."

So I did. I went to learn mechanics. After I got my certificate, I went to different car dealers but they wouldn't hire me. I don't have to tell you why. Believe me, I'm not bragging, but I was number one or two in the class. My grades were As and Bs. I could take an engine, take it out of a car, set it on a table, dismantle it completely, and check the cylinders. If there was a way, the specs showed you could roll the cylinders, you could put oversized rings in it. That's one thing I learned. You could put it back together and make it work. I was damn good.

I went into body and fender work at school. Again, I was one of the best ones. Again, I tried to get a job with dealers and they wouldn't hire me. I had learned roofing from my brother. So these fellows were putting up wood shingles and I went to work with them as an apprentice. We had subdivisions they were putting up wood shingles. I started working with different contractors. I did that until I retired. I did all kinds of training. I fixed everybody's car.

I joined the union and told the agent what kind of roofing I could do. Ninety percent of the members were colored and the officers were colored. The guy said, "You sound like you know what you're talking about." I said, "I know what I'm doing. I want to get out as a journeyman." They hired me as a journeyman's helper. "How long before I can get a raise?" "It'll be up to the company to see how you do it."

From that day on that man called me saint until the day he passed away. I worked there for two years. It didn't take me long to become a journeyman. You get top wages then. He didn't want to let me go because he wanted to get me a crew. I was one of the best.

A few years later they wanted to hire me as a business agent's assistant. There were a lot of people here from Latin American countries coming in here and getting into the shops without being union. They took less money. They hired me as a business agent's assistant. Back then I used to drink a lot and I used to hang around with lots of colored guys because I knew a lot of them from the union.

My wife said, "Honey you do what you want to do." So I went ahead and got that particular job and was signing up people left and right.

We had fourteen kids, two born dead. Ophelia Leal was my wife's name. Naturally, on the budget report they would see all these new members with Spanish names. I knew the treasurer, but he didn't know me. He said, "Rob, who is this assistant you have now—Reyna—Have I met him?" Rob said, "He probably knows you."

Cesario became a successful union man. Then, after retiring from that job, he volunteered to assist in veteran burials.

I retired in 1991. The reason was that my arthritis knees hurt; at the airports I had to walk so far. I joined this post here, VFW (Veterans of Foreign Wars). George Chavez talked me into getting a detail, and that's what I do now. Tomorrow we have a service. They are dying left and right. Another Tuesday. We stay pretty busy.

Antonio Torres
80th Infantry Division
Company A
318th Regiment

First Rejected and Then Accepted
Antonio Torres of Kingsville, Texas, lost his father when he was six years old. Antonio wanted to fight for his country, but he was rejected at first. As the war became more fierce, the restrictions once applied to recruits were relaxed, and Antonio was allowed to become a soldier.

When our father died, my mother was left with the challenge of raising two boys and two girls. She worked as a domestic and the children who were big enough picked cotton to help the family.

In 1938, I went to New Mexico and worked in the CCC (Civilian Conservation Corps) and earned thirty dollars a month. At that time soldiers who heard of the salary the CCC boys were earning became jealous because they were only earning twenty-one dollars monthly.

In 1940 I attempted to volunteer for the army. I was rejected because of my low weight and the condition of my teeth. So instead of joining the army I worked at different jobs, including the railroad and an apprenticeship.

Although I had been told that since I was the only man at home I wouldn't be called by the army, I volunteered again. This time the army accepted me. Like many young men, I wanted to join the Army Air Corps but was assigned to the infantry. Other young boys were given thirty-day leaves, I did not have time to go back home.

Because my mother worked for a priest, she asked me to go to the priest to receive a blessing before I left home. I went to Father Álvarez for the blessing. As I knelt, the priest advised, "Now don't laugh!" Then he gave me the blessing.

I was sent to Dodd Field, which was part of Fort Sam Houston in San Antonio, Texas. After a week at Dodd Field I was sent to Camp Forrest in Tennessee. We spent two months in maneuvers.

Nashville, Tennessee, was a place where we would go to relax. I had a friend, Alfredo Rentería from Los Angeles. He and I would go to a drugstore in Nashville. Some girls would actually come in and look at us because they had never seen Mexican American people before.

We spent two months in maneuvers in that area. Later we would note that the mountains in Tennessee resembled the mountains we would run into in Europe. In Camp Phillips, Kansas, we spent three months. There we did a lot of marching.

In Yuma, Arizona, we participated in desert maneuvers for three months. We were given an assignment. After being given a compass, instructions with coordinates, and information about the stars, the platoon leader told us to go find a certain locale, which would be marked with a stake with a red cloth on it. We looked all night and never found it. Finally, the lieutenant asked me to help the sergeant. I found the stake. The umpires who were the judges noted that I could find anything.

Before long it was time to ship out. I was sent to Fort Dix, New Jersey, by train. After that it was Camp Kilmer, which would be the POE, point of embarkation. The men were watched carefully and they were not allowed to go to town. However, across the way there was a park. We could not go, but we noticed that prisoners of war were allowed to go to the park while supervised by guards.

In late June 1944 we sailed to England on the *Queen Mary*. For two weeks or so the Americans were running, marching, and participating in other maneuvers in England.

We were taken to Omaha Beach, which had already been secured by the Allies on D-day. We had been trained to get off ships by using ropes. This time they let us off on small boats. We were scared. A man who isn't scared is a man who is dead.

We rode trucks to the front lines, and on the way we saw lots of dead Germans. Airplanes would fire at us at night. We had antiaircraft that would fire back at the German airplanes. I was shocked, because we were right in the middle.

I first saw action in Argentan, France. We were waiting near a field of turnips and a field of wheat. A colonel and a captain were trying to decide on which way to go. I was a first scout, a point man. David P. Curry was the second scout and was to follow fifty to one hundred yards behind me. Yardage always depends on the terrain. He has to be able to see me. After that the squad would follow.

I decided to go a certain way. Then I saw some tracers and decided that there were Germans not far from us. So I immediately hit the ground and just lay there. After a while David Curry said, "Let's go back."

I didn't want to get up. The firing was about two and a half feet up from the ground, but they couldn't see exactly where I was because of the wheat. I told David that if he wanted to go back he could. After a long while I ran back to the company.

The lieutenant came up to see how we had done. He said, "Torres, you mean you made it back?" Then I found out that the colonel had been killed by German bullets. I guess he failed to hit the ground when the firing began. Also, I found out that my good friend, Alfredo Rentería from Los Angeles, had died from bullet wounds. When he was first injured, a friend of ours had stayed with him for many hours waiting for things to calm down before seeking help. He didn't even call a medic. He just lost his power to think when the firing started. My friend might have lived if a medic had been called.

The English troops were supposed to help at Argentan, but the Germans gave the English a hard time and they didn't get to help us.

The Fourth Armored Division broke through the lines. I saw hundreds of tanks and artillery. Then the Americans made a mistake and started shooting at US soldiers. Finally, that was stopped. At night, again, American artillery fired at our men. The American soldiers were called back and returned in trucks.

At some places people would come out and give us wine. One soldier wanted me to drink with him, but I told him I wouldn't. He asked me why and I told him that I didn't want to get too happy. I needed to be alert. Before long someone started firing in our direction, and the boy who was drinking was shot and killed.

Someone started shooting flares so that the Americans would know that we were returning. A major told us, "When you reach the bridge, don't stop. Keep moving."

The sergeant told the squad, "You're going to go out there." One of our men said, "Antonio, we're always in front. We are going to get killed."

I told the sergeant what the man had said and so the sergeant put other men to do the job we had been doing. He said I would be in reserve. They went out there and some of them were killed. The Germans began firing at us and I hit the ground.

Then a young German surrendered to us. The captain wanted to shoot the German. The young boy kneeled and begged for his life. The captain aimed for the young boy and couldn't hit him. A sergeant arrived and took the captain with him.

Kenneth Foster from Kentucky had invited me to his home when we had trained in Nashville, Tennessee, but I had never gone. One day a barrage occurred. Kenneth and I jumped into a hole. Kenneth's lips were trembling and he said, "They're going to kill us," and I jokingly said, "Let's just go home!"

We saw lines and lines of German vehicles and tanks that had been hit by American airplanes, even though the Germans had good anti-tank and antiaircraft 88mm guns.

When I was really scared I would pray, "*Virgin Mary, cover me up with your cape.*"

We kept on going to the front, and while we were close to Germany, I was hit. That was October 8, 1944.

A medic came to help me. I told him to go away or he would get hit. I began walking to the Aid Station and decided to take the highway. German artillery started firing at me. So I crawled into a hole. When the firing stopped, I went to the heavy artillery section. There was a Hispanic from Chicago there. He said, "*Cuñado, que le pasó?*" [Brother in-law, what happened to you?] The medic then took me to the aid station. At the aid station the doctor couldn't see me right away because some German artillery was firing at them. So I had to wait until the firing stopped.

Meanwhile, the second scout was hit. He was patched up and given a tag. Then he was put in a jeep and was being driven to the aid station. The jeep ran over a mine field and the two men were killed.

At the field hospital I saw lots of men. The medic wanted to go get the chaplain. I told him I wasn't that sick. In Nancy, France, I was operated on. I went from France to England and finally to Charleston, South Carolina. A guy from New Mexico said, "Let's go into town." We went and enjoyed ourselves, but on the way back I fell and hurt the arm that had been operated on. The nurse made a new rule for me, "No more trips to town." Then on Christmas Day everyone could go to town.

In 1946 I received a disability discharge.

Amadeo J. Sanchez
7th Army
63rd Division
1st Scout

A Mother's Promesa
Amadeo was born on January 1, 1926, on Javelin Ranch near Cypress, Texas. He lived with his mother, two brothers, and two sisters in Edinburg. He received his draft notice on Mother's Day, May 10, 1944. The letter he received from the selective service broke his mother's heart. Amadeo's mother made a promesa that if Amadeo returned alive, she and her son would make a long walk to a church and then walk on their knees to the altar. Amadeo had

some close calls, but when he returned, he and his mother made the long trek.

I was trained in Fort Hood near Waco, Texas, and then at Camp Van Dorn for infantry training. There we heard that the Sixty-Third Division had been wiped out, and that our group would replace the Sixty-Third.

I was given a ten-day pass back home. Before I left to go back to rejoin my unit, my mother had me kneel in the living room of our home so that she could give me *la bendición*. "*Te encomiendo en Dios,*" she added. [I commend you to God.] And my letters to me in Europe always said, "*Que Diosito te ayude.*" [May God help you.]

Finally they sent us to Camp Shanks in New York, our point of embarkation. We knew we would now be sent to Europe where the heavy fighting was going on.

[December 1944] we went to Marseille, France. We marched through the city and people lined up on both sides of the street to look us over. Their faces looked happy. Some knew to ask for chocolate and cigarettes; they had learned that soldiers usually carried those two items.

We marched to the top of a hill and set up our tents. The next day they loaded us up on trucks and took us to the railroad so that we could travel by train instead of by truck. All of our gear was in the trucks and would be given to us later.

At the railway station we were assigned to travel in boxcars. We were insulted because these cars had been used to transport cattle, and we thought the trucks would have been more comfortable. At night in the train we saw lightning through the cracks and heard thunder, so we knew that rain would fall soon. By early morning we saw dead people by the railroad tracks.

We were taken to Nancy, France, then to a wooded area, which was the front lines. Then we found out that the "thunder and lightning" we had heard were the sounds and sights of fighting at the front!

Because we had left our gear in the trucks, we wore only light parkas. The news that shocked us at this time was that German airplanes had strafed the trucks with our duffel bags. The drivers were killed, and we knew that we would have been also, if it hadn't been for the smelly cattle cars! Then we were thankful that someone thought to transport us in the dirty box cars! After all, we did have our rifles and bandoliers and belts with shells.

I was to be the first scout in my platoon, the first man out in front, and I was supposed to look for anything that looked unusual. If I saw anything that could be dangerous to the rest of the men, I was to motion for them to get down. The second scout is to do the same, but he is supposed to be ten to twenty feet behind the first scout. The artillery observer who carried a walkie-talkie was to walk with me and notify artillery if they were needed.

In training we had hated our helmets. They were heavy and didn't feel good on our heads. On the front lines we appreciated our helmets. In fact I wished that I could bury myself inside my helmet to keep from getting hurt.

We walked over so many hills that some men just passed out. I was walking with a group and a tall, strong guy from California, Bob Sanchez. He was carrying a Browning Automatic Rifle, a heavy weapon with feet for standing it up known as a BAR. Another fellow who was also carrying a BAR just passed out. Bob Sanchez took his BAR, placed on his shoulder along with his BAR, and helped carry the man to where we were going. I heard that later in the war Bob Sanchez wanted to destroy a machine gun nest. He got up to take action and a bullet hit him in the forehead.

I may have passed out, too, because I was walking along and the next thing I remember is that I am digging a foxhole. The rest I don't remember.

We were constantly attacking, and then we knew that there would be a counterattack. The first and second scouts are supposed to take turns sleeping. I was so tired that I fell asleep during a short lull. They woke me up and I started running forward again.

The first lieutenant and sergeant decided that I had "battle fatigue," and they sent me to the nearest town to rest. They told me that at 4:00 a.m. a truck would come by to take me to the hospital to rest. Although I was on the floor I was so tired that I slept about twelve hours straight. So I missed the 4:00 a.m. truck. The next night I was back on the front lines.

After one attack there was a lull. I didn't see the second scout so I began digging a hole for myself. The counterattack began but it was a quieter one. A soldier with blood all over his face was walking around as though nothing was happening. I pushed him down in the ditch and called a medic to tend to him. I continued digging when the sergeant and corporal called me over. They asked me about the second scout. No one knew where he was. They asked me to dig with them.

We dug a hole big enough for the three of us. It was big enough that two people could lie down and the third person could stand watch. It was a long, rectangular-shaped hole. We covered three fourths of it alternating with wood and dirt.

The next day I volunteered to guard first. I squatted down in the hole while the other two men slept. The Germans began an assault. All of a sudden I blacked out and was thrown into the hole and the two men sat up and woke me up. They asked me what had happened. I told them that I was hit on the head. They looked at me and said there was nothing wrong with my head.

Now it was very cold outside and yet something on my leg felt warm. I looked at my left leg and found it bleeding, and my left foot was twisted in the opposite direction. It turns out that we had broken a rule and I was paying for it. We had dug our hole near a tree. An 88 artillery shell had hit the tree, burst and sent shrapnel flying all over.

I immediately took my "wound pills" to prevent infection. The sergeant wanted to call a medic, but I told him to wait because he would just get killed getting over to see about me. The German fire was heavy at this time.

Later in the day two short medics came to see about me. When they tried to carry me, my leg dragged causing me much pain. So I told them to lay me in a ditch. At this time a communication jeep came by and he volunteered to take me for help. When I sat in the jeep, I let my hurt leg hang over it. Then I noticed that the jeep was driving very close to a truck. I picked up my leg and put it in the jeep. Otherwise I would have lost my leg.

I was taken to a large barn which had been set up as a First Aid Station. They used a stretcher and put me on the floor. The barn was full of soldiers. I saw men with faces blown away and men with their stomachs opened up. Everyone looked so bad that I told the medics to take care of them. I could wait. The medics were running back and forth trying to help everyone.

Finally, some men came and put me in an ambulance. Although I had been wounded early in the morning I was just now taken to an aid station. It was 3:00 p.m. There was a long line of stretchers waiting for the doctor who was seeing the soldiers. I was hurting so much by now that I told the medic, "Don't touch my leg."

A medic took me to the front of the line. The doctor said, "How can you complain? Don't you know that there are men much worse off than you? When did you have your last shot of morphine?"

When I told him that I had not had a shot of morphine, the doctor looked embarrassed because he knew I was going through a lot of pain. So he gave me a shot of morphine and I immediately felt better.

In the next ambulance ride there was a buddy named Rodriguez who had been hurt. He asked me if I would write his mother and tell her about him so she wouldn't worry. I agreed to do it.

We were taken to Nancy, France, to a hospital. I woke up the next day and saw a cast that started at my waist. I thought I might have lost my leg. Then I saw my toes and wiggled them. I knew then that I had my leg and I was so happy!

I wrote my mother and also Rodriguez's mother to tell them of our injuries, because we were both afraid that a telegram from the service would scare them. Then I was sent to a hospital in Paris, France. They removed my cast and told me to walk and not to use the elevator. My leg swelled up to a very large size. So they reversed their instructions.

The Red Cross took us on a tour of Paris. We saw the Tomb of the Unknown Soldier, Napoleon's Arc de Triomphe, Notre Dame, and the Eiffel Tower, which was still covered with barbed wire to keep the Germans from damaging it.

They flew me to England and then to Halloran General Hospital in New York and finally to Beaumont General Hospital in El Paso, Texas. I had lost my appetite and felt depressed. A pass into town meant nothing to me.

Finally, at Sam Houston Convalescence Hospital in San Antonio I began feeling better mentally. I exercised more and felt good. I was allowed to take the bus home on October 22, 1945.

When I arrived home my mother cried. And now we had to fulfill my mother's *promesa*. She had promised our Lord that if I returned home safely, we would both walk from our home in Edinburg to the shrine of *La Virgen de San Juan* [normally a ten-mile drive]. Then we would enter the doorway to the church on our knees and walk on our knees all the way to the altar. And although my leg was still stiff, we fulfilled our *promesa* to God!

Jesús Luís

1st Infantry Division
26th Infantry Battalion
Medical Detachment

Soldier without a Gun

Jesús "Jesse" Luís was born in Robstown, Texas, on October 25, 1924. When he was eighteen years old he was drafted. On May 5, 1943, he was sent to Camp Berkeley in Abilene, Texas, to be trained as a medical technician. No guns were assigned to the medics. As a medic he was supposed to land before the soldiers, but many things went wrong at the landings. At one point the Nazis decided to fire at the medics, and Luís was a victim.

The medical technicians were to work in field hospitals, which would be located about five miles from the front lines. We couldn't carry a gun, so I never carried one throughout the war.

On the last day of training a lieutenant gave the men a farewell speech. Since he had been overseas and was experienced, he knew how fierce the fighting had been. So as he talked to us, he cried. Afterward we were divided into groups.

We were given furloughs to visit our families. Although I knew I was going to Europe, I didn't tell my family anything. Just before boarding the bus to leave, my mother gave me *la bendición*, and then I left to go to Europe.

On November 17, 1943, we arrived in New York City, New York, to be shipped out to Europe. We crossed on the third largest passenger ship, *Quarentino*, and we were unescorted because it was supposed to be faster than a submarine.

We received more training in England. As medical technicians we were to give shots, look at broken bones and wounds, and make the patient comfortable. Then the doctors were to take over.

Meanwhile we were living in pup tents. Although we were shown movies, we couldn't go into town. On Saturdays and Sundays we would go to the park. I remember it was often foggy. In Dorchester we ate lots of fish and chips.

My best friend at this time was James Malone from Terrell, Texas. We double-dated together. Once we had an idea: we asked the girls if they knew of another girl who might be interested in dating an American soldier. They said they did, and so we matched the third girl up with our sergeant. He was so happy that he never again gave us KP or other duties. Sometimes the guys would ask us, "How come you never have KP?" and we would tell them that we had guard duty at night.

We had plans to go into London and we had been approved. Suddenly everything was cancelled and we knew that this was it! When we found out we would be going to where the fighting was, I wrote my parents and sisters, but I couldn't really tell them anything.

We went to the boats and a priest said a mass as we prepared to leave. Then we heard General Eisenhower give a speech and finish it by saying, "Good luck!"

Because we made up the medical detachment, we were supposed to land several hours after the infantry, at 11:00 a.m. There was lots of commotion, and that threw things off. We were transferred to a barge because of all our medical equipment. James and I saw gallon containers full of orange juice right below the LST. We grabbed one apiece and tied them to our belts. So we landed on Normandy at 4:00 p.m. instead of 11:00 a.m. Meanwhile we could see the whole battlefield before us. Bullets were whizzing by, and airplanes were flying over us to drop bombs on the Germans.

Finally we hit the beach. When we got off the barge with all our equipment, clothing, blankets, raincoats, etc., we began to sink. So we had to take out our knives and release the gallon containers of orange juice. A German plane dropped a bomb five hundred feet away from James, but it was a dud. We just watched it sink into the sand.

It appeared that the infantry had traveled about a mile. We went up a small hill and dug foxholes for ourselves. All night we heard the firing of machine guns, which meant that we slept off and on.

Saint Lo in France was a town nearby, which the airplanes had bombed. The hedgerows were problems for the infantry, but finally they solved that problem, and the infantry moved on. After the breakthrough, the Germans were on the run.

In August, the air force caught a German convoy and bombed it. The Germans had horses pulling the artillery. That night we set up a hospital. We treated both injured German and American soldiers, eight hundred in all. Among the captured German soldiers there was a Spaniard. So I spoke Spanish to him. He spent his time cursing the Germans.

Before long we heard that we were going through Paris, and we were so excited. Then the route was changed and we were disappointed. One evening, while traveling through France, we had set up camp when we were approached by a Spanish family who came down from the hills. Because they spoke Spanish, they brought the family to me. The family was happy that I knew Spanish. They said to me, "We came to tell you that the war is going to end."

I asked them what they meant, and they told me that they had seen a bright light flash in the sky and that that was a message from God. I had to explain that what they had seen was antiaircraft fire hitting an airplane, which had exploded causing the great flash of light.

We marched through Belgium and through the Siegfried Line which had already been broken through in places. In Aachen I didn't see any civilians. The next day I decided to look around, and while looking in the direction of an old church, a sniper shot at me. He missed me, and then an American infantry man killed the sniper.

When we arrived at the Hürtgen Forest, we were told that the Germans were now deliberately killing medics on the front lines. So they decided to send people like me to substitute for a medic at least for a month. On November 29, 1944, I was injured. A shot had entered my body right below my left shoulder and exited on my left side. A medic came and gave me a shot of morphine.

An ambulance came and took me to a field hospital where my buddies worked. From there I was sent to a Paris hospital and from there to a hospital in England. On February 28, 1945, I was sent back to the US. While I was in a Denver hospital in rehabilitation, the war ended. I was so happy but wasn't allowed to go celebrate.

Then finally I was on furlough with the idea that I would be sent to the Pacific where we were still fighting the Japanese. Then suddenly we heard that Japan had surrendered.

I was discharged in November 1945. Peace at last after two and a half years of war!

Hector Mendez

1st Army
8th Infantry Division

An Observant Soldier

Hector Mendez, from San Marcos, Texas, joined the service after one year of college, thus making him an unusual GI—a college boy in the army. He used his skills to assist a young boy who could neither read nor write. He also managed to make many observations as he fought the enemy.

After graduating from high school, I began attending college. I volunteered for the draft after finishing the first semester of my sophomore year, thus pushing my number up.

I trained right outside San Antonio. A winesap apple was always included with my breakfast, which was served at 5:00 a.m. From there I went to St. Petersburg, Florida. The air force had commandeered luxury hotels for the training of the men in that Florida city. The Vinoy Park Hotel had beautiful flowers—hibiscus, oleanders, and other beautiful flowers all around—and the men stayed two to a room.

The training included marching through residential areas, and retreat was held every afternoon. On the first day the men were assigned to the hotel rooms, my roommate, a young boy from West Virginia, walked in and after saying "Hello" asked me, "Can you read and write?"

I told him I could, and he asked me if I would write letters to his girlfriend back home. He told me that his girlfriend couldn't read or write either, but that she had a girlfriend who would write for her. So I wrote letters for my roommate. The boy told her about what we were doing, the training, the weather, etc. I decided to add more to the letters to make them love letters. I added phrases like, "Darling, I love you. I wish I were holding you in my arms right now." When I read what I had written to my roommate, he cried saying, "That's exactly what I wanted to say."

And so it went during basic training. The young boy seemed to fall more in love with his girlfriend through letters that he began a strategy to get dismissed from the army so that he could go back home. I never knew what happened to him after basic training.

We were taken on a train to Salt Lake City, Utah, to a clerical-type school located on the site of the State Fair. While there we took technical training. Because there were no barracks available we were put up in barns in which horses were kept during the fairs that were held there. Even though it was March the temperatures were low, and I remember the cold. This was a different type school. Every day we worked on different typewriters and every day a new teacher walked in to instruct us. The teachers always asked, "Where did you leave off yesterday?"

In Idaho we trained the crews of the B-24 bombers. Ten-men crews for airplanes were chosen from large groups. They had to undergo three months of training before they were ready for action. We worked with ground-to-air communications. Charts were in front of us. The seasoned veterans helped train the new recruits, who had to practice different kinds of missions on the airplanes. I kept records of the men's missions. For example, a trainee might ask me, "How many gunnery missions do I need to finish the training?" When necessary the instructors and I went up to check the weather plane. Each time we took parachutes so that we would have them if we needed to jump.

By November, in Idaho, the temperature was well below the freezing point. A mess hall sergeant decided to make a warm porridge to warm us up. He cooked *champurrado*, a porridge made with corn flour, cocoa, cinnamon, and sugar. I felt like crying, because it was like the wonderful-tasting *champurrado* my sister made back home in San Marcos, Texas.

In November of 1944, the army sent out a call: more men were needed in the infantry! My captain liked my work in training airplane crews and tried hard to keep from losing me, but it was to no avail. I had to go fight in the infantry.

I ended up doing my basic training in Tonopah, Nevada. What a difference from the glitzy hotel accommodations I had experienced in St. Petersburg, Florida! Whereas in Florida we had our own baker, in Tonopah we sometimes ate canned tomatoes with bread. And it was so cold! Finally, after the training was over I was given a ten-day furlough. Now I was in the First Army, Eighth Infantry Division.

After my visit back home I shipped out to Washington, DC, and then New York for embarkation. Ironically enough, I remember a band playing the song, "Saturday night is the loneliest night of the week."

It was a rough trip overseas. As the company clerk I had to use the bathroom as my office and the commode as a desk. I kept the service records of two hundred men. All the while the ship is rocking. And no garbage could be thrown overboard because the ocean had German submarines, and the garbage would indicate that we Americans were nearby. The English food was not tasty, either.

From Liverpool we went to London by train and finally ended up in Southampton. The train was cold to everyone. After arriving in London, the Red Cross had large containers on the platforms of the train stations; they poured hot tea and milk into our canteens to warm us up.

A boat carried us across the English Channel to France. From there we traveled in boxcars and slept on straw all the way to Belgium. From Belgium they took us in trucks to Aachen, Germany, a trip which took four days. In Aachen we slept in a barn.

I was taken aback when I saw a sign in a store window which advertised caskets and actually published death announcements in the window. Somehow in the midst of war with so many people dying, death announcements seemed out of place.

After the Battle of the Bulge we went from house to house, fighting Germans all the way. Replacements came often. I remember a new lieutenant saying, "You guys go in front and I'll cover you from behind." He was scared to lead. Those guys were called "Ninety Day Wonders."

The Remagen Bridge was a major bridge that the Germans wanted to blow up; the Americans wanted to save it so we could use it. The men crossed on a pontoon bridge. When confronted with German soldiers, we were surprised to see that the enemy soldiers were from fourteen to sixty years of age.

In Cologne, Germany, we fought near the Ruhr River. Also, there was a cathedral that was of great interest to the Catholics in our group of soldiers. We decided to take a risk and run and look over the cathedral. When we entered we found an old German man who cried when we appeared. He took us down into the basement and showed us large, beautiful, stained glass windows that the citizens had taken down in anticipation of being invaded.

As the war continued, and the Germans realized they were losing, they began surrendering in large numbers. In addition to giving up, they began leaving their dead fellow soldiers just lying by the side of the road. When they thought it was safe, civilians came out and took the dead Germans to bury them. The Germans were industrious people. Although the towns and cities were shelled by us before the infantry came in, by the time we went in to continue fighting, the citizens of the community were already stacking up the fallen bricks and were cleaning up.

In spite of the fact that it appeared that we were faring better than the Germans, the dying, injuries, damage, etc. caused some of our soldiers to get depressed. I, too, felt sad. Then one day I received a letter from home in which my sister told me about her husband reading to their daughter. The humor in the letter brightened my day and I felt cheered for a while.

On April 2, 1945, in Cologne, we captured a business that had cold beer and cigars aplenty. The soldiers drank plenty of beer and filled their pockets with cigars. Later that day five of us were victims of a mortar shell from an 88mm gun. Three men died instantly; another soldier and I were injured. I felt certain that I was being punished because I had drunk beer. I was hit on my thigh, knees, leg, feet, and on the right side of my body. I lay there waiting to be helped. No one came. Finally, since I was near a river, I had an idea. I rolled over as best I could and placed part of my body in the river to stop the bleeding. My idea worked. At around 11:00 p.m. I heard voices. I began yelling again. The voices belonged to paratroopers. First they asked me if I were American. Then very gently they placed me on a stretcher on top of a jeep and took me to a Red Cross tent. I stayed there three or four days. While there I heard of the death of President Roosevelt.

Finally, I was taken to the Chester Hospital in England, where I underwent surgery. On May 8, 1945, Germany surrendered, and the war was over. Those of us in the hospital received a shot glass of rum, compliments of King George VI of England. English female soldiers came to visit the hospital. I saw films, which were being offered as entertainment. It turned out that the films were about the king of England.

In June 1945, I returned with other soldiers to the US by ship. Even though the war was over, paratroopers guarded our ship—just in case someone hadn't heard that the war was over. Now there were two soldiers to each stateroom. There were also many refugees from concentration camps coming to the US from Europe. I noticed that the women wore red wigs and the men wore hats.

I went to a hospital in El Paso, Texas, where orthopedic cases were treated. While there I heard of a bomb being tested in nearby New Mexico. I was discharged in August 1945, right after the Japanese were defeated.

After returning to college and graduating, Hector Mendez became a renowned teacher and counselor in San Diego, Texas. He also worked at Del Mar College in Corpus Christi, Texas.

Johnny Martinez
765th Battalion

A Musician in the Service

Johnny Martinez, born in Rosebud, Texas, moved to Houston, Texas, when he was eight years old. Johnny came from a long line of musicians. His father, who had earned a living as a musician, had taught him how to play various instruments. However, when they moved to the United States from Mexico, they found that in the United States a musician could not easily earn a living. The only occasions that required a paid musician were the weddings and baptisms of folks in the Hispanic communities. Johnny wasn't content with music as a pastime, however. He wanted to join the service and see action. Some folks thought him crazy for wanting to do that. He ended up driving a jeep.

My father, Anastacio Martinez Sr., a citizen from Mexico, was an accomplished musician. My father couldn't make enough money to support his family through music. As a result, he joined a circus so that he could work at what he enjoyed, making music. And he took me with him. Finally, we both returned to Houston after several years.

In 1943 I volunteered for the service, leaving behind my wife and two daughters. A drum and bugler corps was formed in Ohio, and I became the instructor, thus becoming a member of the third generation of musicians in my family. Battalions went through the camp on their way to the war. They also had a band and often they invited me to play with them. Then they asked me to join their battalion. This happened often. Once I went to my commanding officer and asked if I could join a battalion that was going through the camp. The CO said, "Are you crazy? Get out of my office!" He figured I didn't know what I was asking.

Another battalion went through the camp and again I was invited to join them. This time when I asked my CO, he said yes. I am not a technician, but I became attached to the 765th Battalion, which had people with technical training. They also had people who knew about railroads.

We went to Camp Kilmer in New Jersey and from there to New York, where we boarded the Monterrey. On December 24, 1943, I went up to the top deck to watch the celebrations in New York, but I had to go to bed at 10:00 p.m. Early the next morning the boat was swaying. I went to the top deck. It turns out we had traveled all night long, and when I awoke it was December 25, 1943. The ship was swaying because there was a storm on the coast of Africa, and we had taken another route because a submarine was nearby.

We docked at Southampton, England, where we spent some time. A train took us to another place and after staying there a while we boarded a ship. It was after D-day and the ship took us across the channel to Le Havre, France. A train took us to Paris, and from there we were taken to Thionville, where the soldiers were crossing the Moselle River. I was finally at the front lines.

My first job was to guard train cars, which were full of ammunition. My new CO called me to his office and asked, "Which technicality do you have?" I told him that I didn't have a technicality, that I was a musician. He said, "Well, what in the hell are you doing in my outfit?" I didn't have an answer. Finally he decided to give me a jeep and make me a "runner" who carried messages to the front and medications to the field hospitals. I even carried medicines and messages to Luxembourg. In January 1945 I carried officers to Liege, Belgium.

We crossed the Moselle River, and General Patton came in with tanks from Italy. I had to lead the tanks to where they were to be positioned. I spent two months at the front.

We crossed the Rhine River in my jeep over the pontoon bridge that the American engineers had built. Ike stopped Patton from advancing so fast, because he wanted the Russians to get to Berlin first.

The roads were in bad shape. There were tanks on the roads, and the roads were torn up and muddy. Once when taking an officer somewhere in Germany I met up with a car which had three stars in front. I thought it was General Patton, but I never knew for sure.

Patton decided to give every company one pass for one person to go for R&R. There were supposed to be passes to London, Brussels, Paris, and the Riviera. I wasn't interested, so I went to bed. The men in each company put everyone's name in a helmet and drew. In my company the men urged me not to go to bed, but to put my name in the helmet. I did and my name was chosen for the pass. The CO said that my pass was to Brussels, Belgium. He said, "Do the best you can to get there."

I caught rides with columns and stayed fifteen days. It took me longer to get back and when I did, my company had moved. It took me two weeks to find my company. Now I had been away for a month. I went back to driving the jeep. A week later I was stopped and was informed that President Roosevelt had died.

Another time I was driving my jeep down the road when an MP stopped me. He said, "The war is over." I went to Ike's office to pick up the travel orders for the whole outfit.

I was driving my jeep to pick up a soldier from a hospital in Paris to take him back to his company. Thirty minutes outside of Paris, two officers joined me in my jeep. I spent two days in Paris. I met a column coming back to Le Havre.

I spent seven days on a ship back to the US, and we landed in Boston. I was sent to Ft. Sam Houston. After a month of R&R they called me to report to Ft. Sam Houston. I boarded a train headed to Arkansas. While I sat waiting for the train to move, cars began honking and finally someone said, "The war is over. Japan has surrendered." When I arrived in Arkansas, they sent me back home. I was discharged in November 1945.

My wife and I ended up having four daughters, and I gave each one of them a home. I also taught music at the Southern College of Fine Arts.

Julian Flores
487th Bomb Squad
839th Bomb Group

A Handshake and Two Friends Join the Army

Julian Flores was born May 20, 1924, in Goliad, Texas, a small town located south of San Antonio. He was one of seven children born to Carlota Salinas Flores and Angelino Flores. While he experienced prejudice in his hometown, he was proud of his country and was eager to do his part to defend it. He and his best friend joined at the same time. A dairy man who delivered milk from Goliad, Texas, to neighboring Victoria gave the two boys a ride to the recruiting station. They rode on the back of the truck with milk cans filled with fresh milk so they could do their patriotic duty.

I was an altar boy in the local Catholic Church. There were three Mexican American boys who attended the same school. At lunchtime when we took out our lunch of tacos, the other non-Hispanic students made fun of us. So, we took our taco lunch out behind a water tank; there we hid and ate our lunch without any criticism.

I felt that I didn't have the right clothes for school, so I dropped out. I worked at the Five and Ten Cent store on Saturdays for ninety cents. At the theater I sold popcorn so that I could get in without paying. My mother made tamales, which I sold for fifteen cents a dozen.

I worked with the CCC. While there I occasionally listened to the radio owned by the supply sergeant. It was through that radio that I and the other young men heard of a place that had been bombed. The place was Pearl Harbor.

[After leaving the CCC on January 12] I re-enrolled in high school. Then in November 1942, my best friend Raul Martinez and I shook hands and vowed to join the army.

On November 4, 1942, Raul Martinez and I were sworn in at the post office in Victoria, Texas. From there we went to Fort Sam Houston in San Antonio. We did our basic training at Brooks Field.

A troop train took us to Camp Kilmer in New York. Married men with children cried because they were leaving their families and didn't know if they would ever see them again.

At Camp Kilmer all the men gathered in a large building. A captain spoke to us. "You men are going overseas. You will be stationed in Britain, and you will see things you've never seen before. You are going to see Negro men with white girls. Don't say anything and don't get into trouble. One half of you are not returning." It was a scary talk for us, the new recruits.

Forty English boats filled with troops took us to Liverpool and finally to Lavenham, which was ninety miles from London. I would be there sixteen months. We worked on B-17s and B-24s. I was a mechanic, and our crews' specific assignment was to work on "The Big Drip."

In England the Germans were strafing the fields. The Germans used buzz bombs and then rockets, which you could see early in the morning. The Luftwaffe bombed London nightly. England had search lights which they used when they fired antiaircraft artillery guns. People slept in bunks in the underground railways.

We went to a dance one night and there was a blackout. The girl I was dancing with hit the floor. I learned I was supposed to do the same thing.

We slept in Quonset huts and burned gas for warmth. Near us was a large round concrete wall about four feet high. When we heard the siren we ran outside our huts and jumped in the round concrete structure. The vibration from the bombs would cause our large hangar doors to vibrate and then fall.

Our airplanes flew early in the morning to different locations in Germany. We could see about a thousand airplanes going to Germany. Members of each crew had certain assignments. Some men loaded the bombs; the guys wrote words on the bombs. Others warmed up the planes. We gassed and worked on the engines and often times had to change the engines. When an airplane returned from a job the pilot told the crew chief what had happened such as oil pressure information, etc.

Besides the pilots each airplane had the following gunners: one in front, one in the tail, one in the top turret, one in the ball turret and one on each side. The B-24s were called "box cars" and the B-17s were called "flying fortresses."

Upon my return I flew back in a B-17 to Iceland. I could bring back only fifty pounds. We had a bad storm and stayed there. Then we flew to Newfoundland and from there to Connecticut. I kissed the ground when we got off the plane in Connecticut. A bus took us to Tampa, Florida, where we were discharged. A troop train took me to San Antonio. Then I took a bus to Goliad. They gave me the tools I had been using on the airplanes.

All the time we were in England working on airplanes, we never had to salute. Our captain said, "Now you have to salute and polish your shoes." When we returned, things were still being rationed.

Not long after that, the bombs were dropped on Japan. The war was over. Women from town walked all the way to the Bahía Catholic Church, located a few miles outside of town, to give thanks to God that the war was over.

I had thirty-six war bonds at $18.75 each saved up. I cashed them and opened up a beer tavern at age twenty-one. I was in business for forty-six years until my wife became ill. At that time I closed up my business so that I could take care of my wife. We had a son and a daughter. I now have three grandchildren and two great-grandchildren.

Joseph Lawless
7th Army
42nd Rainbow Infantry Division

Going to War in Spite of Problems

Joseph Lawless was born to an Irish Catholic family in East Orange, New Jersey, on May 2, 1926. The men in his family were pilots of ships and belonged to the Sandy Hook Pilot Association of New York. These boats brought in the ships that would dock in the harbor and then led the ships back out to sea. It was expected that Joe would follow in the family tradition and would one day be a boat pilot. In WWII these same pilots became commissioned by the Coast Guard. Joseph expected to become a maritime or ship pilot like the rest of the men in his family. This was his plan until he was drafted in 1944. Although he experienced respiratory problems, he denied it so that he could pass the fitness test and be approved to fight for his country. When he became a priest, Joseph Lawless worked in barrios in California. After being assigned to a church in a Hispanic neighborhood in Corpus Christi, Texas, José Ángel Flores, also a veteran, helped him at the church utilizing his carpentry skills.

I was drafted in August of 1944. One of the questions on the application was, "Do you suffer from any respiratory diseases?" I answered no because I wanted to go. I got two [asthma] attacks in basic training in Florida. Two of my buddies took over my duties. Two weeks later on the parade grounds I had an attack. During my furlough to visit my parents, my doctor came over and said, "Just let me know and I'll get you out." I said, "Don't you dare, Dr. Kessel. I'll never speak to you the rest of my life." During the war I had an attack in Germany right before the war ended. I was in a barn with the hay underneath. I was upstairs with my squad and I started getting an attack. They were covering my mouth. When it came time to leave, they left me there. I waited and left and joined my outfit. In Austria I got an attack and I was dying to get home. Do you think they would send me home? No.

My uncle Nini who was a ship pilot told me of his sadness in seeing so many young men in the troop ships, which he led out of the harbor with his boat. Six days later my uncle saw me on the boat he was escorting out of the harbor. He had a sailor call me up to him. He gave me $50.00, which I didn't want to accept; my uncle gave me much advice. As soldiers we were told that if we had any money on us and we were captured, the Germans would take that money and spend it. So, I kept the money my uncle gave me for ten years before I spent it.

During the war I applied to the US Merchant Marine Academy, but was placed on a waiting list. While I waited to hear from them, I was drafted into the army.

We landed in Liverpool, England, Jan. 14, 1945. We took a train across England to Le Havre on an LST. We proceeded across France in a train called "40 and 8s" because the train was designed to carry forty men or eight horses. They loaded us up in that train and took us to join our group. The train had a small window at the top and hay on the floor. Very uncomfortable. It stopped only two times a day, once in the morning and at night for food. It took several days.

We landed in Alsace-Lorraine. There was still fighting going on. We went to a replacement depot—"Repo-Depot." They would pick you as replacements. You were just cannon fodder.

Other divisions would pick you to fill rank. I was lucky in that I joined an intact division, the Rainbow Division. They were like family. They had fought in the Battle of the Bulge. They had pulled the men off the lines to recover, and I joined them then. The Bulge started in Belgium. Alsace-Lorraine was the southern boundary of the Battle of the Bulge.

The Germans had been defeated. The fighting was very fanatical at this point for obvious reasons. Women and children were not in the front ranks, but they did subversive kinds of things like shooting you from windows and putting land mines out on the road. The Germans did have women in their army in service units like driving trucks.

The Russians didn't have any regard for life. There was no agreement after WWI between the Germans and the Russians. When they fought it was no-holds-barred, because they didn't respect rights. That's why the fighting was so fanatical between the Germans and the Russians. Their war was so brutal.

We went through two weeks of intensive training in Alsace. The whole Seventh Army made up a whole line. Our purpose was to wait for the last great offensive. The move started in March 1945. It was one concerted effort. We had infantry, tanks, air support, everything. All our Allies were involved. The rest of the war we spent going from city to city in Germany. Intensive fighting for obvious reasons.

They said, "We're going on a special task force." We rode for fifteen or twenty minutes, and all of a sudden we saw the railroad tracks coming out. Highlight was that my division liberated Dachau, the concentration camp. On the outskirts of Dachau I saw thirty-three boxcars on some tracks. They told us to go see what was in the train cars. When we opened up the cars some bodies fell out. The sound the bodies made when they fell on the ground was like the sound of wood hitting the ground.

The cars were filled with bodies, still frozen. One person lived through that and became a tailor in New York. When we found them, the people had been moved three days prior to escape from the Russians, and the Germans didn't see them and so they starved. They smelled. There were children. Mothers and babies. The pain they must have gone through. There was human excrement and vomit. They were in twisted contortions. Mothers were trying to nurse their babies. At that moment we developed hatred. Then we moved into the camps and we were full of hate.

They had people from every country the Germans had fought. The majority were Jews. They had French, Italian, Polish, political prisoners, Gypsies. One of the things that hit me when I went into Dachau was that they had five hundred Polish Catholic priests. They would tie them to donkey carts and take them down to the railroad and fill the donkey carts with loaves of bread to bring back to feed the prisoners. The priests pulled the donkey carts. If the priest dropped as much as a crumb of bread, the priest had to get down on the ground and lick it. Other things they did, they stripped them and tied them to a barbed wire fence in a crucifixion form and they took cattle prods and stimulated their genital organs and they had mean dogs and the dogs would tear them apart. I killed one of those dogs while I was there.

Schoenstatt fathers. Some of those priests were in Dachau.

Most were Jews. They had significant symbols indicating what kind of prisoner you were. If you were a political prisoner, you had a certain symbol and color code. The Gypsies had a symbol and the Jews had the Star of David. Thirty thousand.

Most of the guards had slipped away. Either the American soldiers killed them or the prisoners killed them. The American soldiers gave some prisoners guns. Most of the guards had run away.

What bothered me about that—we saw reporters and media people from the major media publications such as *Life* Magazine. They took pictures of American soldiers shooting the guards. They destroyed the pictures; the Army censored it. I've always regretted it. They were worried about the impending Nuremberg trials coming up and they didn't want to mess it up. I saw Clare Boothe Luce.

We had Harry Collins, our division general. We liberated Munich, where the Nazi party was founded. When you go in the army, the best and the worst comes out of you. I was raised as a Catholic. I picked up one of the prisoners, an elderly man. They had cholera and tuberculosis in the camp. We were inoculated against it. I picked up this man to take him to the medics; he was dying. He smelled so. Vomiting. Doing things in his pants. He looked up at me and in perfect English said, "What faith do you hold to, my son?" He was a rabbi. I saw the Star of David on him and my first reaction was "I'm a Catholic carrying a Jew," and you know how we're trained as kids that Jews were Jesus's killers? I said, "I'm Catholic" and he said—I'll never forget the words—"Never forget this day."

Basically, the Germans did follow the regulations. But some Germans would put a mine by a wounded American so that when the medics went to help him, the mine would go off. The SS didn't adhere to anything.

I knew that Nazism was founded in Munich. When we went there, it was quite a feeling. We rode on top of the tanks for protection. I said to myself, "Wow, I liberated the town where Nazism started." The infantry rode on top of the tanks. Of all the emotions I've had in my life, you can't describe the feeling you get riding on top of a tank. When those engines start and the whole tank backfires and it lurches like this, like a rifle top, you feel like you have all the power in the world. And you are only eighteen. Nobody can stop you. You're not afraid of anything. I can't describe the feeling. Exhilarated. I've never had that experience since.

Dachau is just seven miles from Munich. After we stayed two days in Munich, we went from city to city until the conclusion of the war. In Munich they greeted us with open arms because we were going through on tanks. There weren't any men in these cities unless it was a man with one leg. The cities had mostly women, and they were coming out and giving us baskets of food and bottles of liquor. They were inviting us. We went into one home and had lunch. They wanted to see us rather than the Russians. They told us that.

In one town—I have the picture—there are Russian slave laborers in Schweinfurt, Germany. Our faces are down because they had notified us that President Roosevelt had died. We had just known the one president. The Russian slave laborers also have a sad look on their faces because now that they are liberated they were to be put on trains and sent back to Russia to die in Siberia. The Russians had this philosophy that you didn't dare get captured. Weakness.

We were not supposed to talk to civilians. You would be fined a whole month's salary if you talked to a girl. No one paid attention to that.

Fürth. Nuremberg. We kept going south toward Bavaria. Hitler came from there. We were in Austria when the war ended. There was summer snow on top of mountains. People were un-Germanic. They had no concept of time. Germans were perturbed with Austrians.

We were informed of the end of the war by the BBC. We had the radio on. We used to listen to them. We didn't experience the joy you would think, because we had to go to Japan. Instead of being elated, we were put through training. In Austria the Germans who had been released, they'd be sitting on guard rails and look at us and laugh because the war was over for them, and they knew we had to fight some more. We started cheating. When we were supposed to have two men on guard, we just had one.

Infantry training. It bothered everyone. It was just to keep us busy. We stopped training when they dropped the bomb on Japan. We stayed there until the following February. They had a point system, and I didn't have enough points. They tried to reenlist us. They promised advancements. All I wanted to do was to get home. Our sergeant asked, "How fast can you pack your bags?" I said, "I can do it in one hour." He said, "They will send you back to the states and give you forty days; then you have to come back to Europe." While at home, the point system changed.

We were guarding a train with badly injured German soldiers who had been wounded in Russia. They couldn't move the soldiers; they stayed there all summer. They were afraid the civilians would steal the medical supplies. That was the first time I had seen the German soldiers on a peacetime basis, and we learned they were just like us. We were sitting at night bored to death and you'd hear the soldiers come out at night to urinate. They'd go behind you, and you wouldn't even know they were there. All they wanted was a cigarette or to talk. I never smoked, and I used to give packs away. This one soldier who was 90 percent burned—he had been in a tank—spoke perfect English. I asked, "Where did you learn English?" He said, "Before the war I worked with the Hamburg American Shipping Line in New York. I was a steward and got drafted."

Toward the end of the war I came upon a stream of water. I reached down to fill my canteen with fresh cold water from the stream, because they used to put Halazone in our water to keep us from getting sick and it tasted awful. A young girl said, "Don't touch that water, soldier." It was a young German woman and she said, "That water will make you very sick." "Why would you tell me that?" She said, "I spent all my life in America. I was born in Germany. This is my hometown. I've lived in America, but before the war I came to see my mother and then couldn't get back [to the US]." She handed me a letter and asked, "Would you mind posting this? It's to my sister in Philadelphia." I posted it. Human things in the middle of the war.

There is a priest in this diocese. He was stationed in Monte Casino where they bombed. There is a big Benedictine Monastery on top of a big mountain. The Germans were using it as an observation post. I was still in high school when this happened. The US bombed it. This priest was a seminarian in that Benedictine Monastery. He said, "One day the Germans took all the seminarians out and the slave laborers into the field and they were getting ready to shoot us. We could understand enough German. Just as the Germans picked up their rifles, this German jeep came up with an officer. The officer said, 'No, no, don't shoot them.'"

They stopped. We found out that the German officer had been in that seminary. Bavaria is mostly Catholic.

The Northern Germans are the darker ones. Prussians. Bavaria with the Alps are the most beautiful. Fairer skin there. Influence from the Spanish. Italians have the Greek influence.

We were taught to hate the Japs. Poor soldiers. Poor eyesight. So fanatic. If you died for the emperor, you went to heaven.

I went to college on the GI bill. University of Georgia, School of Journalism. It was ranked number three in the country. I worked on the student newspaper. I never wanted to interview people to embarrass them. I was in business with my sister. It dealt with the maintenance of shopping carts for a huge chain in New York—Grand Union. The Korean War broke out. I was in the Reserves. I got out of it because I was in ROTC. We could do it in half the time.

I was thirty-nine when I went into the seminary. With a degree in college I could get out in six years instead of eight. We underwent Franciscan training. Phil Donahue was in my parish. There was a summer camp for affluent kids and poor blacks, Camp Dakota. I ran it. I was ordained in 1971.

I went to Los Angeles, California, in the *barrio*. Then I went to a Black neighborhood. I was there during the Watts riots in Compton, CA. Then I went to a succession of parishes in Texas. I didn't want to go.

Father Joe Lawless ended up in Corpus Christi, Texas, where he was greatly loved.

Manuel Del Llano
82nd Airborne Division

Guarding the Boss
Manuel Del Llano was born on March 13, 1927, in Corpus Christi, Texas, to Dolores Diaz and Enrique Del Llano. Dolores and Enrique Del Llano were born in Mexico. Manuel vividly tells the stories his mother told him about

the time they lived in Mexico and had to fight off the revolutionaries. His parents, like so many Mexican citizens, fled their country to seek peace in which they could live and raise their families.

As a young girl my mother Dolores ran upstairs to the roof of the hacienda where her family lived to give her brothers and uncles guns to fight the revolutionaries who were attacking haciendas. The revolutionaries perceived the owners of the haciendas as profiting from the labor of the poor people of Mexico. And so my mother and her family, like so many other Mexicans during the time of the Mexican Revolution, fled their homeland for the security of their soon-to-be-adopted country, the United States. It cost all of five cents to cross over.

I remember that times were hard during the Depression. I made my first Holy Communion at Sacred Heart and then got in the car with Daddy and Mother. We drove and drove until we arrived at a hacienda in Mexico near Linares. Although the revolution was over and it was in the 1930s, things were still rough. We were picking strawberries and people started shooting each other. We ran inside. They fired all night long. The next morning there were dead people lying on the ground.

I attended Sacred Heart because my grandmother believed in a Catholic education. Then I went to Northside Junior High School and then Corpus Christi High School. I volunteered for the service in February of 1945 before I graduated from high school.

I trained at Camp Hood. Then for paratrooper school I went to Ft. Benning, Georgia. I joined the paratroopers for foolish reasons. When you are young, you take risks. And it was an elite service. We were known as a Special Bastard Regiment. We were trained to assault behind the lines. That group was dissolved and we became attached to the Eighty-Second Airborne Division. I had to jump at least once every four weeks to get paid the extra money each month.

I arrived in Germany just as the war ended and became part of the Occupational Army. We were assigned to guard Eisenhower's Headquarters in Frankfurt, Germany. Although Frankfurt had been bombed really hard, there were a few blocks that hadn't been destroyed. That included a building with beautiful gardens. That is where Eisenhower's HQ was located. We didn't let anybody get close. We had to stop anyone that approached the place.

At night you didn't go out by yourself. The Germans were glad that Hitler was gone. They were starving to death. Another soldier and I rented an apartment from a German and paid him a pack of cigarettes every two weeks.

Manuel Del Llano returned to Corpus Christi where he obtained a high school diploma and then graduated from Texas A&M in Bryan, Texas. He and his wife Raquel Del Llano had three children.

Oscar Flores
Recipient of the Distinguished Flying Cross
8th Air Force
447th Bombing Group, Squadron 708

An Eighteen-Year-Old Hero
Oscar Flores was born in San Antonio. After living in the Rio Grande Valley, where his grandfather had a general store, his family moved to Corpus Christi, Texas, when Oscar was nine years old. In Corpus Christi, his uncle who came from Mexico, owned a dry goods store. Oscar began helping him by selling and doing other odd jobs. A young man when he entered the service, Oscar became a ball turret gunner.

I remember that there was a couple—the wife was Mexican and the husband was German—who ran a store of imported leather goods and shoes. After the war started the German merchant was picked up and never seen again.

I attended school in Corpus Christi and was drafted into the Army Air Corps in 1943.

All the training I received in the Army Air Corps was geared toward the day when the Allied Forces would invade Europe. I ended up flying in B-17 bombers. They were large airplanes, 103-foot wingspan and 74 feet 9 inches length, which could carry heavy loads and travel far without refueling. My job was to be a ball turret gunner with a .50-caliber gun. I had a checklist to follow closely before I could do my job successfully.

The ball turret on each plane was a round-shaped attachment located on the belly of the airplane. And it accommodated only one person. I used a screen known as the "Norden Bomb Sight"; if an enemy plane came on the screen, I would fire the gun. That was known as "framing the plane." The ball turret could turn 180 degrees in either direction, thus allowing the gunner to be able to fire in any direction. It was a small space in which a person would sit for a long period of time. Not only that, but because of the location on the airplane, before the airplane landed, I had to get out of my position in case the landing was a rough one. If the landing were not smooth, the ball turret would be in danger of getting smashed.

Because the airplanes flew up to twenty-five thousand feet up, the airmen on the B-17s had to endure cold temperatures. We wore suits, which were plugged in like electric blankets to keep us warm, and we used throat microphones to communicate with one another. We had to keep gloves on our hands to prevent freezing.

Each B-17 carried from ten to thirteen men. The jobs on the airplane were as follows: chief pilot, copilot, navigator, engineer, radio operator, ball turret gunner, waist gunner (2), tail gunner, bombardier.

The men named our B-17 The Milk Wagon and painted on her a milk bottle for each successful mission. At that time, the average life expectancy of an airman was thirty days! Because the lives we were leading were so dangerous, the ground crew was ecstatic when an airplane returned after a successful mission. Upon arrival the ground crew would run up to us yelling and screaming and hugging all of the crew from the airplane. The Red Cross would give the arrivals something to drink. In short, everyone was grateful that one of the planes had returned safely.

When an airplane was lost, the buddies would cry and scream in anguish over the lost lives, but they would go back to their jobs and fly again.

On two separate occasions bombs, which were supposed to be released by a switch, the usual way, were hung up. There was only one way to release them, and it was a risky business. A mask which carried only five minutes of oxygen had to worn by the person willing to crawl into the area where the bombs were located and then release them by hand. I was willing to do it, and I did it successfully both times. For this heroic service, I was awarded the Distinguished Flying Cross.

The British and Germans would sometimes fly at night and do carpet bombing, which meant that targets weren't always certain. The American airplanes would fly in the daytime to do precision bombing raids. Also, the B-17s flew in box formation, which meant that they looked like a square with four planes flying in each corner. It took eleven hours to fly to and from Germany. When the airplanes were loaded, they could fly at the speed of 225 miles per hour. After the bombs had been dropped, the rate of speed of the airplanes rose considerably.

When confronted with American airplanes, the German Luftwaffe would aim at the belly of the airplane, attempting to hit the gasoline source. In 1944, the Germans were using rockets, which no one else had at that time. The British used the underground train tunnels to keep their citizens from being killed during the German raids.

For the duration of the war, I spent my time training other young people for active duty.

The Milk Wagon, Oscar's airplane, made thirty-two successful missions with the same crew. In October 1944, Oscar traveled back to the United States on the Queen Mary, *which had been converted to a troop transport ship.*

Guadalupe Valdez
M Company, 3rd Battalion
78th Infantry Division

Guarding an Important Person
Guadalupe Valdez was born on July 14, 1917. In 1932, when he was in the ninth grade, he dropped out of school. In 1933, he moved to the outskirts of Ricardo, Texas. At first, Guadalupe was rejected by the armed services. Then in 1944, when the war had reached a critical point, he was drafted. After seeing action, he was assigned to guard Axis Sally, the German version of Tokyo Rose.

When war broke out everyone was joining up to fight the enemy. I was no exception. I volunteered but was rejected. I finally worked with the Civil Service in O and R—Overhaul and Repair.

Every six months the army called and checked on several men and on me, but because I had an essential job with the Army and Navy in Civil Service, they would not release me. And they kept me in this situation for two and a half years. In 1944, things were looking bad, and so they called me. I became part of the Seventy-Eighth Infantry Division.

I was sent to Camp Hood [IRTC-Infantry Replacement Training Center] and trained for seventeen weeks. It was rumored that the training was to lead up to the invasion of Japan. Among the many different kinds of training was walking many miles per day. After the basic training, I was given ten days to visit my parents in Kingsville. I left Kingsville on December 15.

I reported to Ft. Sam Houston in San Antonio, Texas. From there I was sent to Camp Shanks, located in the outskirts of New York. Now it looked as though the fighting would occur in Europe and not in the Pacific theater.

We stayed there for ten days and prepared to go overseas. We left New York on December 26, 1944, on the USS *Montclair*. During the trip a hurricane with fifty to seventy-five foot waves hit the ship. In addition to the severe weather, we were told that German submarines had been sighted in the area. We landed in Le Havre, France, and stayed at Camp Lucky Strike, named after the popular cigarette.

Our goal was to march to Berlin, Germany. We soldiers traveled by walking, on trains, and in trucks. It involved a month of traveling. Although the Americans were making progress and had the German army on the run, there were nonetheless pockets of resistance. The German soldiers who hid in old buildings and fired at the Americans as they traveled toward Berlin were outnumbered and were usually killed or had to surrender.

We remained at Frankfurt for ten days. Then on February 1 we continued our march to Berlin. Berlin was to be divided into four sections: Russian, French, English, and American.

The Eighty-Second Airborne Division, which had seen much action, was leaving Berlin. There yet remained much bitterness in their minds as they had seen their buddies die at the hands of the German soldiers. The young American soldiers were perceived as being disrespectful toward the German populace. The army decided to send these young men home.

The Seventy-Eighth replaced the Eighty-Second Airborne. The Germans were still angry at the American soldiers and threw rocks and bricks at them. The American officers told the soldiers to act like gentlemen toward the defeated people.

At this time the soldiers were just allowed to carry their rifles as they guarded American headquarters and German prisoners. I had the opportunity to guard "Axis Sally," a popular propagandist heard by American soldiers during combat. She appeared to be a friendly person and was reputed to have been born in Boston, Massachusetts. She was later put on trial.

After the Germans surrendered, I remained, along with many other American soldiers. During that time I had eight-hour duty shifts. After that I was on my own. I took advantage and took radio courses from teachers who had been officers in the German army. When I wasn't going to school, I played ball on teams and was even in a league. One of the men I played with was Red Schoendienst, who was later to play with the St. Louis Cardinals.

In August of 1946, I came home for good!

Julio Aldape
1st Division
26th Infantry, Company L

Guarding the Nuremberg Defendants

Julio Aldape was born on December 20, 1927, in Pearsall, Texas, to Gil and Paulina Aldape. The family lived in Crystal City. Two other brothers fought in WWII. Santiago became a prisoner of the Germans. Isabel fought in the Pacific theater. Julio was the son of a preacher. His father did not like violence of any kind. When Julio became a guard at Nuremberg, he was astounded at how ordinary the Nazis who were put on trial appeared to be.

Our father was forced to fight in the Mexican Revolution. My father saw Pancho Villa when he came to Saltillo. He had a bunch of men with him. Everybody was just looking at him. He was an idol to them. At one time he lived in El Paso.

Our father Gil had to join the revolution in Mexico at age fourteen. The forcing was known as *la leva*. He played the coronet. At age seventeen my father was wounded. As a result, he hated violence of any kind, and he became a preacher.

Before leaving home my mother Paulina administered *la bendición*. I went to San Antonio for induction on October 2, 1945. After training for four months at Camp Robinson, which was an Infantry Replacement

Training Center, as a cannoneer, I was shipped out to Europe. Although I joined after WWII was declared over, I became part of the Army of Occupation, and I served as a guard during the Nuremberg trials.

In Germany I was with the Third Division but returned with the First Division. In small towns I guarded between the Russians and the Americans. I remember Allendorf.

When we were told we had to go to Nuremburg, I had to get a special ID card. I noticed at the trial that the Germans looked like everyone else. They did not look especially evil. My brother Santiago, who had been a POW in Germany, advised me to treat the prisoners well.

Anthony Quinn's father and Pancho Villa were friends. Quinn reportedly said, "Whatever you say about the man . . . I knew the man. He was a friend of ours. He came many times to our house. We were not afraid of him." Then I have heard of others—when he [Pancho Villa] came, they trembled.

Julio became a preacher like his father. Most of the children he raised became educators.

Macario García
Staff Sergeant, Company B Battalion
22nd Infantry Regiment
4th Infantry Division

Not Yet a Citizen
The following text was drawn from interviews with people who knew Macario García, who had died several years before I began these interviews. His story is an important one.

Macario García was born in *Villa de Castaño*, Mexico, in 1920 to farm workers who were parents of ten children. The Mexican Revolution ended in 1920, and times were hard for people like the Garcías. Three years later, like so many families in Mexico, they migrated to the United States. The Garcías settled in Sugarland, Texas, and lived in that vicinity when the draft notice for Macario arrived in 1942,

After being wounded in Normandy, 1944, Macario rejoined Company B, First Battalion, Twenty-Second Infantry Regiment, Fourth Infantry Division, and experienced action again.

For his actions Macario García received the Congressional Medal of Honor. The citation reads:

Staff Sergeant Macario García, [then Pfc.], while an acting squad leader of Company B, 22nd Infantry, on November 20, 1944, near Grosshau, Germany, single handedly assaulted two enemy machine gun emplacements. Attacking prepared positions on a wooded hill, which could be approached only through meager cover, his company was pinned down by intense machine gun fire, and subjected to a concentrated artillery and mortar barrage. Although painfully wounded, he refused to be evacuated and on his own initiative crawled forward along until he reach[ed] a position near an enemy emplacement. Hurling grenades he boldly assaulted the position, destroyed the gun and with his rifle, killed three of the enemy who attempted to escape. When he rejoined his company, a second machine gun opened fire and again the intrepid soldier went forward, utterly disregarding his own safety. He stormed the position and destroyed the gun, killed three more Germans and captured four prisoners. He fought on with his unit until the objective was taken and only then did he permit himself to be removed for medical care. Private García's conspicuous heroism, his inspiring, courageous conduct and his complete disregard for his personal safety wiped out two enemy emplacements and enabled his company to advance and secure its objective.*

Macario became a hero. President Harry S. Truman awarded him the Congressional Medal of Honor on August 23, 1945. Even Mexico honored him with the *Mérito Militar*, Mexico's highest honor.

However, when Macario García returned to the US, an interesting occurrence in his life merited being told in the *New York Times*. Although the story has more than one version, the end result was the same. A month after Macario had been honored by President Truman, Macario and some friends decided to go eat at a restaurant in Richmond, Texas, near Houston.

When Macario, who was proudly wearing the uniform of an American soldier, sought to order some food, the owner told him, "We don't serve Mexicans." One of his friends said, "You can't refuse him. He's a Congressional Medal of Honor winner." The owner responded, "That don't mean anything here. We don't serve Mexicans."

His remarks did not set well with the feisty veteran.

He had killed the enemy and had been wounded and through his efforts had saved the lives of Americans. And for what? Is this the way it was supposed to be? Hadn't he paid his dues? He just wanted to buy a meal like any American citizen. He began fighting with the owner of the restaurant.

Someone called the police and Macario García, winner of the Congressional Medal of Honor and defender of America, was arrested. Hispanics everywhere were greatly offended. And as for the Anglo community—well, there was the dirty laundry for the world to see. The story was told and retold in major newspapers in this country.

LULAC Council number Sixty and other groups in the Houston community sought to assist Macario in every way they could. Two outstanding attorneys—Gus García [no relation] and John J. Herrera represented Macario. An acquittal was the result.

Macario García married and became a counselor for the Veterans Administration and served in that position until his death in 1972.

*María-Cristina García, "MACARIO GARCIA," *Handbook of Texas Online,* accessed September 05, 2018, http://www.tshaonline.org/handbook/entries/garcia/macario. Uploaded on June 15, 2010. Modified on February 20, 2017. Published by the Texas State Historical Association.

PART II

The Pacific Theater

Humberto Valderas
United States Navy

Island Hopping

Humberto Valderas was born on March 25, 1923, in Los Ojuelos Ranch. From there his family moved to Las Albercas Ranch. When Humberto was six years old, his family moved to Hebronville, Texas. Humberto was a most modest veteran. He volunteered and was not surprised about the toughness of boot camp. Reluctantly he told me of his experiences in the Navy. I assured him that technology had advanced so much since 1945 that nothing he could tell me would reveal any secrets.

Before I left my family to join the service, my mother gave me a religious cross to carry with me so that I would always be safe. After the war I returned to my family with the cross my mother had given me.

In 1942, I went to San Antonio to volunteer for the navy. I was nineteen years of age. On July 2, 1942, I ended up in San Diego, California, in boot camp. It wasn't any different from hard work. I liked it. I was there eight weeks.

I was assigned to the USS *Chauncey*, a combat destroyer. We arrived in Hawaii while it was dark. The destroyer was loaded with all the supplies we needed. From there we were taken to Wake Island. *Chauncey* at times escorted large ships including the *Lexington* [docked in Corpus Christi, Texas] and assisted in destroying Japanese aircraft.

I was a gunner's mate. We fired forty and twenty-millimeter guns. I was a loader and a trainer whose job it was to get the guns in position to fire. The destroyers had a "sound" element, which detected submarines hidden under the surface of the water. Thus, these smaller ships were of great use to the large ships, which did not have the equipment to detect the deadly submarines.

After Wake Island, *Chauncey* headed back to Hawaii and then south to the Gilbert Islands and Tarawa atoll. The marines made a landing there, which the *Chauncey* supported by bombarding the island.

Then, I went to Ravel Island. En route aircraft fired at us, and we fired back. Meanwhile the Japanese were holding Eniwetok. The *Chauncey* escorted the *Lexington*. The ships decided to go between two islands and fight the Japanese from those positions.

From there the ships went to Guam in a convoy. They surrounded the island and bombarded Guam for six hours. Then, they situated themselves between Rota and Saipan Islands.

After that it was on to the Philippines and right into Leyte Gulf. We hit two or three islands and tried to destroy the Japanese ships in Leyte. Then, on to New Guinea. The *Chauncey* stayed in New Guinea and was given three months of supplies.

Chauncey escorted a carrier to Okinawa. A typhoon hit close to Kyushu. The destroyer moved violently up and down. The kamikaze planes were expected to hit. When they came, our ship was able to shoot down a few.

Admiral "Bull" Halsey had a task force under his command. He was known as a tough leader. *Chauncey* escorted the carrier, USS *Franklin*, out of Shikoku after the Japanese had hit it.

I ended up in close proximity to where the surrender document was signed. The destroyer went on to Shantou, China. Meanwhile North Korea began activity, which received worldwide attention. Another war would soon begin.

On December 10, 1945, I was discharged from the navy. I missed being in the service so much that on April of 1946, I joined the army and stayed with them for seventeen years. Of the two, I preferred the army because I liked the feel of ground under my feet.

I trained as a paratrooper in Ft. Benning, Georgia, and became a soldier in the Eighth Army. I wish even now in 2002 that I could be in the army. I liked the training, the equipment, and the order in the army.

In November 1963, I happened to be in Washington, DC, when President Kennedy was killed in Dallas, Texas. I was able to go to the Capitol rotunda to pay my respects.

I love this country. There is no other country like this one. I have been to other countries, and this one is the best. If I could, I would serve my country again!

Santiago Jaramillo
E Troop, 12th Cavalry
B Troop, 8th Cavalry, Mechanical

Knowledge of Spanish, an Asset in War

Santiago Jaramillo was born on December 19, 1920, to Rafael and Anita Jaramillo in Kingsville, Texas. There were six children in the family with Santiago being the only male. Rafael Jaramillo worked with the post office for twenty years. Santiago said he and his friends wanted to join the service, and he dropped out of school so he could volunteer. His knowledge of Spanish became quite handy as the Filipinos who worked with the Americans on the Philippine Islands could speak Spanish.

Every day I walked to school I would see a large billboard that featured Uncle Sam's picture, which said, "I want you to join the army and see the world." About thirty guys from Kingsville wanted to join the service. After the service I got my GED (General Educational Development). I volunteered on August 5, 1940. Although I was to graduate in December from H. M. King High School, I dropped out of school and volunteered in the army.

Fort Ringgold in Rio Grande City was the first stop. From there I shipped out to Ft. Riley, Kansas. My pay was a dollar a day or $30 a month. You could buy a whole bunch with one dollar.

My family was reluctant. They wanted me to go to college. Since I was the only boy, I got on my mother's good side and everything. I had already gotten the papers. I went on to San Antonio to Fort Sam Houston and I got the papers and told my mother to help me go in there. I had to go before I got drafted. So she talked my father into signing those papers because I was twenty years old then.

I wanted to select what I wanted. I selected the horse cavalry. I love horses. I enlisted in San Antonio. They asked me where did I want to go, and I said, "All my friends were going to Ft. Ringgold, Texas, neighbors." So I went there. When you volunteer you get to select. I wanted to go to the Air Force [Army Air Corps] in Denver, Colorado, but none of my friends wanted to go, and I wanted some company.

I did my basic there [Ft. Ringgold] on horses; in other words, the regular basic training. Then they sent me to Ft. Riley, Kansas. My present wife was my high school girlfriend. I came home on furlough and my take-home pay was $19.25 from the $1 a day deal. We got married and I took her with me. We married in a church in Kingsville. We went to Ft. Riley, Kansas. After work I was working at the service club. I got my wife a job out there. And so we worked; I worked with her. I did alterations on over-coats for five dollars apiece. We managed to save $1,000 in six months. We came home on furlough. We had lots of fun with our friends.

We were living in Junction City, Kansas. She was going to have a baby, and I said, "I want my baby to be a Texan." I brought her home and shortly after that they called me. I was going to go overseas.

I was in a restaurant having lunch and I had just started eating when they had a radio advertisement, a recall of all military personnel to report to the camp immediately. So I left my lunch. They wouldn't take my money. I went back and we were restricted to quarters until further notice.

We were briefed on what to do and all that. Keep a tight lip about operations there. Don't talk to strangers about military things and all that stuff. Report any suspicious characters around the camp. That was part of the briefing.

I left my wife in Kingsville with her parents. When I came it was very sentimental. We went to the church. They said a prayer for me, the priest. He's the one that married us. He gave us the blessing; so did my mother and my father. They placed their hands over my head. Everybody was crying.

I got my orders. They didn't tell me where I was going. [The papers said] "You have your shipping orders and you will be notified on the way." We had a troop train. Everyone on there was going to Fort Ord, California. We got our orders on the train. She [his wife] was with her family. I called her and said I was going to an undisclosed place. "I'll call you know when I get there." She said, "Okay."

I was at Fort Ord. We had indoctrination on Field Combat. Live ammunition over our heads. We were crawling. They had a fire hose with water making things slippery and muddy. We were going to the Pacific and it rains out there every day. We made that part. Fort Ord was a very sandy place and it was very hot. We had to go with a full pack and a full day of maneuvers. Back and forth. We had intensive training like that training for two to three weeks. Finally, we got acclimatized to that weather. We got used to it.

Then we got our orders. We were going to go to San Francisco. Finally, when they did tell us where we were going . . . Let me tell you one thing. We were issued winter clothes because actually we were supposed to go to the Aleutian Islands. They gave us heavy overcoats and heavy woolen clothes. But there was a school of loose small Japanese submarines. They were patrolling the Hawaiian coast. They were chasing us all over. So they changed the course and told us we were going to . . . They said, "We have to change course now, but you'll know where you are when we get there."

So we landed at New Guinea, Milne Bay. I was sent to the Admiralty Islands. They are in the Bismark Archipelago. While there we were still combat training. And as a matter of fact, we got the Japs out of there. We were foot soldiers. When we got there our unit was doing mopping up operations. We were holding the land there.

We went to the Admiralty Islands and we were at *Los Negros*.

We were fighting from island to island. You couldn't see them [Japanese soldiers]. They were good at camouflage and everything. They tied themselves with their machine guns on top of the coconut trees. We couldn't see nothing, but they saw us.

Let me tell you how close . . . .I had many close ones [close calls]. Sgt. Leonard had a cigarette in his mouth and he said, "Jerry, give me a light—I had a big cigarette—and when I was lighting his cigarette, this sniper shot him right between the eyes. He froze—like this—[rigid]. And he was just frozen. He didn't move; he was just leaning against a palm tree. And he [the sniper] shot the antenna—from my side—of the radio. The radio was in my backpack. He [Sgt. Leonard] died standing in front of the tree; he froze.

When I saw him I was trying to help him. I said, "Medic! Come on down." And I stayed with him. Somebody got the chaplain over there. They [Japanese] were strapped to the palm trees. So they [the Americans] said, "Spray [with guns] all the trees."

When we got to the islands we had to go on mopping operations. At *Los Negros* [in the Admiralty Islands], we had to chase the Japs up into the mountains. Up in the mountains there was a little stream. We found a school of Japs there but they were unarmed. We had a field day. They had a fire going. We spotted them because when you see smoke, they say somebody's out there. We went up there very silent, and some were taking a bath in the river, stuff like that. To this day I am really shocked. They [the Japanese] had—the Koreans—they were their prisoners and their servants. One of the Koreans, he got smart. He would hardly eat anything. He was skin and bones. And that's why he survived, because they [Japanese] were eating—cannibalizing—eating some of those Koreans. That skinny guy told our interpreter. He told our G2, which was intelligence. They asked him what happened to him? He said, "I refused to eat. I haven't eaten in I don't know how many days." He didn't want to eat because as soon as they got fat, they [the Japanese] eat them, too. See what I mean. He was just skin and bones.

And in one of the mess kits this guy says, "Look what they've been eating." They were eating the Koreans. They had a steak about this big [Santiago demonstrated with his hands indicating approximately 6X6 inches round] from the leg. It was cooked and everything. This guy who was going to eat his lunch—a Japanese had his lunch in his mess kit. He [the Korean] showed us what they were doing to them. He said the reason he was saved was because he would not eat. And they didn't want to eat him, because there was hardly anything to chew on, only skin and bones.

We shot them [the Japanese]. The G2 took the Korean and took care of him, fed him and everything to restore him.

After that we were on standby for a few weeks. They transferred one of our squadron to a little island called Howe, Lord Howe Island. Beautiful island. About a mile long and half a mile wide. We stayed there. It was so beautiful, the water. We used to go swimming every day and catch some fish and all of that. It was just a paradise.

The natives there were called aborigines. And we called them "fuzzy wuzzies." They were short guys with kinky hair. They had betel nuts that looked like a green pecan. They used to chew it, and they used to grind seashells into powder. And they had some sort of weed. They got that weed and soaked it in that powder and chewed it with the betel nut. Their mouths get red right here, and their teeth were red. And they used to dye their hair red with that stuff.

We went to Samar, which is in the Southern Philippines. When General MacArthur said, "I shall return." We went to Tacloban, capital of Leyte. We went to the next island, Capo Logan. We waited until October 19, 1944.

I was in Manila. I shook hands with MacArthur. "I shall return" was there with us. He came back into Manila. I had my radio. I was transmitting all my messages in Spanish to my outfit. You see we had squadrons all over and I was right in the headquarters in the Malacañang Palace. I was in the First Cavalry. It was the central point in the Malacañang Palace.

We were transmitting in Spanish because the Japs could not pronounce the Rs. And we have a lot of Rs in our language. Transmitting to the other units like Baker Troop and Charlie and all of those.

We got our orders to go to Luzon. That was on October 19, 1944. We landed at San Fernando, Pampanga. We had to make a hundred-mile dash in one day and capture Manila. We liberated a whole bunch of political prisoners at Santo Tomás University right there in Manila. Those poor guys were skin and bones. The reason they were like that was because the Japanese used to let them grow their victory gardens there. They said they would eat anything that crawls, roaches and anything. The prisoners ate worms and anything that crawls. The Japanese ate the garden produce. When the stuff was ready to be harvested, if they [the Japanese] caught anybody out there, they'd cut their head off. Some of the guys sneaked at night and got some of those vegetables. They had Russians, Germans, a lot of nations, white guys as prisoners.

Before we entered Manila or when we entered Manila . . . in *El Cementerio Del Norte* [the Cemetery of the North] we went through there and the Japs took out the bodies of the dead and they were using those [graves] as foxholes and were shooting at us.

All around there, The Japanese captured all the priests and nuns from the churches. They used to lock them up in the churches, and then set fire to the churches. They captured a lot from a convent or someplace that had a whole bunch of them. They had their heads cut off. The nuns, you know what they used to do? We saw a lot of them. They [the Japanese] put their bayonet right here [gestures to the groin area] and ripped their belly open from right here on up.

I saw one of them, a nun. She was alive. Let me tell you what was so gruesome. I saw a thing that looked like leather that was hanging from a piece of wood—you know right there [points to groin area]—and part of the belly and she crawled just a little further on down and all her guts and stomach was right here. She said, "*a-g-u-a, a-g-u-a.*" [water, water] And I heard that and I said, "*Quieres agua? Aquí traigo agua?*" "*Sí.*" And I gave her a drink from my canteen. *"Gracias, hijo mío."* You know what? She closed her eyes and she died after that drink of water. *Cementerio del Norte.*

From there we went to Santo Tomás University. From there we went to the palace. I was a radio man, an advance, what they call a point man. I was transmitting what I was seeing, you know. I was with a squad. We had a squad leader. A second lieutenant. Young kids from the states. There was one . . . They were new guys, but they were officers. They didn't have experience, so they wanted us to give them some experience in the field. There was one poor kid. He had just made second lieutenant and he got killed the first day.

After that we slept right there, right around the palace. We had foxholes all around it. And here was the Pasig River on this other side. And the wall of Manila. Old Manila was a walled city. It was across the river. The fence was twelve foot wide; you could put a jeep on top of it and it was about eight feet high. The Spanish built those fortresses, the walls.

We met President Riojas; he was the president of the Philippines and lived inside the palace. They brought me coffee all night out there to the foxhole. They had a young Filipino girl, and she took care of me all night long. She listened to the radio to see if there were any messages. I had the transmitter.

My code signal was "Baker 1 calling Baker 2" or "Charlie." Charlie Troop is another troop. Fox was "F Troop" and so on.

After we landed General MacArthur heard me making a transmission in Spanish. "Hey, Trooper, I want you to transmit this for me." He gave me five letters like Z, 5, Baker, EZ, Charlie or whatever and then he said, "ASAP." About five minutes later here comes one of those big jeeps with all kinds of whistles and bells and everything and a big, tall antenna. That was his personal transmitting thing. The antenna was eight feet long, maybe longer, all over the place. He had some operators and guards all around it.

That was General MacArthur's transmitter or communications center. He came over and said, "Where're you from, Trooper?" I said, "From Texas." He said, "You guys did a damn good job." And he shook my hand.

I said, "Thank you, sir." He was very nice.

And President Riojas . . .you see the official language in the Philippines was Spanish during that time. They changed to Tagalog. I had a time. They treated me royally, President Riojas. I went into the palace, and they brought me coffee all night long because I spoke Spanish.

After the palace we went into the hills. We went to Antipolo. That's where I got wounded. It's way up in the mountains. It was two o'clock in the morning. It rained there every day. It was like throwing water with the tub. Those typhoons out there are mean. So, I felt something like hot breath in front of my face about two o'clock in the morning. Those guys [the Japanese] are pretty smart. They attack you during the silence of the night while many of the guys are asleep. When I did like this (arose slightly) my helmet hit his helmet. And I had a submachine gun with me. I cut him loose. [he imitated the sound of a machine gun]. We had orders not to fire unless it was necessary. I let out a burst, and cut him in two, guts and everything on me.

And as soon as I did that—we had strict orders not to do that unless we had to—somebody, the Japs, threw a hand grenade with dynamite. My buddy who was with me, I think he got it, and when he picked it up, that thing cut him in two. Both of us were in a foxhole. It was raining and the foxhole was full of water. My buddy picked up the hand grenade with the dynamite. He was going to throw it back, but he didn't get the chance. It cut him in two. I was knocked out, unconscious from about two in the morning until about six. I had sandbags and I had sandbags on top of me. I fell like that. Some of the other sandbags fell on top of my head. One of them fell right on top of me, and I was breathing through a little opening. There was water underneath me and blood and guts and everything. About daylight, dawn, I felt someone playing around with my dog tags, and I got up. I saw someone, the chaplain and his assistant. They had a tablet and they had gotten my dog tags, and they had written my name on the tablet. When they saw me, they saw the dog tags and they scratched my name. And the chaplain—I couldn't hear what he said, but I could see them moving their lips. He shook my hand and I heard him say, "Congratulations. You are still with us." Something like that.

I was sent back to New Guinea to Finschhafen to a general hospital there. I was out there, but they didn't do nothing to me. I was staying there and they gave me some APC tablets which are like aspirin. They gave me the APC for pain, and I was there for a week or so. The grenade and dynamite ruptured my ear drums. Therefore, they didn't do anything. I got tired and I went to a little airfield out there. A friend of mine was out of

Manila. I said, "Let's get the hell out of here. You want to go with me? Let's go see if we can hitch a ride." He said, "Yeah."

They used to bring things out here for repairs. They had planes going back and forth to Manila. So we went out there and told one of the guys we wanted a ride back to Manila. The guy said, "You go talk to the crew chief over there." So I went to him, "Hey, I need a ride back to Manila." He said, "When are you going? When do you want to go? We have aircraft going every day." [I said] "I'm ready but I have to get my gear all ready." He said, "I'll tell you what, the best time is tomorrow morning. Be here by six or seven if you can." I said, "OK."

Out there you see a jeep, anything that you see nobody using, you take it. The jeeps, they didn't have a key; they have a built in key. So we turned that thing on, took off with it. This other guy went with me. We went to the airport. We left the jeep over there.

I rejoined my outfit outside Manila in Antipolo. Right where I was wounded. We went to other places from there. Because I was just one week in the hospital, they were still going out there. I went back in and I located Baker Troop.

They gave me a rifle. I became an infantryman. I went out there. They had shot a bunch of our boys. We had a skeleton crew. We had a perimeter and they had so few people [American soldiers] that the foxholes were about ten feet apart and sometimes even more than that. Before that the foxholes were closer, every five feet.

No replacements until we got to the point that we had secured the place. As new replacements came in, they put them up. After we did all that hard fighting they sent us to a place called Santo Tomás. A little town. There was not much activity. . . . Our outfit went to Lucena, a rest camp. When we were at Lucena, it was a rest. You didn't do anything else but rest, run around, drink coffee.

The second Sunday we were attending an interdenominational service. Our theater or church—they cut the palm trees, the coconut trees, and put them right alongside each other. And they had a movie screen, we sat on those logs and you know what? Funny thing was that one night we were watching a movie and they showed Babe Ruth, the famous player, and we had some Japs that came in and sat close to where we were. They came in from the jungle. They said, "Hey Baby Luth, Baby Luth." Before the show was over, they'd take off.

We got a few of them. An American came over with his gun, hit him [the Japanese] over the head, and knocked him out. They interrogated him and everything. The Japanese would sit down and say. "Hey, Joe, give me cigarette." We thought they were Filipinos. We knew exactly, because they called us "Joe." "Hey, Joe." They'd just sit down and enjoy the show. And they'd say, "Baby Luth. Baby Luth."

Our password was "Lucky Lady." And one time, one of those Japs came. We said, "What's the password?" And he said, "Rucky Rady." We shot him right away. They [the Japanese] couldn't pronounce the Ls.

Somebody would be coming in and they [Japanese] were sneaking around listening. We'd say, "Who is that?" Some of the guys [Americans] had to go to the woods for the restroom. They would say like, "Joe Gonzalez coming in." "What's the password?" "Lucky Lady." "Advance and identify yourself." Or something like that. The Japanese were listening to everything. So they tried "Rucky Rady."

The movies are in the boonies, in the jungle where we were. We had Bob Hope and Tony Romano. He played the guitar. We had a lady (Frances Langford). She went up there and sang for us. This girl told us this. They were talking about hobbies. She went to the kitchen. The guys were making cookies. And Tony Romano said, "You know how they put in the raisins in there?" "No."

"They get the little cookie like that, put it on their . . . And put a little hole in there and then put the raisin in." I don't think it was true, but he was crazy enough.

Jack Pepper used to hang around with Tony, Bob Hope, and this gal. They would joke and sing. Very nice people who would go and entertain us. We appreciated that.

I was at the theater sitting down attending morning church services. Here comes one guy and says, "Jaramillo, they want you at the orderly room."

"What did I do?"

"I'm not supposed to tell you, but you're going home."

"What? You better not be kidding, because you're getting me out of service. And it is not nice to play jokes."

"They told me to come and tell you. You don't want to go, okay."

"If it's not true, I'm going to be looking for you."

"Okay. Do whatever you want."

So I went and reported to the staff sergeant. The sergeant said, "Hey, Jaramillo, congratulations."

I said, "Thank you."

He said, "You're going to Australia."

"What?"

He said, "You're going out there for indoctrination for a briefing. You're going to be a second lieutenant before you come back."

I said, "Wait a minute. Wait a minute. That's not what they told me. Is this some kind of a trick?" [He said] "Why?"

"The guy told me I was going to go home."

"That big mouth SOB. He was not supposed to tell you."

"Well, what is it?"

"We were hoping you would go out there for a briefing and you'd come in as an officer because of all the field training you've had."

"I want to go home. I have a daughter and my family, and that [promotion] don't mean nothing to me. My family comes first and I haven't seen them in twenty-six months. And I have a little girl waiting for me and my wife, too."

"Okay. Whatever you wish. I'm gonna get that guy for squealing."

I don't know what they did to him. I would have been a second lieutenant when they sent the soldiers to Japan. Probably a captain or something when I was out there.

From there they sent me to Lucena City or one of those assembly points. It was in August 1945.

You know what? When I was coming back . . . it was in the middle of the Pacific when we heard something about an Atomic Bomb. We said, "What in the world is that?" "I don't know." Nobody knew what it was. They had dropped a bomb on Hiroshima and Nagasaki. They said it was a powerful bomb and it had knocked out the whole city with everything. We had a briefing and they called an assembly. They said, "The war is going to be over. They dropped an atomic bomb."

We asked, "What is that?" We were out there on the deck during the briefing. And they told us what it was. We had a powerful bomb that can knock out a whole city with everything in it. So we've already won the war.

So when we got to San Francisco, some of the people out there had gotten the news. I was starving. I went to a whiskey store, a liquor store, and the doors were closed. I knocked on the door like this, you know. They saw that I was skin and bones. I weighed 126 pounds, and I had malaria. My skin was yellow, because I took atabrine tablets. They make your skin color yellow. Little yellow pills and I was taking those things because of my malaria and I was yellow all over. And when they saw me—somebody did like this [closed signal].

I said, "Let me in." Somebody opened the door. And I said, "Hey, I want to get something to drink because I haven't had a decent drink in twenty-six months." And you know what? That lady—she was so nice—said, "I'll tell you what. You deserve it." She gave me a fifth of Scotch. "You go and celebrate and have a good time."

Okay. Bells were ringing and everything. Bells were ringing because they declared a victory. VJ Day. I went out there and girls were throwing keys down. Keys from their rooms. So I went up there and we celebrated. I took my booze and they had plenty, too. To make a long story short, I stayed there about a couple of days.

I got my orders and got on a train to Ft. Sam Houston in San Antonio. I reported in and I was looking for that little piece of paper. I had enlisted there. He says, "Here's your orders. Now you are going to receive the officially signed piece of paper you want."

They gave me a little money—it wasn't too much—and my walking papers. They gave me enough to go buy me a suit, a civilian suit. I went home to Kingsville and oh, I tell you.

I called them. My family was at the train station. My little girl was six months old when I left. She was three years old when I came back. Beautiful little doll. Anita.

I had four kids. I was in the Naval Hospital. My ears hadn't healed. I went to the hospital. They didn't do anything. They just gave me two APC tablets. Actually what it was—I was shell-shocked. That was one of the things. And I had malaria. Actually, what they wanted us to do was to relax and take it easy. Gave us good food and good entertainment and everything. Free passes to the theater. So we rested a lot in the hospital, but they didn't do anything. Doctor came by in the morning, recommended two APCs. "See you in the morning." I was there about a week or so.

There were some people they were recruiting for somebody to go to work for them at the base. They approached me. I told them my name. They said, "Do you have a job?" "What are you going to do?" I said, "No, I don't have a job. Sure would like to have one." "What kind of work did you do?" I mentioned them. "Also I was a supply sergeant before I went overseas."

He said, "I can get you a job with supplies." He told me to report to Building Ten. I went out there and they hired me on the spot. They had mostly women. The women—with all their hearts—wanted us to have their jobs. They would rather give them to the veterans. With five years military and thirty years at the base makes thirty-five years with Uncle Sam.

I went to work out there in supply and there was O & R navy. Overhaul and Repair. They hired me out there and I went to work in supply. When they opened up O & R, I went to work in the upholstery shop.

I learned about sewing machines in Horse Cavalry. They had horse blankets. I was to patch them up. They had a big investment in sewing machines. They sent me to school in Kansas City, Missouri, to the Singer Company. They trained me how to tear them apart and put them back together. I went to sewing machine repair school out there. And then I came back. Anytime they had any problems with them, I fixed them. And when I was discharged and came back, I took my MOS [Military Occupational Specialty], and then I mentioned sewing machines. They had forty-four sewing machines in the fabric shop at the base. Mostly women were working there. They were sewing soundproofing for the aircraft. They used to make covers from—like linen-like sheets made covers for airplanes and they would spray them to waterproof them. And sent them overseas. I got into that.

For a while Santiago and his family lived in Arizona while he worked at Williams Air Force Base. Santiago and his wife had four children: Anita, a Methodist minister; Jimmy, a mechanical engineer; Gloria, a school principal; and Alma, a nurse, deceased.

Tom Cantú

Aerial Engineer 2750

Flying over the Hump

Tom Cantú was born in Robstown, Texas, on February 23, 1923. A young man from a small town, Tom observed his father in business dealings, something he would do in the future. During the war he was part of a group that flew supplies from India to China. Though it might sound simple enough, the job was fraught with dangers.

I was raised okay. We lived in Nueces County, but we moved to McAllen. I must have been a couple of years old. Then during the Depression in 1929, my father repatriated. We went to Mexico.

He came from Monterrey, Mexico. My dad didn't come to Texas. He went from Mexico to Louisiana. Father was named Tomás. Mother was named Caritina. He went to New Orleans in 1920. My father had businesses all the time. He had a bingo business for all the people who used to work in the fields. We then moved to San Antonio.

He ran a taxi cab business. He had two taxis. From there he moved here to Corpus Christi in 1922. He opened up a business in Alice, Texas. He had *molinos* [mills] to grind corn. He moved from here and he had eighteen *molinos* in the valley. He also had a frito company. They were corn chips called "Corn Puffs." I used to go with him to collect from all the businesses. I was not in school yet. I must have been about five years old, and we lived in McAllen. He always had someone, a helper with him. It was very common in Europe or in the Latin American countries. People with business always had a man to do everything. Anyhow, I remember he had collected in money bags from all the businesses he had, and when we got to the bank there were a lot of people in front of the bank. He said, "What happened? It's not a holiday."

And they said, "No, the bank is closed because they went broke." And he had all his money.

So he had to sell everything, and he saved enough money to move to Monterrey and open a grocery store. And he had or so I hear one of the first people who had a shuttle, a bus running around Monterrey. We didn't stay long. We came back to McAllen and didn't stay there long.

He opened up a business here in Nueces in the early 1930s. He opened up a *molino*. He did very well and opened up a grocery store. Later he owned the Cantu Packing Company, meat company, like Sam Kane. It was at 1427 Antelope.

In my family there were five girls and four boys. All the boys served in WWII. Gilbert Cantú, Navy on the oil tanker *Monongahela*. They would go out there and put oil in [vessels]. If you get hit you don't have to worry about anything. Frank Cantú, Intelligence G2, Ft. Nix, New Jersey; Henry Cantú; Cantú, Army Air Corps.

I volunteered and went in November 11, 1942. I served in what is called CBI, China, Burma, and India (also referred to as The Hump). I was the flight engineer. I was only a corporal. They wouldn't give you promotions. I would take care and make sure that the plane was ready to go. It was only a four-member crew. We flew Liberators. The crew had a pilot, copilot, radioman, and a flight engineer. They are called B-24s. These were B-24s and B-17s. C-47s are cargo planes. C is for cargo. The reason we flew B-24s and B-17s is because they had brought some of those planes from Europe and they converted them into cargo planes so we could fly cargo. And we would fly—most of the time we would fly two things, either bombs or the B-29s to bomb Japan. Also, gasoline.

We had different pilots and flew twenty-four hours a day. Sometimes you were called the next day. You had to go back. We would fly cargo from Assam, India—fly from there to China and sometimes . . . These are the places: Jorhat, Kunming, Chengdu, Luliang, and Chabua.

These are the decorations. This one here is the most important one, the Distinguished Flying Cross. This tells you where I was, like the American theater, the Pacific theater, three bronze stars.

It was beyond the call of duty. I flew over five hundred combat hours. The Air Medal was for 150 hours. The DFC was for 350 combat hours. The worst enemy we had was the weather. I've got at home how many planes we lost. We lost eight hundred planes. We were very fortunate. We came so close to getting killed.

First of all the weather. The wings would get ice, and it made the plane too heavy. And the plane can't fly. In those days we had to fly sometimes through the mountains. There are twenty-nine peaks that are thirty-one thousand feet high. [The highest peak, Mt. Everest is over twenty-nine thousand feet high. There are other peaks that are almost as high as Mt. Everest.]

We had three routes. You could fly through the mountains, but the Japanese were in Burma. Normally they would shoot at you. There were three routes—Fox, Easy, and—can't think of the other.

That was the most dangerous part. And the weather. The Japanese would always bomb the bases where we would land on holidays—July Fourth, Christmas, New Year's Day. They figured that we were celebrating. A few times we were coming in with cargo and they would say "Go to the other base." "Go to Kunming or Chengdu" because we were alerted already that the Japanese were coming. They said Japs but we don't say that word.

They would turn the lights off on the runways, and then they would say, "Look, we'll give you ten minutes to land. We're going to turn the runway lights on. As soon as you land they are going to turn off. Taxi the plane and turn off all the lights."

We could hear where they were bombing the other bases but luckily we never got hit.

At one time we had more crew, a gunner, and a bombardier. We were cargo planes. You'll see the B-24 converter is called—it has four engines. Most of the planes would land like this [parallel to the ground] and this one landed forwardly like this.

They were called Liberators. They used them in Europe to bomb Germany for many years. Recently we were using those where we were, because you could fly longer distances. We would fly eleven hours sometimes. They didn't fly as fast as most planes do.

Three hundred miles or so. That was one of my jobs [to refuel]. I had to make sure how many gallons. Sometimes they would get upset with me because I said, "Man, that ain't enough. We need more gas."

We flew a priest one time. We used oxygen masks in those days. The planes were not pressurized. A lot of times I had a hose [for breathing] about forty feet long. We were flying bombs on the B-29 and I had to go to the back to see if there was any ice on the wings. There wasn't. I fainted and what happened was the priest stood up. He was stepping on my hose. He didn't do that long or I wouldn't be here. He moved by accident. The minute he moved I could breathe.

This is gross, but I'll tell you. Some people in the Far East believe that if they get close to danger, all the bad spirits go, they die. The Chinese believe that.

We were taxiing and this guy—I don't know if he was Indian—he got real close and we cut him in half with the propeller.

I did this for two years. I was stationed here in the states. I was stationed in San Antonio; Biloxi, Mississippi; Las Vegas; and Kansas City, TWA Aircraft School. Aircraft Engineering mechanic. Basic training in Biloxi.

They didn't know where I was going to wind up. I was trained. Basic training in Biloxi, Mississippi.

I volunteered. Thanks to my father. Here is where I was trained: Kansas City, Missouri, Aircraft Mechanic. That's when I was in the service. . . . I went to an aircraft school here in Corpus Christi before I went into the service. My dad said, "You want to be in the air force [Army Air Corps]." I quit high school to go to aircraft school. They teach you mechanics. When I volunteered I put down on the application that I had mechanic experience. They needed mechanics so I had an advantage.

These are the qualifications of Army Air Corps. Technician, and badge of Airplane Mechanic. Army Air Force Crew Member.

When I came back I was at Love Field, and I wasn't feeling too good. I had been in the hospital with a nervous stomach. When I was in the service overseas, I was very nervous. I was afraid I was going to die. When I came back I wasn't feeling well, and this sergeant wanted me to go out and do something. I told him I wasn't feeling well. I just stayed in the barracks for two days. He wrote me up and said he couldn't find me.

I went to my own doctors. It was just nerves. One day I came back from the flight. So they needed someone to go again and they asked me. I said, "I just got back so I can't go again." I was the youngest in the squadron. There was another gentleman, I can't recall his name. He went at midnight. We used to fly twenty-four hours a day. Then about six o'clock a.m. they came back. I heard some noises. I said, "What are you doing?" They said, "We are picking up his belongings," because they got killed. And it was sad, really, really sad. They hit the first ridge. See, we had so many mountains. The guy that got killed was probably in his early thirties.

We had long flights, about nine hours up in the air. In order to pass the time the radioman played the radio and we heard Tokyo Rose. We listened to her all the time. She said things like, "All you Mexican boys should not be fighting for the United States, because in the United States you are discriminated against everywhere."

Then she would say, "And now I dedicate this song to the soldiers who are over here from the state of New Mexico."

Other times she would put out false information. One time we took off from Assam on our way to China. There was a small village, Jorhat, near our base. On this particular flight Tokyo Rose said, "The Japanese army has taken over Jorhat in Assam." We knew it was totally false because we had just left there. Our pilot jokingly said, "I guess we'll have to land somewhere else when we return."

We met with three other guys. We got together and we got to drinking. We took a rickshaw. Actually we took the one with a horse, like they have in Mexico. We told the driver to take us somewhere so we could get something to drink. So he got money. There were only two of us left then. We waited thirty minutes, forty-five minutes. He never came back. He took the money. So I said to the other guy, "You know I'm from Texas. I'm going to take this old horse and make him take us somewhere." So we did. This is at one o'clock in the morning. The people in India—lots of poverty. They sleep on the street and on the sidewalk. Well, we hit a cow. So he and I got out. There was like a funeral procession. They were taking a body to the river or something. So he and I started walking, and they started running after us. We didn't know where we were going. We were running. It was dark. I told him, "Joe, don't stop, Joe."

'Cause I looked back, and there must have been a hundred people running behind us. We were very strong then. I remember one guy heard the noise—he tried to grab me and I hit him and knocked him down. We went finally to a dead-end street. There was a wall. I went and jumped and grabbed him, Joe, and I pulled him up. Some of the Indians were trying to get him down. So we jumped . . . and there was glass on top, but I didn't cut my hands. I don't know why. So, we heard some noises. I don't know what you call them, the group that was after us. There were two gates, the wall, and about fifty feet. But we didn't see the gate. We jumped the wall and as we were walking we saw these two gates and all these Indians trying to get in there.

So we hid under some bushes. Then we saw three men with lanterns and *unos garrotes* [some big sticks]. I told Joe, "Joe, let me handle this." I knew a few words in Hindu, and I had some rupees. I said, "Sahib, Rupees, paani." (Paani is water.) So they took the money and brought us some water. Then I realized where we were. It was a temple. The other guys who were after us were outside. These guys didn't know what was going on.

They took us to the next street. And about a half a block from there, there was an MP station. I have never in my life been so happy to see the military police. Nobody likes them. I told them, "Look, we got lost. We're supposed to go to base and fly in a plane." They gave us a ride in a jeep. I'll never forget. I tell that story every chance I get.

There was an older man, probably in his forties. We had this pilot, Captain White. He had been a pilot with a big company. He was experienced, but he was not experienced in B-24s. On takeoff, something happened with one of the engines. We were loaded with bombs. And something happened to one of the engines. I was standing right between the pilot and copilot. In front of me there are four red buttons, called feather buttons. And what this does, if one of the engines—this is a four engine plane—something happens, you push the button, so the propeller will go even like this [demonstrates], so the plane will not shake. But what he did, he feathered the wrong engine.

I hit him with my hand and I pulled the button. We are taking off. At take-off you need all the power that you can [get]. I am watching all the engines. When one of the engines went out, instead of pushing the red inside button, he pushed the right outside button. That meant we were flying on two engines, with all that cargo. So I automatically pushed it back. And we turned around.

I hit him. He was a captain. He pushed the wrong button. I was watching him, so I hit his hand and pushed the right button. And then of course when you are flying like this if one of the engines is out, you bank, you bank the plane. So we went back and we landed. It was okay.

What it is on planes, the wings have little flaps. So when you are taking off, that little flap is supposed to be about twenty degrees down. When you land, that flap is almost eighty degrees down. It holds the plane. When you are landing the plane it is eighty degrees down. Say this is the plane. This is the wing. This is the flap. It comes out like this and goes like this. [demonstrates].

To me most air flights are very safe. The most dangerous is on takeoff. You taxi the plane and then you take off, you are climbing and then you cruise. When you cruise, everything is lovely.

I was one of the very first to come back on the point system, because I was there two years. I was a holder of the Air Medal, 250 combat hours, holder of the Distinguished Flying Cross, which was 350 hours. And I also have, which I never got and I didn't care because I just wanted out. I was supposed to get Oak Leaf Clusters for my Air Medal and my Distinguished Flying Cross.

When the war ended, when the Japanese surrendered, then we flew home. I flew from India to North Africa, Casablanca, to Accra; we flew to *Acensión* Island between South America and West Africa. The planes couldn't fly that far. It was a long strip, maybe like a block, two blocks, two blocks wide and a mile long because when the plane would take off the sea is here [close by]. From there we flew to Natal, Brazil, and from Brazil we flew. I could have taken a ship, but it would take about two weeks or something like that and I wanted to get home.

What happened was what you would call hitchhiking. You would wait for a plane. That's the way I went overseas. From Miami to Puerto Rico to Brazil to Acensión to Accra to North Africa. I stayed in North Africa a month. We landed in Egypt—Cairo. And we were there a week.

[On his return] When we landed I kissed the ground in Miami. I wanted two things. I wanted a glass of milk and a big steak, because in India they don't have that; we used to eat water buffalo.

From Miami they flew us to Dallas, Love Field, and from there we took the train to San Antonio. My parents went to pick me up.

I was almost nineteen when I went in. I was twenty-three when I got out. My mother and one of my sisters went to pick me up. They had a car and we got home. I was quiet and didn't want to talk about it. I was short-tempered. I was in the hospital for two weeks with a stomach virus I had gotten in India. When I came back the priest told me to go to the hospital, because they had all my records. I didn't want nothing to do with the service, mostly because a couple of people make your life miserable. Like this acting sergeant in Dallas in Love Field pushing people around.

I figured I had done my duty, and he wasn't going to push me around. And that is why I was AWOL. Absent without Leave.

I got married a year later. My wife was also in the service. She was a sergeant. She volunteered. Her name was Claudia Ramirez. She went in '43 maybe. She went to school here. She took a test, and they called her. She was supposed to go to Officers Candidate School [OCS]. She joined. She made sergeant. She was stationed in San Francisco. She was in basic training in Florida. She was a clerk. She volunteered two times to go overseas, but they wouldn't let her. She graduated from Corpus Christi High.

I went to Del Mar and took some business courses. I helped my dad. My brother went to live in Chicago and the other went into business. I wound up with my father's business, the meat packing business.

Reynaldo Álvarez
US Navy Coxswain

A Promesa and Ten Battles

Reynaldo Álvarez was born on November 22, 1924, in Riviera, Texas, to Paulo and Angelita Ruiz Álvarez. His father worked for the Southern Pacific Railroad, and he also farmed and took odd jobs. Like most servicemen, Reynaldo did not get to pick his assignment, which was to pilot an LST, a landing craft that carried the soldiers ashore from their ships. Often the soldiers were rightfully afraid to get off the boat, and Reynaldo tried to reassure them.

After attending grammar school in Riviera, I moved to Corpus Christi, Texas, in 1939. When my father died, I began looking for a job. I became a drugstore clerk and worked in delivery. I also worked for the wholesale San Antonio Drug Company.

My mother gave me *la bendición* since Dad had already died. Then I took the train to San Antonio. There they process you and then send you home for a week and give you a date when to appear at the bus station here and then they'll take you to San Antonio.

I was drafted and inducted into the Navy on May 8, 1943. They had the fellows in a line and this fellow said, "You come over here. You go over there." And they picked me. They were officers. They put you wherever they needed you. I was discharged December 1, 1945.

From there they ship you, put you on a train. I wound up in San Diego, California, for training. I wanted to go to school. I applied for school, but I had been out of school since I was fourteen. You had to pass a small test to qualify for a school. I wanted to be in communications, radio or something like that. I wanted a trade, but I didn't qualify. They said, "They send you out to sea and you can strive for those positions. Work your way up aboard ship."

In San Diego training involved marching, using a rifle, just like a soldier. I was placed in a company for training. When I was through with the training, they showed us how to tie knots, rope, how to manage a gun or a cannon. All about the fire power aboard a ship. They taught us communications, how to read signals with light. The training in San Diego took about two months.

In San Diego at another base they had amphibious training. I was trained to drive those small boats, landing craft. We carried thirty-five men fully packed. We'd hit the beach. That's the landing. We'd drop that ramp. I had two sailors with me on the boat. They handled the ramp. We'd hit the beach. They were alert. They'd pull the lever; the ramp would drop, and thirty-five men ran out and took cover. And they were shooting at you real heavy. You had to crank the ramp by hand to pull it back up.

After a couple of months we were ready. We were on standby. They said, "You and you and you"—there were so many sailors there that got through the training—"are going overseas."

Where are you going to send me? To Corpus Christi? They have a naval base in Corpus Christi. "No, you're not going home, man. I know what you want." We were two hundred men. "This group is going overseas and this group is going to the Great Lakes." They had a naval training station there. We stayed around there a couple of weeks to get ready. Finally, we got on a draft going overseas to the South Pacific. That's where the action was.

They sent us over there in a troop cargo ship. When we got to the New Hebrides Islands there were ships in that harbor waiting for men from the United States to put them on as regular crew. So we got off at this place. This island had a big camp. Sleep in tents and all that. They called it our receiving station. From there the ships would send a message on the beach, talk to the commander and say, "We need a hundred men" or "We need fifty men." There were fifty men getting off those ships, which never came to the US. They just transferred the men out, a sailor who had been gone from the US. The ships in the harbor would send the messages over to the beach(es). "We need so many sailors for ship's crew."

I was assigned to a troop transport, The USS *Fuller*. Everybody works on the big ships. They give you an assignment from eight to four. Nobody lays around on the bunks or nothing. I painted. The ships had to be clean, painted. And then we manned the guns. We had four hours on and four hours off. We used to carry two thousand men and the ship's crew is only about five hundred men. We carried two thousand troops and got them ready for the landing on those Japanese Islands. We took marines and army, whoever they told us.

We could get our small landing crafts down in the water and the men that are going to land on the beach came down the side of the ship. The men came off the side of the ship hanging on nets. My job during the battles: I was assigned to a small boat, a landing craft. We hauled them on the ship, cleaned them, and got them ready for the next landing.

After I was through with a landing, my assignment was—I was assigned to drive the captain and the officers in a boat—captain's gig—to carry officers. The gigs are called captain's boats. I had to get that boat down and take the officers to another ship for meetings. I had to maintain it, polish it. Every time they came on board everybody stands at attention. We had a pipe and we had to pipe them aboard every time they came aboard. That meant the captain was coming aboard and going to the beach. Everyone stands at attention. When the operation is over, we come on board back to the ship. They haul those boats up and secure them. Then we went back to our duties because we might have to go back to Pearl Harbor and take another load of troops.

So we had to stand watch twenty-four hours aboard a ship because the Japanese enemy was all around us. So we had to stay on watch. We were all assigned because there were guns mounted all over that ship. All the sailors had to man, so many sailors per gun, four hours on and four hours off around the clock. Our places were called battle stations.

You had to stand watch. The back of the ship, the bottom deck, was called "sick bay." It's like a clinic with doctors. So you man a station in the rear of the ship. To maneuver that ship by hand, it had a big wheel. The main wheel is on the bridge where the officers are. In case we got hit up there, we already had a sailor back there. And [you could] tell him to go ahead and maneuver the ship by hand in the back because the bridge had gotten hit and the control was all torn up. In the back we had one of those big [steering] wheels. With the four hours on and four off back there also, around the clock.

One night I had a watch from 12:00 midnight to 4:00 a.m., and the guy I relieved didn't tell me nothing, just, "Everything is okay." So I got the earphones on and I called the bridge and told them the station had been relieved. So I sat down on a stack of rope there with my ear phones [on]. Everything was quiet sailing. After a while the sailor on the bridge would call once in a while to make sure you weren't asleep. He'd say, "This is the bridge calling." "This is the ear of the ship." I used to answer, "Hi, every-thing is quiet." He'd wait a little while. Everything was dark. There was no light because the enemy would see it and say, "There are some ships over there. Go take them." So then this guy [who had called from the bridge] says, "How do you like all those dead people around you there?" "Where, Man?" "All around you where you're at. They were on the top deck. If you walk around there, you can feel it with your feet." And I said, "Aw, you're kidding me." I was sitting on the rope and started feeling around the deck. And sure enough there were several dead persons.

We had brought them in wounded and they had died. The other guy found out and had told the man on the bridge [about the bodies]. He had asked, "Who brought all the dead people up here?" He said, "The oth-er ship that was here." So he told me and sure enough, there were about twelve bodies up there.

They are buried at sea. They have a ceremony. They have the chaplain give a prayer. If it's a marine or sailor, they bury them at sea. The army guys we have to put down there in an icebox until we get to the next island. We get the bodies off and they bury them on the ground at the island. Soldiers are buried in the ground.

We have duty while we are sailing. They don't let you just lay around. And I have my landing craft all along. When I am not sailing, I am making a landing. That was our duty.

We had buddies who used to stand watch with me on the bridge with earphones and they handled a lot of stations. Four hours. This other fellow used to take the other four hours. The last battle we had we got hit with a Japanese five-hundred-pound bomb after we made a landing. They hit a section on the rear. My partner got killed, so that night I was there by myself, and I didn't have my partner with me. It is sure a bad feeling. A bad feeling. Three sailors got killed and seven soldiers—we were carrying soldiers—got killed because they were down in the hold unloading ammunition and putting stuff in boats on the side to take to the beach.

Islands that I went to: Guadalcanal, Bougainville, Luzon, Leyte, Guam, Mariana Islands, Okinawa, Oahu, and Palau. Another group was heading for Iwo Jima, and they separated us. We went to Okinawa. We made the first landing, the beachhead.

In Palau we almost got killed because we made the landing; we had a crew aboard ship that was very well trained. Our idea was to make the landing and then come back and start taking supplies and hurry, hurry, hurry because we had a system that everybody got together and worked and unloaded the ship.

If we unload the ship we have to steam out a little bit away from the beach and lay low until the other ships got unloaded. Then we can all sail back as a convoy back to another island that was secured to pick up more soldiers, supplies, or whatever. In Palau we almost got killed because we had to lay around there for about eight days because the other ships hadn't finished unloading their stuff. They were messing around or something.

We went out to sea a little bit and got away from the beach, because the Zeros [Japanese airplanes] used to come at sundown over the mountains and spray [strafe] the beach. [This time in Palau] everybody on the beach got killed. We were getting ready to steam out and here come the suicide planes. We were behind another troop transport, the *John Land*. We all had to stay together. We were behind there and here comes the suicide plane and hits that boat in front of our boat. We just saw fire and sailors jumping. And of course we were steaming right behind that ship. You can't stop. We had just gotten through making those landings out there. They yelled, "Hey, Hey." We throw life jackets and life savers with a rope on them and everything.

Behind us are destroyer escorts. They move around easier, fast. They are the ones that do the picking [saving] of whoever is overboard. They get there fast and they throw a rope and pick them up. We leave those people there because if you stop, you are a sitting duck. I saw two kamikaze pilots.

[Responding to a question regarding waves] You load up your people. They'll tell you what wave you are going to go in. I used to tell them, "Put me in the first wave." And they used to tell me, "You're crazy. You get there first and you get hit." They're shooting at you. Nothing is protecting me. There are snipers. The landing craft had a ramp. The two sailors with me drop the ramp and then crank it back up. As soon as those people ran off, they'd crank it back up. A lot of people got hit there on the beach. They'd say, "You're crazy for choosing the first wave. Why do you do that, Rey?" I said, "I caught on to this thing. You get some lighter fire when you're in the first wave, because the Japanese are waiting for the second and third waves so they can get more people. They don't want to waste [fire] on the first wave." The Japanese hide in those caves and in the trees and all of that, and if they start shooting, they'll [American soldiers] know that they are there. So they really start shooting at the second wave, because there are more soldiers [to kill].

As soon as those people got off, I was back on my boat. The worst problem we had was those soldiers that freeze on you. They start to cry. Everybody got off running, but one or two would remain in the landing craft. We'd say, "Hey man, get out." I'd tell the sailors who were with me, "As soon as they get out let's start rolling that thing back so we can leave." And those soldiers [who didn't want to get off] would hold on and cry and cry. So I had the sailors who were with me to pick up the [reluctant] soldiers and put them on the beach. I told them, "You stand a better chance out there if you dig into a hole."

Those big ships would lower the boats. We would get instructions from different ships; we would put our sailors down with the boats with the men and they'd say, "You're going to go in the first wave," so the men would get prepared. They'd put the boats down. When they'd give the signal, everybody in the first wave would take off to make the first landing. Our ship carried fifty landing crafts. Each big ship sent men on the first wave. It was a big invasion.

The marines are crazy. They had daggers, grenades hanging here [on their bodies], flame throwers; of course they had rifles. They'd go in there [the islands] with flame throwers in the bushes and in the caves, forcing out the Japanese. Not the army. They'd let the marines go in there and soften the islands first. The army went in there with a kitchen and stuff like that. The army soldier has a rifle and bayonet.

The marines take over an island; then they leave and take off for another place. The army pulls in and gets settled there to maintain the island and clean up, make a cemetery and all that.

What's funny aboard ship: three days before we make a landing, they put us sailors to work. They won't let you do nothing [be idle] when you are aboard ship sailing to another invasion. You always work on a ship. You've got to work from eight to four. There were a bunch of sailors on the top deck making crosses out of lumber and painting them white. They did that because a lot of people are going to die on the island. When someone was killed they used a cross [at the grave], and they'd put a helmet on top of the cross. Somebody was assigned to keep records of who was killed. The first thing a sailor wants to do is find a spot so he can go to sleep. That's why they are always [giving them jobs] working.

They said the Philippines were going to be the worst because they had towns. We hit those islands, island by island, Luzon, Leyte, and Manila; they didn't find too much resistance. A lot of those Japanese had split from there.

We weren't stationed in those islands. Those islands make you nervous. When we'd come back after the landing, in our compartment, you'd see a sailor over there and he wouldn't talk. We were like in shock. We'd been busy since 5:00 a.m. in the morning. We had soldiers who were left inside the island and sailors that came back aboard ship took a shower. We had cooks in the kitchen, and they had a warm supper. We had a change right there. We had very few Mexican Americans.

I was aboard the ship, the *Fuller*, which got commissioned in New York. When they picked us up there in the islands, we brought people from Brooklyn, New Jersey, Boston, and Chicago, and they had never seen a Mexican American. Really good people. They're funny. They would never get depressed. They were making whiskey.

They would get "torpedo juice," they called it. It's a kind of alcohol they used for torpedoes and they put raisins, potato peelings. They get fermented. We had wooden kegs and we had them in the life rafts, tied down and full of water in case we would get hit, they'd get the life rafts, unhook them and we'd have fresh water. They would put [the fermenting alcohol] in them, tied them back in the rafts near the first aid kits. They'd put another raft on top. They'd stack about six of them. They would stay there to ferment and it would ferment pretty good.

Once a month they had a ship inspection. It was the captain, the first lieutenant, and a couple of ensigns, and an officer coming up from the ranks. He was following, and they'd all come in line inspecting the ship. We had to stand by our stations. If they found something wrong with our station, they would tell us: "This thing needs to be painted." The captain would go and rub his hands on the boat—it would whistle—you're supposed to keep those boats clean.

They'd go from one end of the ship to the other and look under lockers and stuff, ship inspection. There were four of us guys that used to man one of those stations. The officers came by our area and kept on walking. That last officer was a young guy. He was trailing the inspection crew. We were standing at attention and he was passing by those rafts. He could smell the liquor. He leaned over and said, "When is it ready?" They told him, "In about two days." The others didn't smell anything. They knew. They let us have some fun to keep us happy.

I used to tell those guys. "Don't drink that stuff. It's pure alcohol." That was what they used on the torpedoes. Torpedo juice. They used it to run the motor at the back of the torpedo just like you use gasoline.

Okinawa and Palau were close together and I picked up more dead and wounded from those two islands.

The admiral is usually on the flagship. He calls the shots. He tells the convoy where to turn and all that and all the other ships obey orders from the admiral. We had captains and first lieutenants. Officers are used as navigators and they have to answer to the captain. The officer stands on watch on the deck. They will tell you, the men on the ship, how to turn so many degrees right or left. And he gets his instructions from the navigator who is in a little room. There is a big compass up there.

It's funny; you run into things. There at Midway it was so overly secure and we are going with a load of troops or to pick up some troops to take them to another landing. We had to stay there about two to three days. Here comes Sunday and we've got to go to church. Everyone that's going to church needs to go to the quarter deck; there's a boat there that will pick them up and take them to church, to mass. We had a protestant minister, but at the USS *Dixie* they had a priest and they held mass on Sundays.

There are about thirty guys and there's a boat down there so we got on it. We went to the *Dixie* to hear mass. As we are going up there on the gangway from my boat and as soon as we get up there we salute the flag and the officer of the deck. I looked down and there was a soldier kneeling down painting. You're always painting. I looked at the man and kept on going. I took three or four more steps. Then I said, "That looks like somebody I know." So I stopped and came back and took another look at that man working. And it was Uncle Pete Álvarez, my father's brother. He had been drafted and I didn't know. He was on the USS *Dixie*.

I wanted to work on another ship to come back to the States. I asked for a transfer. They said, "We're not going to send you back to the States. They don't need you in the States. They need you out here."

They put me in a submarine tender. It supplies submarines. It was named the USS *Holland*. We would load them with supplies, torpedoes, all kinds of supplies. The submarines used to come alongside us and tie up, and we used to load them up with torpedoes, supplies, groceries, fuel, all that. That's why they call them submarine tenders. We tend to the submarines. That's the last ship I was on before I came home.

We stayed in a secure island most of the time, and the submarines used to come by to be filled up. I had been with the USS *Holland* for about a year when the war ended.

I had gotten off the *Fuller*. We were in Guam at the receiving station waiting for a draft. That's when somebody asks for some sailors to be on ships. Some of the sailors got off the *Holland* and came back to the States. They had been in for about three years. They were due to come back. Then they asked for the drafts, the guys waiting for ships. I was in a camp in Guam. It was in the morning, and I had to go in the showers. I got up and went to the showers.

As I was coming back with a towel around my neck in a pair of shorts, here comes a sailor running with a copy of a paper. It had come in from the teletype. It was little. It said that the war with the Japanese was over. That the Japanese had surrendered. It was August 1945. Everybody was running wild. We were living in tents waiting to be shipped out to fight some more.

I said, "Man we're going to go back home." No. I met an officer and I said, "I understand the war is over. The Japanese have surrendered. We get to go home now."

He said, "That's what you think, Sailor. Who's going to run the ships if everybody goes home? You've got to wait."

I waited another year before I got discharged. I got aboard the USS *Holland* and finished my duty there. We went to Japan and I got to know Tokyo. It was destroyed. They had been bombing that thing all these years. The Japanese people treated us all right. I went to town with other sailors. They would tell us not to bother those people. They were glad the war was over, too.

I was discharged December 1 in Camp Wallace close to Houston, Texas. We [he and his future wife] had been writing back and forth. Mustering out pay, which was $300, so you could buy clothes and stuff. They check you out physically. If something is wrong with you, they won't let you out. They would ask us, "Where does it hurt?" You would say, "I'm okay," because if you tell them you're sick they'll hold you.

I was involved in ten battles. I steered the fully loaded boats that carried thirty-five men from the large ship to the beaches. After you land with the men, you go back [to the mother ship] and take a boat full of supplies to the men [you took to the beaches earlier]. Then you take back the wounded and the dead back to the big ship.

I was aboard a submarine tender, USS *Holland*. We used to service torpedoes and stuff. That's the last ship I was on.

According to Reynaldo's wife, Adela, Reynaldo's future mother-in-law "made a promesa that if Rey came back safely from the war, she would order a statue of Jesus Christ and he would have it blessed. When Reynaldo returned he did indeed take the statue to be blessed. We still have it on the staircase. And it only cost $2.00. We had been sweethearts for four years. Then he was gone four years. When he came to ask for my hand in marriage after the war, Mother said that they would set a plazo [waiting period] of six months, because he might come disturbed from the war. He would be used to being back again. We got married June 6, 1946." Reynaldo and his wife of fifty-seven years (in 2002) had three children. All grew up to become professionals.

Facundo Rodriguez
6th Army Company I
1st Infantry Regiment
6th Infantry Division

Jungle Fighting

Facundo Rodriguez was born in Benavides, Texas, on November 27, 1922.
His father died when he was twelve years old. He helped his uncles in farm-
ing and ranching. He went to Robstown as a young man and looked for
work. He picked, washed, and sold vegetables at sheds and packed crates to
put on trains. He remembered, "I made thirty cents an hour." He learned
what it was like to fight in a jungle setting and fought along with some Mex-
ican citizens who became American citizens after fighting for the US.

I heard about Pearl Harbor and knew my time was coming. I was drafted in February 1943. Before I left, I received a *bendición* from my mother
and my aunt and uncle. My Catholic church gave me a special medallion
to take as I went off to war. The church was giving a medal to all of us
[soldiers].

When they drafted me from Robstown, they were taking eighteen year
olds from Duval County.

Camp Wolters in Mineral Wells, Texas, was the first training site. I remember lots of KP duty. It was a rough terrain. Fast marches took five
miles in an hour with a light pack. In the evening we had the twenty-five-
mile hikes with a full pack. Started in the evening and we got to the camp
at daybreak. We ate breakfast in the woods. For training we crawled under
machine gun fire and barbed wire with charges like dynamite on either
side. When they blew up, we had lots of sand in our faces. We crawled on
our backs to keep our guns clean. The forced march caused two casualties;
they passed out. The problem was with people from the city. We were used
to it since we worked so hard on the farms.

In May we were sent to Camp San Luís Obispo, California, with the
Sixth Infantry Division. We trained on the beaches of California. They
usually had a ridge and water underneath from the ocean. Two ropes,
cross one rope to step on and two at the top to hold on to. Hiked along
the mountains. There were American Indians there who talked to me in a

language I didn't understand. I finally told them I was a Mexican American. My buddies still called me "chief."

In September they put us on a troop train with the shades pulled down so that we couldn't see out and no one could see us. They took us to the dock. Never knew anything. USS *Howard*.

From San Francisco to Honolulu on the island of Oahu in 1943. We had jungle training. Instead of rifles they gave you Thompson submachine guns, mostly the Mexican Americans, because we were the scouts. The Mexican Americans were mostly chosen for scouts or second scouts. And the squad was behind.

I was a scout for a long time. And if I wasn't a scout I was a flanker. The scout was at the very front. On one occasion I had athlete's foot, so they sent Silas, an Indian. He replaced me as first scout and was shot and killed on that mission.

I was the only Mexican American in that platoon. We had two more, but they worked in the kitchen and they were from Mexico. They were Mexican citizens. They were given citizenship for joining the army.

The division before us had trained with Patton in the desert in California and thought they were going to Africa.

We took jungle training in Oahu with the pop-ups. We would be walking along and these things in the shape of a human being would pop up and you had to be ready to fire. It was kill or be killed.

We were going to invade some islands in the Pacific. And our division was in reserve. That's when we sailed. It must have been January 1944. Division in front went in with no problem. Our convoy was diverted and we went to Milne Bay, New Guinea. That's the Australian part of New Guinea. New Guinea was divided between the British and the Netherlands.

We did more jungle training there. Boats came and left us rations. We had meat and fresh eggs, too. After training, we were relieved by a regiment of Puerto Ricans, regular officers, and American Indians.

They took us in the HMAS *Manoora*, an Australian troop ship. Gave us a bunch of lamb chops and tea. Took us to the Maffin-sarmi Bay Area of New Guinea. First Combat.

We were trying to take a hill. We lost First Lieutenant Pedro Rodriguez from San Antonio and our sergeant and platoon leader. He and assistant platoon leaders were killed by friendly fire-artillery shells. We used "creeping artillery fire." It went just a little bit ahead of us when we were advancing. When shrapnel was close to us, they [the platoon] would call back so they could lift it just a little bit.

Morales from El Paso had a radio on his back. They called back. Usually we had an artillery observer; he gave the coordinates of where to fire.

The Sixth Division was an old division. The commanders and the non-commissioned officers were regular army men. They trained the draftees.

We landed in Sansapor, the extreme end of New Guinea. The Japanese left, and we surrounded the area, and secured it so we could build an airfield. We were closer to Leyte. This place had cannibals. So neither the Americans nor the Japanese would go inland for fear of being eaten. There were also crocodiles in the rivers.

We didn't patrol at night, but the First Cavalry fought at night. They had foot soldiers and tanks and they advanced that way.

In 1945 we invaded Luzon. You could look in any direction and see boats as far as you could see. There were three lines of troop ships, and on the sides you could see cruisers and destroyers protecting the troop ships and the carriers. The "ducks" [DUKW—amphibious vehicles] went in the first wave. The TLSs [troop landing ships] made up the second wave. Each boat carried thirty-six men. The LCVs were in the third wave. These vehicles fired rockets from the sides as we landed.

It was rough. Four divisions landed at the same time. Two divisions moved west of the river, and the other two divisions located themselves east of the river. They planned for us to move seven miles the first day, but we stopped after five miles. The soldiers closest to the river met with the most resistance from the Japanese. Our group had less resistance.

The bombardment of the beaches by the American airplanes was awful. But in the middle of all this the water buffalo kept on pasturing under the coconut trees. In the morning we could see the Japanese airplanes. They looked like small dots in the sky.

When we landed we went to a small village. The people were happy to see us. One family gave me three eggs. I carried them until we got into a fire fight with the Japanese. I handed the eggs to a Filipino and never saw the eggs again.

Once when we were attacked we [several soldiers] fired continuously at the Japanese. One soldier froze and just watched. When it was over, the soldier said that he was amazed at how hard we were fighting, but when we stopped firing, our bodies shook violently.

I got mad once only for being on a patrol, one after another. Some had a bunch of excuses and they wouldn't go. The same people always went out on patrol. They told us, "You have more experience and we have more confidence in you."

Some families hid in caves. We slept in slit trenches, which we dug close to one another. A soldier could lie down and sleep in one of these. The slit trenches were two-three feet deep, and tanks could drive over the trenches and not hurt you. But you slept with the rifle on your chest so you could fire if necessary without looking for your weapon.

We got on the road to Manila and fought our way to San José. Headquarters stopped us. The Thirty-Seventh Division was sent to Manila to divide it into halves, the Sixth to the east. At this time the Rangers went into the Bataan Peninsula and liberated the Bataan March survivors. Some divisions like the Twenty-Fourth went North. Manila had already been taken by the First Cavalry and the Thirty-Seventh Division. We were sent to Manila for some rest, but we had our guns with us.

We were east of Manila and found pockets of Japanese in the mountains we had to fight. On April 18, 1945, I was walking along a trail when my sergeant yelled, "They've thrown a grenade at you." I backed out. The sergeant was killed and the other man was wounded. The sergeant saved my life. I protected myself and when I did, they shot and killed my sergeant. Then when I tried to get him out, that's when they shot my helmet off.

I was a scout and they sent me on the trail. There was a ravine. They were going around trying to get on top of a hill. The funny part is I had the helmet on backwards so he could see me but I couldn't see him. If you had the helmet on the right way when you are crawling, it would come off. All the back of the helmet was bent in.

The people behind me thought I was dead. They said my head was shaking up and down on the ground. That was the closest call I had.

I went to the hospital and then went back to the front.

We continued fighting in Luzon in the east from 3:00 a.m. until 9:00 a.m. That was a fire fight. That was when the Japanese attacked us. We were on top of the hill. Some soldiers on another hill later said that when they heard the Japanese yell "Banzai," the whole hill exploded. Everything lit up. I had a sergeant on my left and on my right. We usually had one person awake during the night. We had a guy from Ohio, Richardson. He was supposed to be awake. He went to sleep. One of the Japanese soldiers was next to him. It was a miracle that Richardson wasn't killed. When the Japanese yelled "Banzai," the guy next to Richardson woke up and with his tommy gun he started firing while lying down and he got up that way, firing, and he cut the Japanese down. We brought the artillery right next to us. The company came out okay. We lost a few.

We used M1s in open country and used the tommy guns in the jungle. The scouts had the tommy guns in New Guinea. We used 60mm mortars. On top of a hill we did like the covered wagons and made a circle. In the middle were the company commanders. Artillery is usually behind us.

The Japanese hit a tree near our company commanders and injured several of our officers. One time shrapnel hit Richardson on his belt and just burned him. He acted like he was dying. The medic went to see him and all he had was a burn. The belt was cut all the way.

From there they sent us to Bataan. We were trying to take Bataan back.

When we went west and the Thirty-Seventh went to Manila, there one night we were out, and they sent us a mile ahead of the company. That night they told us, "Don't shoot at anybody coming toward you, because the Rangers will be coming toward you with American prisoners that are being liberated." The Rangers went ahead of us. I just saw the men passing by in trucks.

Eastern part of Manila. We went to clear the area of the Japanese. Ponds there. Shrimp farming. Big tanks. Raised soil. Reed was shot. We usually carried the cartridge belts for our M1s across our chest. Knocked him out. Hit the clip but didn't kill him. Five caliber. We learned our lesson and began putting our cartridges across our chests.

Second Battalion passed by us and took another village. The Japanese came in [disguised] as Filipinos with carts full of things they needed. They let the Japanese inside the town. Once inside the town at nighttime the Japanese started attacking the Americans. Many men from the Second Battalion were killed, and some of them took off. They were not coming from the front but from the back. The Americans had a circle around the town to protect it, but the people got inside the town.

MacArthur came to see what had happened. He traveled with a platoon and he rode in a jeep. The men in that platoon had to be over six feet tall. That's when I saw MacArthur. Our Third Battalion was sent to help them out. We tried to get the stragglers, the people who had run out.

We took over the Bataan Peninsula. Then we went to Clark Field to protect and also went looking for Japanese stragglers who were scattered all over San Fernando. We also rested. They were trying to rearm us, to get us new guns and equipment, because we were supposed to attack Japan.

We had some replacements. We had a forty-five-year-old man as a replacement at Clark Field. He was gray-headed.

We left for the Northern part of the Philippines to the mountains to clear it of Japanese. In April '45 after the death of my sergeant, I was acting sergeant.

I was the lead scout and Reed was the second scout. On the left we had Filipino scouts. They were shot and killed. The company stopped and called me to come back, which I did.

The tanks wouldn't go in unless we were around them. They had to have a squad protecting them.

In the Northern part of Luzon, the Filipinos were short but well-built. It's a tribe of Filipinos. Short and stocky. You didn't mess with those people because they'll kill you in no time. You just left them alone. One of our soldiers had to go back.

We took those hills. I got sick at my stomach and I was sent back to the hospital. A sergeant took my place. When I went back, two or three days later, my lieutenant was sick, too. We had some soldiers bringing supplies for us on their backs. When I was returning, the lieutenant said, "Don't go back. We're pulling out and by the way, you're a sergeant. Again. The guy who took your place was demoted by the colonel."

That was in August, and the war ended.

After that, we could see American trucks with a bunch of Japanese POWS and nurses. Those were American trucks.

On that hill the fight was over food. The planes would drop rations for us. Sometimes the packages landed between us and the Japanese. They would go after the food, and we would fire at them. When we went after the food, we would fire at them.

In Sansapor the Japanese would come in, and we had pillboxes right along the coast with logs on top and with just a little passageway to get in. Six of us in. The Japanese started bombing us and it was like daylight. We went out and used searchlights looking for Japanese. One of the Japanese planes came real low and we ran to the pillbox and got stuck. Richardson got down and crawled into the pillbox through our legs.

We needed sixty-five points to go home. I was sent to Japan as part of the Army of Occupation. We went to a small village. I had to search every house for guns and ammunition and take it if I found it. I did that between two and three p.m. Between four and five p.m. they told me to get my duffel bag and that I was going home.

I felt great. An Australian troop ship, the *Manoora*, took us to Tacoma, Washington, and we were there on Thanksgiving Day. We were fed on the ship and the Red Cross gave us packages. At Fort Lewis, the Germans served us our food.

I was discharged from Fort Sam Houston on Dec. 26, 1945. In January I became ill with malaria, but I haven't had it since.

I never went through a depression. I was happy to be home.

Facundo worked for the same company for over thirty years. He and his wife had six children, most of whom became educators and administrators.

Frank Schwing Jr.
Army Air Corps

(Told to me by his son, Frank Schwing III.)
Frank Schwing III related his late father's story.

Frank Schwing Jr. was born in 1922 in Corpus Christi, Texas. His father, Frank Sr., was born in Germany and settled in Corpus Christi, Texas. He married Leandra Lira, a granddaughter of a Sicilian. She had arrived in Texas from Spain via Mexico. Frank Schwing Jr. was orphaned at seven years of age. He was raised by his aunt and ran away from home with his older brother when they were nine and eleven, respectively. The two boys lived under a train station in Sinton, Texas. Frank Jr. was modest. After serving his country in the Pacific theater, he told his son to bury him in his uniform. When he died his children found out their father had been a hero.

When the naval station was being built in Corpus Christi, Texas, Frank Schwing Jr. was hired as a laborer. In 1942, he was drafted. After being sent to San Antonio, Texas, to be processed, he was selected to be in the Army Air Corps.

Frank was sent to the island of Tinian, which had recently been taken over by American troops. There were still pockets of Japanese the men had to fight. The Seabees arrived shortly thereafter. Everyone had to rebuild the air strips so that airplanes could fly out of Tinian.

The Americans began building the airstrips, and every morning the Japanese bombed the work they had accomplished. But the Americans had figured out a way to protect men from the bombings. They painted large sheets of metal and threw sand on them. Then from the sky the sheets of metal appeared to be sand. The men placed the sheets of metal on the beaches and hid under them. The airplanes fired on the airstrips but never found the men.

Finally, the Japanese stopped flying over Tinian. B-52s began flying out of the island. Although Frank was a mechanic assigned to one plane, one day he was ordered to go on a mission. Later he told his son, "I thought I was going to die. We were flying in formation and flak was all around us. Our planes flew right through it, accomplished the mission, and all of us returned safely back to the base."

Frank Jr. never said much about his experiences in the war. He told his son Frank III that he wanted to be buried in his uniform. After he died, his daughter went to the safety deposit box and found three Bronze Stars that her father had earned in WWII but had never mentioned. When he was laid to rest Frank Schwing Jr., the son of a German immigrant, wore his US Army Air Corps uniform along with the three Bronze Stars he had earned. A proud American.

Gilbert Mora
Marine Air Corps
1st-4th Air Wings Battalion

Too Young to Join
Gilbert Mora was born on November 1, 1924, near Falfurrias, Texas, on the

Numero Cinco Ranch, which was part of the Lassiter property. His mother and father were Santos S. and Silvestre Mora. Santos, who was from Portugal, came to Texas via Mexico. Silvestre was born in the Uvalde area. Gilbert and a friend joined the service at age sixteen, seeking excitement. His friend, however, couldn't take the hard life in basic training, but Gilbert continued and ended up with a successful career in the marines. His family made the news because seven members were in the war.

There were ten boys and two girls. One of the little girls drowned when she was two years old. However, my mother raised one grandson from my sister. And he went by the name Mora 'til he joined the navy and had to use his father's name, Ramirez.

I'm the baby.
[The children were:]

Ruiz Mora (b. 2-25-05)	became chief deputy in Alice, Texas
Esquivel (b. 12-28-07)	was postmaster in Alice, Texas, for thirty years
Teresa	
Silvestre Jr.	medic, corporal in the Army Medical Corps
Calixtro	Army Air Corps
Robert	worked for the governor and at Naval Air Station in Corpus Christi
Felix	
Alex	first sergeant, Army Air Corps
Reynaldo	Pfc. in the Army
Daniel	infantry in the Army
Gilbert	master sergeant in the Marines
Henry Mora Ramirez	Navy, Third Class

Henry was three years younger than I was and he got me in trouble all the time.

My real birthday is November 1, 1924, but in the Marine Corps it is May 12, 1924, because I went in at age sixteen. I made my mother sign for me. I was the second one to join the service. At the time I used to deliver

All six sons of the Mora family, shown here with one nephew, served in WWII. Gil Mora, top center, lied about his age when he was sixteen to be admitted into the army. Property of author, bequeathed to her by the Mora Family.

the *Houston Chronicle*, and I used to stay up with the war news in Europe. Germany was taking all the countries over. But I always had the desire to join the French [Foreign] Legion.

Two days before I was to leave my mother asked me to give her a ride somewhere. I said, "No, I won't." So my mother spanked me. Before I left she lit some candles in a corner in a room where she kept an altar. She prayed for me. Later she told me that when I was in the service after the war started she felt so bad that she had spanked me.

My first brother [to go into the service] was Alex. He's the only one left alive, and he's the one I've been taking care of. He goes between Felix and Reynaldo. I joined the Marine Corps on October 6, 1941.

I had just finished boot camp when the war started. Alex and Reynaldo were in the service when I joined up. I think Alex was a corporal in the army, and Reynaldo was a Pfc. in the army. I was in First, Second, Third, and Fourth Air Wings [marines]. Just like battalions. In all air groups or air wings with the Marine Air Corps. I started as an aerial gunner. Then I was a flight engineer and then engineer chief. My last duty was as a supervisor of jet training schools.

First place was from Corpus Christi to Houston for a physical. From there I went to boot camp in San Diego, California. If you live east of the Mississippi you go to Parris Island. If you live west of the Mississippi you go to California.

There were three of us guys from Falfurrias—Pete Garza and Oscar Salinas [and me]. Oscar Salinas gave up in boot camp. He told his mother to tell the government the truth, that he didn't want to stay in the Marine Corps. They discharged him because he told them that he was only sixteen. We were all sixteen, but I told him, "Don't say anything about me. I'm going to take it even if it kills me." I think Pete stayed in.

It was very rough, nothing like today. At the time it was good for discipline, because even though at that time I figure that the people's behavior was very good, it still wasn't good enough for the Marine Corps. They would be your mother, dad, and teacher. You learn a lot in the Marine Corps. You learn how to do your own laundry. I got slapped around one time. My instructor [slapped me]. They were punishing another boy, who from all information [had problems with] the rifle. He was getting so weak—this kid from Alabama. I smiled. He [instructor] came over and gave me a warning. He said, "Mora, you don't smile when I punish." He turned around and I thought that was it and POW! Of course I wanted to return it. When you get hit you want to hit back. He said, "Yes?"

The Second World War was the roughest it gets. Even in the service we were a little hungry. Overseas I'm talking about. [Boot Camp] was a tough eleven weeks. It was a marine recruiting base in San Diego.

From there some were going to the infantry and others had to qualify for aviation, take a test. I took the test, and I was very lucky. I passed it, and I ended up in the first airfield in North Island, California. We went to Aviation Training School in Navy Pier, Chicago, Illinois, to learn about aviation.

At about this time my father was pretty much retired. In his young days he used to run guns for the Mexican Revolution. He supplied guns to whoever bought them. He worked for a small group.

I was born in 1924. I remember—I have a good memory—back in '31 he had already been working for the Lassiters. He took care of the stock, making sure they had water. My mother raised chickens on the side. It's a shame like I tell people now, this generation. You would look and wonder what you were going to have for supper. You didn't have a refrigerator but you had a garden with all kinds of vegetables and chickens. She canned food in jars.

After I graduated from aviation school I went to a training squadron in Hawaii. At Pearl Harbor I saw a lot of ships sticking out, a lot of damage. They had a bunch of civilians trying to clear the place. A bunch of Navy Seabees.

There I went to a squadron that happened to be one of the number-one squadrons under Major Boyington, called the "Black Sheep Squadron." He was the commanding officer, and he shot down twenty-six Japanese planes. He was one of the aces. He was flying with the "Flying Tigers," fighting the Japanese.

From there we went to an island north of Guadalcanal in late 1942. My brothers joined the services in '42 and '43. [By 1943 there were six brothers and one nephew in the service, all from the same Mora family.]

We were on an aircraft carrier, the USS *Nassau*. At the time I was a gunner. There are only two people on the plane. Mostly like a Torpedo plane. More of a fighter, but they used it for bombing, for torpedoes, for support of the troops on the ground. Troops provide close support. Like if you land we try and clear the place before. It's called ground support.

You don't care when you're young. We were bitter because of what they'd done to us in Pearl Harbor. I got $10,000 insurance. [At Munda] the Japanese had been there a long time. They lost a few people. I transferred into another squadron. We did a lot of bombing. When I transferred I was land-based. From there you fly at night to all areas in close distance.

As we took the islands we moved, you know. Then Green Island. At that time my time ran out—after twenty-seven months. What happens is that after two years they try to rotate you or send you to Australia for a rest. So I took a choice of being rotated back to the States. I went to Memphis in 1944 to learn about the new Curtis Dive Bomber, the Curtis Hell Diver. I went to school for nine weeks. They accomplished two things. You learn something about a new aircraft and you also express your knowledge to the new marines.

I was the youngest top sergeant at one time. You have to carry the authority. In other words it was hard because I was a lot younger than some of the seniors. I mean some of the older people. They didn't mind after they knew what you were talking about. At one time I was 5'10" [tall]. Sometimes they wouldn't let you join the Marine Corps if you were short. We used to be very strict. I remember when they were talking to me in the recruiting office. When you left Texas, I never had a problem.

The only thing they hated was the Japanese. I never saw so much hate. The marines hated them because of Pearl Harbor. I just saw marines attacking. Your job is to spray [strafe] and try to clear the area.

When I was training in Hawaii, they showed us what kinds of tunnels they [Japanese] had already made in Hawaii. They even had reading materials and everything in there. They had a lot of spies there. They had caves and all. Normally spraying with a plane is a surprise. And if you drop bombs, the tunnels are not going to protect you 100 percent.

The last years I was a flight engineer, a maintenance chief, and my last job was as a supervisor of all the jet schools in Memphis, Tennessee. In 1944 in Memphis I spent my time training, and then I go back to California. I joined a squadron with a new type of aircraft. I got a hernia. When I went to the hospital, the squadron pulled out. At the time they used to clamp hernias. They were experimenting with some clamps. When they cut in there, they just blew it. The clamps were about one half inch apart. After so much time they just cut them and pulled them out. They were wires. Like little staples.

I went to another squadron, number 312, and they sent me overseas. We were going to go aboard a carrier. *Bunker Hill* was the name of carrier.

On the morning of May 11, 1945, while supporting the Okinawa invasion, the Bunker Hill *was hit and severely damaged by two suicide planes. Gasoline fires flamed up and several explosions took place. The ship suffered.*

I tried to help. The ship went to a port. We went back to the squadron.

I was reassigned to another squadron, number 223. I came back to the States and I joined the squadron number 223. We got transferred to . . . Cherry Point, North Carolina. It was a training squadron. We were about to train and join the Seventh Fleet in the Mediterranean.

About that time the war was over. I was in the States. It came over on the radio. Everybody celebrated. I was in a town, Cherry Point, North Carolina. Little bitty town but we celebrated.

I have a lot of respect especially for the people here in WWII because in fact, I wrote a little statement on that to the newspaper that we had some great supporters in the States. They didn't mind having some of the stuff rationed, and they would do without so we could have it.

All seven members of the Mora family in the Armed Services came back. There were several articles written about it. I, myself, was in the Navy newspaper that goes all over the world. Then I got a letter from the secretary of the Navy.

Gilbert Mora received the Navy Commendation Medal. He became a career man in the service and served two tours in Korea and two in Vietnam. At one time Gilbert's job was to deliver soldiers' remains to the US and to contact families of the deceased servicemen. The bodies arrived on airplanes and at railroad depots. He had to make all the arrangements. Gilbert did not like this job and asked to be reassigned. He became a rifle and pistol coach on Parris Island. He taught officers to qualify with the use of hand weapons.

In 1940 Gilbert Mora and Emma Salinas were sweethearts. They married in 1944 and divorced in 1945. Emma then married Lorenzo Aguilar, a soldier who unfortunately was part of the Bataan Death March. He returned to Emma, however. Gilbert and his second wife adopted three children. Gilbert heard through the grapevine that Emma was widowed in 1993. He contacted her, and after fifty years of being apart, they remarried in 1994 and are very happy together again.

Of the seven Mora soldiers, Gilbert, Alex, and Henry are the remaining veterans. Gilbert was discharged in 1971 after thirty years in the service. He operated a feed store in Tennessee from 1971 to 1982. He retired and volunteered by helping veterans in the hospitals. In 1997 he and Emma moved to Corpus Christi, Texas. He still has a home in Tennessee.

Gilbert has served on five Aircraft Carriers: the USS Saipan, Bunker Hill, Franklin, Leyte, and Nassau. While in Korea during his second tour he delivered airplanes to the French army.

Ralph Villanueva

Antiaircraft Artillery

10th Army

From a Still in Texas to a Still in Okinawa

Ralph Villanueva was born in Corpus Christi, Texas, on May 25, 1920. He dropped out of school after the seventh grade and worked at different jobs. Finally, when managing a service station at age twenty-one, he was drafted. It was October 29, 1941. As a young boy Ralph learned about making alcohol illegally. This information allowed him to build his own still while he was assigned in the Pacific theater. His commanding officer appreciated it, but there was a group of soldiers who could not handle it. Ralph's obligation as a soldier would last no more than one year. Or so he was promised.

I was glad to go. I thought I could learn something since I had dropped out of school at the seventh grade. My father gave me *la bendición*, and he added *"Te pongo en las manos del Señor. (I place you in His hands)."* My grandfather walked me to the bus station. It looked to me like all the boys going were Mexican American. At least 90 percent of us were. Fort Sam Houston in San Antonio was our first stop.

I had been friendly with the captain of a fire station. He told me not to join the infantry but to choose the artillery. So when I was given a choice I took the captain's advice.

From Fort Sam Houston I went to San Diego to Camp Kearny and trained for artillery using cannons. In January they took us to the Mojave Desert in California. There we trained and drilled using machine guns. "Obey and Listen" were words drilled into our heads. Although it was a hot, horrible time for us, my buddies and I went into Barstow, California and Los Angeles to have fun.

The Ninety-Eighth Battalion became my assignment, and Hawaii was the next stop in May 1942. I trained using a 90mm antiaircraft machine. I saw sunken ships in the harbor, evidence of the damage the Japanese caused at Pearl Harbor.

Several of us were assigned to guard Pearl Harbor with the antiaircraft weapons. It was not until later that we found out that if at the

Battle of Midway the Japanese defeated the American Navy, it was generally thought that Hawaii and the California coastline would be the next Japanese targets.

I was given a test to see if I had the aptitude for radar instruction. When it was decided that I qualified, an investigation into my background began. Officials interrogated my parents, family, neighbors, and acquaintances.

At first the radar machines were operated manually. So the radar and the antiaircraft guns worked in conjunction with one another.

The Marshall Islands were the next destination. The Japanese controlled the islands. The marines entered the islands first and secured them, followed by the infantry. Once a beachhead was established, the soldiers with the antiaircraft guns positioned the guns and the radar/electronic equipment.

I really thought I was going to die there on the Marshall Islands. There were four antiaircraft guns in each battery, and there were four batteries. We were not close together. I saw a bomber plane coming toward us, and there wasn't anything we could do. Another antiaircraft battery saw it coming and fired at it, which saved us. After the United States took the Marshall Islands, some soldiers were sent back to Hawaii to rest.

I became a crew chief on radar. In Hawaii we had to be trained to use the new radar equipment, which became even more sophisticated. The airplanes sent the IFF [Identification, Friend or Foe] to the radar people. The men then fed the data, such as speed and direction of the target, to the computer, which actually directed the antiaircraft guns from the information given to them. Out of the 150 men in our battery, nine people were working on the radar doing the job on two different shifts. A staff sergeant was in charge. Twelve to fifteen men manned each big gun. Four crews took care of the 50mm machine guns.

We shipped out to Okinawa, a big island. That trip from Hawaii to Okinawa took forty-one days. The marines went in, followed by the infantry. Then the artillery battery went in and set up the guns. The pillboxes on both the Marshall and Okinawa Islands were impenetrable. The ships that fired their big guns at the islands before the marines went in couldn't damage the pillboxes. Neither could the airplanes. But when the flamethrowers went in—and they could shoot the fire far—they killed the soldiers in the pillboxes. The thing about a flamethrower is that when he fired his weapon, the fire burned all the oxygen around him for a while, too.

There were lots of civilians on Okinawa. We would go fishing with dynamite. Then we'd pick up the fish and they would cook for the whole battery. We gave the fish heads to the natives and they made soup with them.

The kamikaze pilots crashed on our carriers. We shot them down. Some of the guys had just one job, to load the guns.

A trick the Japanese did to scramble our radar was to throw tin foil, which drifted in the air. Our radar couldn't deal with the tin foil, which confused it. At that point, we would throw the machine on to manual. We had a lieutenant who would look through an eye piece that strained your eyes. He'd say, "You do it. I can't stand that." It was hard on your eyes because of all the interference from the tin foil. We could still track the planes manually.

There were American Indians with us, and I heard them speak another language but I didn't think anything of it. I heard talk of a code but no one knew exactly what that meant. [Navajo Code Talkers were used throughout the Pacific. The Japanese never broke their codes.]

Some of the soldiers who went to the Philippines to take it back joined us in Okinawa. One of the soldiers looked odd. He just sat in a corner and wouldn't speak. We figured he couldn't take it. Some men could take the action and some couldn't. Even though we took Okinawa, Japanese airplanes still flew over us.

While there in Okinawa, I decided to try to make something that an old neighbor of mine had taught me back in Corpus Christi. She was a bootlegger, and she made beer and wine. So I took a keg that nails had come in and washed it out. Then I took the pineapple juice that the army sent us and used that for making wine. I always gave the captain a gallon of it, and that made him happy.

While still in Okinawa I heard that a bomb had been dropped over Japan. Then I heard of another bomb being dropped and that the war was over. I had been in the army four and a half years.

I heard of men who had fought for eighteen months and were being sent home. I had been in for four and a half years, three and a half in action, and they wanted to send me and others like me to Japan as part of the

Army of Occupation. We raised Cain, and they let us go home.

I came home and remained working for the government in Civil Service for over forty-one years. My wife Esperanza, a teacher, and I had two daughters, both of whom became professionals.

Raul G. Vasquez
96th Infantry Division

Three Buddies—to War and Back

Raul G. Vasquez was born on March 23, 1924, in Gregory, Texas. On November 2, 1942, Raul decided to join the service, and went with two friends to sign up together. He never expected to witness the particular horrors of war he saw. During his time in the service, however, he met up with a friend and ended up marrying his friend's sister.

I went with my friend Armando Cardenas and his cousin, Oscar Campos, to register. Airplanes looked attractive to me, so I requested duty in the Air Force. I was told that I was needed in the infantry. Then the sergeant said he would send me to Camp Crowder, Missouri, and all of us three buddies would end up together with me as a radio operator.

The three of us took a train to Camp Adair in Oregon, where we trained before going to Yakima, Washington, for additional training. I was selected to be a liaison sergeant. While still in Yakima, I wrote a letter to a commanding officer in Georgia and told him I wanted to be a paratrooper. I was sent to get a physical because the commander of the paratroopers wanted me. I passed the physical test. Things were getting more desperate in the Pacific, so all transfers were cancelled. Our division was told we would be going overseas.

We were moved to Fort Stockton, California. There we were issued equipment required overseas. The men trained for amphibious landings with the marines. Then we took a ship out of San Francisco and headed for action in the Pacific.

A stop was made in Hawaii. We stayed in a tent city. While there we saw a camp full of Italian prisoners. The men played basketball constantly to pass the time.

All of us were very nervous. The landing craft, vehicle, personnel [LCVP] hit the beaches in Leyte on October 20, 1944. I landed on the third wave with the assault troops. Because we had not seen action before and didn't know what to expect as we came off the landing craft, we heard airplanes up ahead and someone began shooting at the airplanes. Other men raised their guns and fired at the low-flying planes. Finally, the American soldiers noticed that the airplane pilots were dipping their wings so that stars on the navy fighter planes could be seen by the new soldiers.

I was to be a liaison person working with a captain while still being part of the infantry. The small group I was to work with consisted of a captain, a sergeant, me, a radio operator, and a jeep driver. The infantry was in the front and the artillery would be a few miles behind. The mission of our group was to look over the situation; then the captain would give the infantry commander advice on artillery fire.

Since I was a liaison person I was sent to the infantry [383rd Infantry Regiment] to get to know the men, to live with them and to move with them when necessary. Otherwise, I worked closely with Captain Alan C. Poole.

One night while on patrol we had as our objective to go through the woods [using a compass] and meet up with another group. On our way up an embankment, one of the soldiers just disappeared. Finally, we figured out that the soldier had fallen through a crevice. I crawled down the embankment to retrieve him. Also, on Leyte we discovered huge guns that the Japanese had abandoned. It could be assumed that the Japanese didn't have time to install these guns before the American troops landed.

The Japanese Navy tried to surround the island. However, Admirals Kincaid and Halsey separated to attack the Japanese. Admiral Halsey used his carriers and hit them from the sides.

After staying in Leyte six months, on April 1, 1945, soldiers consisting of two army and two marine divisions were taken to Okinawa, which was located 325 miles from the Japanese mainland. We were showed a replica of the island and where it was believed everything was located on Okinawa. The plan was that the two army divisions were to go south and two marine divisions were to go north. We were told that the Japanese would fight much harder now because the Americans were getting closer to their homeland. Also, the Japanese concentrated their forces on the southern part of the island.

Meanwhile, my division happened to be in southern waters when a terrible typhoon hit the island. The waves of water were higher than telephone poles.

The invasion of Okinawa was to involve two thousand ships, two US fleets and one British fleet. However, before the invasion the men were treated to a steak dinner and a shower. No one slept!

There were about twenty men inside the Landing Ship, Tanks [LST], which were used to get the men on the island. Squadrons of US airplanes flying above them along with Zeppelins [balloons] made us feel a little bit better. When a person is highly nervous, it is hard to think straight.

The troops landed. At first we saw railroad tracks. Immediately, a sergeant was killed. We kept on moving. The Japanese were firing artillery and rifles at us. On the third night we had rifles with special night viewing abilities. If civilians came out, they, too, suffered casualties.

Okinawa was rocky, which meant that the infantry had a difficult time digging foxholes. When the men went into caves for cover, they came out with their bodies covered with ticks.

I saw a baby with a dead mother; I picked up the baby and took it to someone who would see to its care. Another time I happened to walk by a trunk whose contents had spilled out; it had been full of beautiful silk fabric. The Japanese left only old people in the huts that were on the island.

We witnessed *banzai* attacks. A group of Japanese soldiers would run through the night shooting at everything and everyone until someone would shoot and kill them. I figured out a strategy to abort a banzai attack. For this effort I was awarded a commendation which stated:

"Sgt. Raul G. Vasquez with disregard for his own safety succeeded in stopping a banzai attack."

At night and in foxholes, the men couldn't sleep very much. The ships shot lights up in the air so that soldiers could see enemy movements. Also, at night the Kamikaze pilots would hit the ships, which in turn turned into bright flames of fire. It was believed that the Japanese sent one hundred to two hundred fighter planes as Kamikazes.

Every now and then I would go see my buddies in the artillery. The guys seemed happy to see me because they could tell I wasn't in the front lines. On June 22, 1945, the Japanese threw a hand grenade that injured me on the left side of my body. A soldier from Arkansas named Pittman and a soldier named Jackson assisted me. As they walked to get help, I collapsed. When daylight came, the men drove me to the aid station.

Upon arriving at the aid station, who should be there but Armando Cardenas, my buddy from home, and a medic who drove me to the next aid station. It was a rough ride, which caused me more pain. I asked my old friend for morphine to kill the unbearable pain, but my friend looked at a mark on me and told me that it was too soon. I said, "Oh, come on, *hombre!*" My friend gave me the extra shot of morphine. I remember eating powdered eggs there, also.

From there I was placed in another ambulance and taken to a MASH [Mobile Army Surgical Hospital] unit. The next stop was a port where I was placed on a ship and taken with other wounded men to a hospital. I looked at three ambulances and noticed that all three drivers were Hispanic.

Tweezers were used to take out shrapnel. Finally, the doctor said to leave the rest in, because it wouldn't bother me. Sure enough, the shrapnel has never bothered me, but the experience resulted in nightmares for a long time.

After I healed, I was taken back to my unit. I was to be a forward observer, and I was offered a second lieutenant field commission.

Preparations were now being made for a land invasion of Japan. One million casualties were predicted. Many meetings were held. Talk about the role of the Kamikazes occurred. Suddenly in August 1945, the war ended. Japan agreed to an unconditional surrender.

In December 1945, my mother died, and the Red Cross sent me home. I went to live with Oscar's aunt Josefina Campos. Two weeks later my cousin and friend arrived home. We three good buddies were reunited, a feat in and of itself!

The three worst things l saw in the war that I cannot forget are the following:

1. At Kakuzu Ridge: The men were in positions while the Japanese were attacking. Captain Newman and others walked around to get a better view when Captain Newman stepped on a mine. Three men were killed instantly including Juan Robles. Captain Newman was seriously injured. I went with Captain Newman to the aid station. Captain Newman said to the doctor, "Awful, isn't it, Doc?" The doctor answered, "You'll be all right." I couldn't sleep all night. The first thing I did the next morning was to go see about Captain Newman. He had died during the night.

2. While fighting the Japanese I ran into a Corpus Christi friend, Gilbert Herrera. In fact, I was carrying a picture of a pretty girl named Margaret Moya. Gilbert convinced me to give him Margaret's picture. In turn, Gilbert gave me his sister's address, and that is the girl [Hope] that I married. [Gilbert married Margaret Moya.] On a particular day I decided to go look for Gilbert. The road was muddy, and the traffic was very slow. Another thing that I noticed was that there was an incredibly strong, bad odor, but the source could not be found. I continued walking and soon saw an American truck driving toward me. It slowed down, and the Mexican American drivers told me that the truck was full of the bodies of dead American soldiers. I noticed that every square inch was covered with flies.

3. Another time my unit arrived at a spot that had an American machine gun squad. The five men were dead but seemed alive because they were frozen in their positions.

George Ochoa
4th Division, 2nd Battalion, F Company

A Veteran of Five Battles
George Ochoa was born on February 22, 1922, in Corpus Christi, Texas. As many young men did during the Depression, George dropped out of school so that he could help his family. His first job was with the Civilian Conservation Corps. George joined the army right before the Pearl Harbor attack. As tough as basic training was, nothing compared to the fight over control of Iwo Jima—the deep ashes, the hidden traps, the existence of tunnels, which

*misled the Allies into thinking that fewer Japanese were present on the island
than were actually there. Then there was that USA flag that went up!*

On November 5, 1941, I joined the marines, but before I left, Mother
administered *la bendición* to me, praying that I would return to her side
safely. I went to San Diego for training and it was tough! At 4:00 a.m. we
were up for exercises. Then breakfast and then more exercises and training, which never stopped. Then there was training for landing on beaches.
It was there in California that I and the other soldiers heard of a place
called Pearl Harbor, and that it had been bombed by the Japanese.

At Camp Razon in North Carolina, I worked with dummies which represented the enemy. And now the training took a more serious turn, for
the boys now knew the enemy.

After my training was completed, I went aboard a troop transport ship.
That ship had a rendezvous with other ships near the Marshall Islands. I
was to learn that the marines' mission was to land on the beach, secure
the island, and then withdraw for the army to go in and continue the fight.
"Battle wagons," actually battleships, would bomb the islands before the
marines would go in. Oftentimes, we noted when we went in that palm
trees had lost the top half of their trunks from the firing of the big guns
on the ships.

It was in the Marshall Islands that I was injured during the fighting and
ended up with shrapnel in my back. I was taken to Hope Hospital located
on the ship. When I healed, I was sent back to my old unit.

We marines never knew exactly where we were being taken. On the
ship on the day before landing we might be told, "Tomorrow we're going
to hit that island."

After fighting in the Marshall Islands, the ship went to Maui for reinforcements, because so many men had been lost in the battles. Then we
were taken to Saipan and then Tinian for more fighting. After that it was
back to Maui for reinforcements.

Iwo Jima was a small island, not a significant-looking island in the least.
Deep volcanic ashes covered the island, and we kept sinking in the pow-
dery black dust as we tried to walk, stand, and fight the Japanese. Along
the landing strip the soldiers could see small holes from which the enemy
could shoot any marine they saw. A marine, in turn, could not shoot back,

because he would have to aim slowly and carefully in order to hit someone through the hole. By then, the Japanese soldier would have shot and killed the American soldier aiming for the hole.

When the tanks came on land, however, the flamethrowers were able to destroy the Japanese soldiers who continued using the peepholes for shooting. Japanese soldiers would throw themselves in the water when the flamethrowers came close to them. Whenever possible, the soldiers threw hand grenades in places likely to be holding the enemy.

Another tactic the Japanese soldiers used was to dig a deep hole and then camouflage the hole. A group of marines might be walking together and then one of them would disappear. The others would turn around, and he would be gone and then killed by the Japanese.

On at least one occasion the marines noticed that the Japanese artillery was firing at them with some degree of accuracy. The accuracy of the firing was a mystery to them. Finally, they looked up and around and discovered a small glare or reflection coming from a smokestack in a sugar planta-tion. It was a Japanese sniper using binoculars. The next job was to get rid of the sniper.

As we struggled on the island, firing at the enemy and trying to keep from getting shot, a group of marines went to a small hill and planted an American flag while dealing with ashes and attempting to avoid getting killed. I don't know where they found the flag to put up.

Some marines found sake in some caves in which the Japanese had been hiding. In their eagerness over their find, some marines drank the liquid without investigating it and went blind.

The foxholes we dug were cold and often wet. It was not a secret that some men cried nightly as they attempted to sleep knowing that tomor-row might be the day that they, like their buddies, would die. American ships would come by and dump supplies on the beaches for the fighting soldiers. One ship would bring troops; another ship would bring ammu-nition, etc.

As it appeared that the Americans might end up taking the island, Jap-anese soldiers began committing suicide rather than surrendering to the enemy. A common way was to take off a boot or shoe and aim the rifle at the head while pulling the trigger with the big toe.

During some fighting, again I was injured. This time I was shot in the leg, and I was taken to Hope Hospital again. The navy took care of my wound. I was sent to Barrington, Washington, to the Navy Hospital. After my wound healed, the doctor told me I had a forty-five day leave.

I was sent to Treasure Island in San Francisco and then discharged from the marines. I had experienced three and a half years of fighting with the only breaks I had were when the ship went back to Maui for reinforcements or my stays in Hope Hospital. In all I was involved in five major battles!

President Roosevelt gave a UNIT CITATION to the Fourth Division! I came home to my parents, who were happy to see me.

Manuel Gutierrez
14th Army Air Corps Depot
AAF Supply Technician

Learning and Respecting Another Culture

Manuel Gutierrez was born to Rosaura and Florencio Gutierrez in Alice, Texas, on October 11, 1921. Rosaura was from Parras and Florencio was from Cuidad Guerrero in Mexico. Florencio, Manuel's father, worked for the Tex-Mex Railroad Company in Banquete, Texas, as a telegraph operator, an occupation he held for forty years. Rosaura went to Alice, Texas, to see Dr. Strickland regarding her baby's birth, so Manuel was born in Alice. Manuel ended up on another continent and observed a culture entirely different from his own. He did his best to respect it. Since cows were sacred there, the Army had meat shipped in so the soldiers could eat food they liked.

I went to school up through the sixth grade in Banquete. Our schools were segregated, and Miss Farmer was my teacher. After attending school in Banquete one year we moved to Corpus Christi the following year. I attended Northside Junior High School and then graduated from Corpus Christi High School in 1941. I played football in 1939-40.

Regarding December 7, 1941, I didn't have a television back then. It was all on radio. I married Carmen Barrera on February 1, 1942. I was drafted in 1942. I was inducted on August 19, 1942, in San Antonio, Texas. I trained there with the Army Air Corps for two years at Kelly and

Duncan Fields as a supply clerk. After going to school in Los Angeles for technical training, I came back to San Antonio. On October 28, 1944, they certified me.

I got on a troop train in San Antonio. There must have been two thousand of us soldiers, and they took us to Los Angeles. They took us to San Pedro Harbor and we boarded a troop ship. We shipped out on February 7, 1945, to the Asian Pacific and arrived on March 10, 1945.

In Sidney, Australia, we refueled and got our supplies and everything. We zigzagged from San Pedro to Sidney and all the way to Bombay to avoid submarines. We were there just one day, and we ended up in Bombay, India. Fifteen hundred of us went from Bombay to Calcutta in a cattle car train all across India. From there they picked us up in a truck and took us out into the jungle sixty miles outside of Calcutta. That's where our place was.

They had all kinds of equipment so that we could repair airplanes. We put parts and airplane wings together to be used in the war.

We were right there in the jungle. We had snakes, monkeys, all kinds of animals. There were, of course, a lot of Indians. The women had no tops. They didn't have any toilets. They just squatted to use the bathroom. They had trenches. The base had toilets.

We sat out in the open to eat. Birds swooped down and took food out of our plates. Sometimes they would take our food as we were taking in our forks to our mouths.

There was no one there from Corpus Christi out of the two thousand men there. I was there ten months, from March through December 1945.

We ended up in New Jersey when we came back on January 5, 1946, from Calcutta on a troop ship. From New Jersey we came to Camp Fannin in Tyler, Texas. We came back to Corpus Christi on a train.

I was making $100 a month and was sending home $75 and keeping $25.

In India we raised chickens, ate them and ate the eggs. All the eggs they gave us were powdered eggs.

On our days off Saturdays and Sundays we scouted around, saw animals and snakes, emus, rattlesnakes, pythons. They sent us meat from the US.

We used to go to Calcutta on leaves sometimes and they had nightclubs believe it or not, a lot of drinking, shows of all kinds and beautiful, fine restaurants or cafeterias. We would eat there something we did not get at the base. You're talking about poverty—oh my God! It's horrible. Begging, mile after mile. Terrible, terrible life they were living at that time. Prostitution and brothels, lots of them. Right there out in the open.

I saw snake charmers. Absolutely.

We were not in danger of invasion by the Japanese, but we had alerts. About one thousand men. We had night guards. We made everything from scratch. We had bunk beds off the ground to keep snakes from going into our beds and to keep spiders off. Monkeys were looking for food.

We were not allowed to have pets. They were wild. Cows were sacred.

We would get the airplane parts together and ship them by flatbed train cars. We repaired engines and propellers for use in CBI (China, Burma, and India). They put them on freight airplanes.

As a technician I wrote down all that was done to the plane. That's where I got the training when I went to school. I was a supervisor.

I saw mothers with babies begging in the cities. You saw cows here and there, but you didn't mention anything about a cow. All the milk we got was powdered milk. But you didn't try to get a cow. Our officers told us about the cows and "not to ever even try anything and no two ways about it." You didn't even think about a piece of meat. The restaurants served chicken and fish. Beef was unheard of.

From Camp Fannin we took a train. They paid for all of that. We went to San Antonio and then I caught a bus to Corpus Christi.

I didn't carry a gun, but we had twenty-four-hour guards. I had guard duty and kitchen patrol.

I cannot remember during the four years I was in the service that I was discriminated against by being a Mexican American. The Blacks had their own; they didn't eat together in San Antonio. They had their own everything.

During that time I knew the owner of Corpus Christi Transfer Moving Company, Mr. Gary Tucker. He and Mr. Hernandez owned CC Transfer. CC Transfer is the same as Mayflower. We moved furniture. I went to work for them as a dispatcher, because I sent people out on jobs. I worked there for thirty-three years.

I was glad to get out of the service. I worked in the engine room at the Driscoll Hotel. Also, I owned a service station. Mayflower offered me a job. I worked as a dispatcher from 1966 through 1996. I had two brothers in the service, Joe and Willie. My brother Raul who had worked with the CCC was too old for the service. In San Antonio the recruits were about 40 percent Hispanic.

We lived at 306 North Alameda right behind our in-laws. It was the last street. We had three boys and one girl. Gloria works with the Labor Department. Richard was a teacher in Robstown, but is now a dean at a High School in Las Vegas. Armando is here in Corpus Christi, and Lewis, a graduate of Stanford Law School, worked for Los Angeles. Lewis is deceased.

Leonel Cristobal Guerra
86th Blackhawk Anti-Tank Division
788th Ord Light Maintenance Division

Born on a Ranch
Leonel was born on May 5, 1926, at the San Teresa Ranch thirty-five miles North of Rio Grande City. As a youngster he rode a horse to a school in San Isidro. Leonel said, "You had to be old enough and strong enough to saddle your horse, get on it, and open and close all the gates—five or six—that led to other ranches. That's why I couldn't start school until I was nine." As a soldier, he was assigned to a camp with Japanese prisoners, and he had to find a way to keep them busy.

My sister was fourteen or fifteen months younger than I was, but my father didn't want her to ride a horse to school. So he built a bus out of a pickup. He built a roof and had canvas to use if it rained. He took three of us and others that went to school and drove us to San Isidro. He did it for free.

The next year the school district hired a person who had a bus. Girls were embarrassed to ride a horse to school. They didn't want to go to school. The boys were tall boys. They would laugh at the girls in class, so the girls quit school. The school district decided to pay someone to go and get the kids and take them to school.

The ones that got the job were the ones who knew the big shots. You went to school if you could. I started driving at eight, because my dad hurt his back. This was a 640-acre ranch. We lived on the south side, and my grandparents lived on the north side. My grandmother got sick and a neighbor came by on horseback and said, "Your mother is very sick." My father couldn't get out of bed. He crawled into the pickup and said, "Get three pillows, two for the back and one to sit on." Then he started showing me how the gears work. "This is a dry run. Now you start the engine. You've got to back it up. This is the brake and this is the clutch." And that's how I learned to drive at eight. But I couldn't drive to school. They didn't trust me. Later I attended San Isidro High School.

I went overseas with the Eighty-Sixth Blackhawk Anti-Tank Division. Then I was separated after I went to the hospital. They attached me to the 788th Ordnance Light Maintenance Division.

I put in four months training in infantry, five months as a rifleman, four months as a Sergeant in Duty Non-Commissioned Officer in the Philippines, and sergeant seven as a parts clerk.

On January of 1945 I volunteered for the army because I wanted to go into the air force and go to Europe. I was eighteen. They sent me in the opposite direction and gave me the wrong branch of the service. There were five of us standing around and one of the sergeants said, "Okay, there will be three for the Navy and two for the Army." Then he said, "Okay, Navy step forward." And I didn't move. I got the army, but it was not what I wanted. I was bitter and I didn't try very hard to do anything.

They inducted me on February 12, 1945, and I went to Fort Hood near Waco. My mother gave me *la bendición*. My father was too much of a man to do it. My father said, "Just be careful, and try to stay away from the bullets."

By this time there had been many, many deaths. The year before that they were bringing in boys [bodies] from the area. The year before they were bringing in bodies of boys from the *ranchitos* [ranches]. I was born in San Teresa, but when I was thirteen we moved to San Isidro. It was closer to the school.

I knew I had to go. First I went to Fort Sam Houston, the induction station. Then we went to Fort Hood where I spent four months. They also gave us advanced training in anti-tank warfare. We were going to Japan.

We went to Fort Ord to be placed on a ship to go overseas. We were there a week in Fort Ord, and then we were on our way to Japan. We had been at sea eighteen days when we heard that the bomb had been dropped [August 6—Hiroshima, Japan; August 9, 1945—Nagasaki, Japan]. They announced that Japan had surrendered over the speaker. It was August 14, 1945.

We had been zigzagging all this time in the ocean because of the submarines. After the surrender they went straight to the Philippines. When we were there our job was to go out with the more experienced soldiers to the jungle and to see if there were any more Japanese. We had two thousand Japanese prisoners in the first camp that I arrived at. "Let's go get more." I never found any more Japanese, but the older guys did. They would give them to us to bring to the compound. Most were in caves. By the time I got there they had passed the word out: "The war is over. Come out." But they had to be very careful, because if they didn't know the war was over they would start shooting at you.

After I was getting ready to come back, the camp trained the Filipinos. When we were in patrol, I found a dagger with a zigzag blade. The handle is ivory and is encrusted with precious stones. Some stones were missing. Beautiful. The scabbard was made of brass. It was half buried. About fifteen-inch blade. Owned by somebody of high rank. Hard steel blade. It's gorgeous. I mailed it home. Anything you brought, the soldiers at Fort Sam took them away. I saw one with diamonds for $35,000.

The Japanese prisoners. We used to take them out to dig six by six by six to keep them busy and to give them exercise. Several of us would take five. It was boring as could be. No one tried to escape.

I used to go around looking at the fence. To make sure they didn't cut it. I walked around the compound and looked at their camp. The Geneva Convention. We didn't mistreat them. As I was walking around tents I heard someone say, "*Habla español?*" I thought, *what's going on around here?* I looked around and several Japanese were sitting on steps looking at me. I moved another step and a Japanese said, "*Habla español?*" I said, "*Sí.*" He said, "*Ven para acá.*" [Come over here.] I sat down with him. He was Japanese who came to the Philippines way before the war, and in the Philippines there are lot of Hispanic men married to Filipino women. He saw me and saw that I was fair and figured I was Hispanic. I sat with him and asked, "Where in the world did you learn how to speak Spanish?" He said, "Here. I came here ten years before the war and there were a lot of Spanish people here. I wanted to learn Spanish." We're talking in Spanish, because he didn't know English and I didn't know Japanese. We're conversing in Spanish like we were *amigos*, and from then on every time I saw him, we would speak for a little while, "*Cómo estás? Qué has hecho? Cómo te tratan aquí?*" [Hello. What have you done? How are they treating you here?] He said, "*En poco nos mandan a la casa.*" [In a short while they'll be sending us home.]

The Japanese were cruel with the Filipinos, burying them and leaving their heads out and cutting them so the ants would eat them. The Filipinos started capturing Japanese and stripping or skinning them alive.

There was a camp called *Los Angeles* at the Philippine Islands where we were training Filipino men to take over our job so that we could come home. Shooting, marching, administrative work, too. Within those men were men who had been fighting the Japanese since it started. When the United States came in, the Filipinos were committing atrocities with the Japanese.

We were told that there were some POW who were Dutch who had been brought in to the Fifth Replacement Depot. They were tall, about six foot two to six foot five, blond, and emaciated. Even their ribs were showing. The Americans were told by the Dutch government to give them anything they wanted. That they would pay for the expense. The Dutchmen took one or two mess kits and a case of beer a day [each case had twenty-four small cans] per person. The Dutch didn't want their men sent back in bad shape. After they had gained some weight, they were sent home.

My trip to the Pacific was from July 27, original date of shipping out, and then August 31, 1945, to Sept 23, 1945. My trip back home was from October 7, 1946, to October 21, 1946. I returned to high school to finish up. Then I attended Edinburg Junior College for one and a half years. In 1948-49 I sold drugs as a wholesaler.

On December 24, 1949, I rode a train to Milwaukee, Wisconsin, to study TV electronics, a relatively new field. I spent fourteen months at the American Institute of Technology in Chicago. I worked with Simpson Electric Company Instruments until 1953. Finally, I worked for thirty years at the Corpus Christi Naval Base as an electric technical engineer. In 1984 I married Nena Guerra.

Lázaro Gonzalez Benavides
Construction Battalion (Seabees)

He Joined the Navy because He Didn't Want to Walk

Lázaro (Larry) was born in Laredo, Texas, on September 14, 1918. His family moved to Benavides, Texas, in 1934. In earlier years his father worked for the Tex-Mex Railroad. Larry decided if he were assigned to a ship, he wouldn't have to walk as much as a foot soldier. Then he was assigned to a Construction Battalion. He became a Seabee. His first assignment was in Alaska, but before long he was sent to the Pacific, where the Seabees accomplished much with their talents and abilities.

On one job into Mexico, my father's brother, Lázaro Tyles Benavides, who was a train engineer, told him to leave the country and go back home because the Mexican Revolution was getting to be dangerous for everyone. So my father quit that job. By 1934, my father worked as a pay master for the Conoco-Continental Oil Company in Driscoll, Texas, and he held that job until retirement.

I married Consuelo Garcia and had two daughters. Although I had a family and was operating a service station, I felt that I had better join the service of my choice before I was drafted into one [branch] I didn't like.

In tiny Benavides, Texas, there was a business, Coronado's Garage, which had a radio. Since the radio was a unique instrument of communication in that town, people gathered around it from time to time to hear the news. It was there that I heard of the bombing of Pearl Harbor, and a day later I heard the president of the United States, Franklin D. Roosevelt, declare war on Japan.

We felt helpless. We wanted to do something, but we didn't know what to do. So we just listened and waited.

I joined the Navy Reserves on May 13, 1942, because I didn't like to walk. I felt that if I served on a ship it wouldn't involve much walking.

I started out as a Seaman First Class and became a Machinist's Mate, Second Class. This group of men became known as Seabees from the first letters of the two words, Construction Battalion.

Before leaving Benavides, Texas, my mother gave me the blessing. I spent two days in Houston where I was tested and I passed the exam.

I went to Corpus Christi, Texas, and then traveled to Norfolk, Virginia, for training.

Then the navy sent me to Fort Hueneme in California. There the navy issued me and the rest of the men clothes for cold weather. We wondered what that meant.

The destination was Kodiak, Alaska, where Lázaro stayed one year. In Kodiak the Seabees took care of construction and maintained the area for a two star admiral.

I was sent to Kwajalein Island, and from there was sent to Engebi Island, which was one of the Marshall Islands. Pillboxes were present in Engebi Island, with signs of recent Japanese occupation still obvious. When the Americans bombed this tiny island, the Japanese deserted it. Beside the pillboxes, the Japanese had built a train track which took them from one end of the island to the other. They had also built a port capable of receiving supplies.

Wyler, an American Seabee, found a four-cylinder engine and built a vehicle that men used to ride on the island. There was a saying that there was a woman behind each tree. The catch was that there was only one tiny tree on the island.

The Seabees cleaned up the place and built desalination machines, which filtered the water, making it drinkable. We also drilled a water well.

When the war ended, I left on *Nehenta Bay*, a baby aircraft carrier. The carrier stopped at Eniwetok.

When I returned home, I didn't know what to do with myself. I didn't know of any rights or benefits I had as a veteran. I really felt lost.

I remained in the army reserve for eight years and then worked with Civil Service for twenty-five years. My wife and I live in Corpus Christi, Texas, and we raised four children.

José Posas
United States Navy
Seabees 66th Battalion

From Willywaws to Typhoons

José Posas was born on September 13, 1924, in Sinton, Texas, and moved to Corpus Christi, Texas, at age five. At age seventeen he joined the navy. His mother was afraid of her boy going off who knows where, but told him that it was okay, if that was his choice. José was selected to be in the Construction Battalion, the Seabees. His first assignment was in the Aleutian Islands, where the snow was so thick they moved from hut to hut by holding on to a rope. Going from that extreme to Okinawa allowed José to learn a bit about the world.

The recruitment officer who assisted me as I signed up promised me that I would be back home in three days to visit. Instead, I was immediately sent to Providence, Rhode Island, to boot camp, and there I stayed for eight months. After that I was sent to Camp Pendleton for advanced training. I was selected to the Seabees, a construction battalion, which was involved in activities such as the following: building landing strips for the marines and the navy; constructing hangars, docks, and buildings needed in the war effort. Many Seabees were older, more experienced craftsmen such as carpenters and welders. They asked me what in the world I was doing with them. I told them that I didn't know.

From Camp Pendleton I was sent to Port Hueneme in California near Oxnard. There the marines taught me and others how to fight; how to use Browning automatic rifles; and how to fire 60mm rockets, "stove pipes." When we weren't learning from the marines, we would go into Ventura, California, to have fun.

Now as a First Class Seaman, I was sent to the Aleutian Islands, where I spent twenty-three months. The snow was so thick we couldn't see one another. To get from one hut to another, we had to hold on to a rope, which would lead us. The snow storms were called, "Willywaws." One of the sayings was that there was a woman behind every tree. The only catch was that there were no trees, only mountains and lots of snow! Daylight wasn't seen until about ten o'clock in the morning. Also, the salmon were beautiful as they swam upstream to lay their eggs; however, they could not be eaten at this time. One seaman from Boston tried cooking and eating a salmon and became very ill.

The Japanese had conquered some of the islands and the marines had experienced some hard fighting in the heavy snow and ice. After my time in the Aleutian Islands I was sent home. I had thirty days in which to go to Corpus Christi, visit my mother, and return to duty.

In May 1945 I was sent to Okinawa. The marines and the army had already taken over the island. There were many dead people lying around when I arrived. The Seabees had many jobs repairing much damage that had occurred. Surprisingly enough, the air strip was in pretty good shape. Although the soldiers were never told of any action in advance, we couldn't help thinking that the next step would be to invade Japan. It was not a pleasant thought.

From what we soldiers found in caves and from the condition and age of the air strip, it was believed that the Japanese had planned for war on this island for many years.

One month a horrendous typhoon hit. The ships had moved out into the water to weather the storm. Even so, the typhoon moved the ships on to the beach! It took a long time and lots of work to be able to get the ships out to the water.

One evening while we were attempting to sleep on our cots, which sat on the ground, a loud bang was heard and our bunks seemed to move. One sailor said to another, "Quit moving my bunk." One seaman from California who had experienced earthquakes said, "It's an earthquake." We tried to sleep. The next day we learned that a bomb had been dropped on Hiroshima. Then some time later we heard that the war was over! Men began firing their bullets up in the air. Unfortunately, one bullet rained down on a seaman and injured him.

I ended up in Camp Wallace, Galveston. Much to my surprise German prisoners were doing the cooking for the American soldiers. I was discharged on November 27, 1945. I knew for certain that I was one of the few soldiers who had seen both extremes in weather during my hitch. It was good to be home!

Baldemar Garza
598th Signal Aircraft Warning Battalion

Working with Radar

Baldemar Garza was born on October 13, 1923, in tiny Benavides, Texas, to Leandro and Vicenta Garza. His father was a farmer. Out of eight children, Baldemar was number seven. Baldemar spent two birthdays while in the service—his twentieth birthday on a train headed for San Francisco. His twenty-first birthday he celebrated at sea, on his way to the Philippine Islands.

I had two other brothers in WWII. Nestor died in maneuvers in Palacios, Texas. Leandro Garza Jr. remained stateside during the war.

My daddy used to tell me that they used to go on horseback to pick cotton around San Marcos. They would get friends or cousins to go. He did farming. He said that he worked at one time for twenty-five cents a day and keep for uprooting oak trees with picks and shovels, clearing fields. I said to him, "How did you ever make it?" He said, "The same way to make it today, with what you make." Everything was very cheap.

During the Depression, before they used to farm, it was very hard on them. Because on a farm you have chickens and eggs and you can raise a hog. Venison was plentiful. Wild boar was plentiful. All we had to do was to go to town for the basics like flour, sugar, coffee. They got it on credit until they raised a crop. Then they got their money back. We had watermelons, cantaloupes, beans, corn. We had more vegetables than what we can buy now.

I attended high school and quit as a junior. Then I finished after I got back. I was nineteen when I was drafted. I worked on anything that came along, working on farms. I went into the service on April 29, 1943. My mom gave me *la bendición*. I went to San Antonio. A piece of paper saved my life—I think so. They woke us up at 4:00 a.m. to ship out. They had the buses waiting, and they loaded everybody except two persons; I was one of them. They were missing the pass books. The pass books keep your shot records and everything else. They didn't have them for me and another guy from San Diego. We couldn't load up. We had to stay behind.

These people were going to Fort Knox, Kentucky, which is mostly infantry. Since we were left behind, two or three days later they called us again. They shipped us to Wichita Falls. That's where I took my basic training, at Sheppard Field. At that time the air force and the army were one.

We were shipped out to Florida, and we were training for radar. Our group was part of a battalion. Our unit consisted of fifty-two men, two officers, one master sergeant, and the rest were control operators, radiomen, guards, and cooks. The guards guarded our unit to make sure that no one got in. We kept everything pretty well safe. At one time we had an infantry platoon taking care of us. That was on the island of Samar.

They test you from the day you get there [San Antonio]. In basic training half a day is close-ordered drill training, disassembling rifles. In Sheppard Field they test you in general.

We were shipped to Alexandria, Louisiana, Essler Field—by mistake. When we got there, they came to pick us up and said, "You don't belong here." That was a training center for pilots. They said, "While you are here, feel free to ride with any of the pilots that were training." We were there two weeks.

From there they shipped us to Drew Field in Tampa, Florida. Everything was related to radar, taking the radar apart, the antennae system and all of that. We used a flashlight with a little slit of light showing until we got the word to ship out. In basic I just went through physical training, exercise, discipline and marching, close-order drill.

While in basic they send you to the gas chambers with a gas mask. You get a whiff of the gas and run through so you can get an idea. I have no complaints. We were lucky out there.

They shipped us out to Camp Stoneman in Pittsburg, California. On my way to San Francisco I had my twentieth birthday on the train. There we played and waited for our orders to ship out overseas. We waited about two-three weeks.

We shipped out to the island of Oahu in Hawaii. The damage at Pearl Harbor had been cleaned up, but the damage of the buildings from strafing was still there. In Oahu it was like being over here. One time we were bragging that we had crossed the Pacific from California to Hawaii with no escort at all. Someone said, "The water between here and the States is just as safe as the Mississippi."

I spent most of two years there. We were training and training and patrolling the skies. I was a guard patrolman. I did a lot of things, but that was my title. We were by ourselves, and we were close to the water. In Hawaii we had everything we had here. There we went to the radar station, operated it, and came back until we got orders to ship out. What they were doing there was making sure that no unknown aircraft would approach the islands. And if they did, why get the fighters in the air. It was quiet.

I guarded some Japanese prisoners on the Hawaiian Islands. They had it made. They ate the same thing we ate. They had good quarters in comparison to what they had in their armies. They never gave us any trouble.

Sometime in '44 we shipped out to the Philippines. On October 8th we crossed the equator. On our way to the Philippine Islands I had my twenty-first birthday at sea. It was October 13, 1944. Leyte was invaded on October 20, 1944, while we were still at sea.

By the time we got there and by the time we unloaded and everything, the marines were about ten miles in. We entered in through the city of Tacloban on the island of Leyte. The marines had it bad, and the army went in behind the marines.

We are supposed to set up the radar station. When we first got there we didn't even assemble or do any radar. What they did was send us around the island of Samar. They sent us to the other side because of the mountains because when the aircraft were coming, by the time they picked them up, they were already at Leyte Bay and you had to fight them there. That's too late. But by going around, you could pick them up way out in the ocean and warn our people about enemy planes. And that gave our fighters time to get up in the air. Our planes had emergency runways of metal that they put together besides the aircraft carriers and the navy. They bombard quite a bit before they let anybody go in. The Seabees did quite a bit of work.

We were classified as noncombats. All we were supposed to do was to patrol the air. The only time we had to fight was if they broke the lines. Our first mission was to destroy the equipment so no one could get their hands on it. Then fight the best way you could but we never got to do that. The largest weapon we had was a .50-caliber machine gun. The rest were just our rifles.

I heard horror stories about the Japanese, but I never saw it. We used to see dogfights every day, usually in the afternoon as the sun was going down or very early in the morning. We couldn't do anything. By the time they were in the air, so were our pilots. You have a plotting board in the shape of a circle, which has names like Mexico, Texas, whatever. The center of the circle represents us, the unit. You pick up a plane here or many and report to a central point by radio. The next time the antenna goes around it'll give you an idea which way the plane is pointing to the right or to the left or if it's coming toward you.

I was strafed with a machine gun four times. The strafing was early in the morning, and they didn't hit anything. One time they almost ripped the tent off, but they didn't hit any persons, and we got up in a hurry. On the island of Samar they assigned an infantry platoon to protect us. If we got attacked, we were defenseless.

One day, coming out of lunch with two or three other guys, I heard an aircraft. If I had had my rifle I could have shot that pilot. He was about as low as he could be, just enough to clear the trees. I could see the writing. The aircraft was a Japanese Zero, a fighter plane. He must have been scouting. He had one bomb. That's all, but he didn't let it go. You can see the bomb underneath the plane. We sounded the siren. At that time we didn't have the radar station on the air. We had just gotten there. We had all the radar equipment, bands, generators for electricity, all in one place. So the first thing we did was to spread them out. He never came back; he just went through.

We didn't have any problems with the Filipinos because mostly the older people spoke Spanish. The younger people, most of them spoke English. So we didn't have any problems there with people.

To me the job was like a gravy train, because we had no physical contact, and no combat. The radar operators had a six-hour shift and they'd get relieved. The radar was on twenty-four hours a day. Each crew had a maintenance man on the spot in case something went wrong.

The Filipinos had guerrillas that went out patrolling. They would warn us in case something went wrong. They were on instant patrol. Their lives were on the line same as ours. They hated the Japanese.

Some of our American planes were shot by our people. Every radar station gets what it calls IFF [Identification Friend or Foe]. Some fighter pilots either forgot to turn on their IFF and when the radar picked them up assumed they were the enemy. So if it was early in the morning or close to darkness, they got shot same as anybody else.

IFF was very secretive. No one knew about it. Even on trains when they shipped men out from one place to another, they had FBI people on there as passengers asking questions to see if they would talk because they [soldiers] were instructed not to talk regardless of who it was.

A lot of lives were saved by radar. They gave them early warnings.

After Samar we came back to Leyte in late '44. We never set up our equipment in Leyte; we stayed in port. A short while later they put us on a ship going to Okinawa. Two or three days later they took us off the ship. We never sailed out. A few days later they put us on a brand-new ship, the USS *General Stuart*. We were on that ship that was ninety days old.

The rumors start. We're going to Japan. We're going to the States. Every kind of rumor. We ended up in the Hawaiian Islands. After the war ended in Japan—shortly after that we sailed back to the United States. We had R and R—Rest and Recuperation. I don't know what we needed to rest from. We were there when they dropped the first bomb and when they dropped the second one. Everyone thought the war was almost over. I give President Truman credit for dropping the bomb, because hundreds of thousands of people would have died.

Not much chance of my going after this beautiful girl. When we got word that we were shipping out, I went to the barbershop there in the same commissary. I told that barber to cut my hair in a crew cut just in case I couldn't get to another barber. So he gave me a crew cut. I left. The next day I came in to buy cigarettes or something and the barber called me over and said, "Was that your girlfriend?" "No." The barber said, "Well, she came over here and gave me hell for cutting your hair." I never tried to date her. Everyone was trying to date her.

There was one occasion in the Hawaiian Islands in the big island; there we had the radar station in operation and they had a restaurant. They had a beautiful Japanese Portuguese girl. Everybody was after her. I used to eat there most of the time and talk to her. One day three of us decided to go have dinner there. We had a few beers. We ate. When it came time to pay, one of the guys said, "Well, I don't have any money." The other guy said, "Well, I don't have any money either." Well, if they don't have any money, I don't have any money. So we walked out. They could have put us in jail right there. Nothing was said. The next day it went to my head that I got out of there without paying. I went back and there she was. "Do you remember me?" She said, "Yes." "Where was I sitting?" "Right there." "I came back to pay you." She said, "I paid for you. The other two I'll catch them when they come by here." And I started with her and I would have married her if it hadn't been against the law to marry a Japanese. She was born and raised in the Hawaiian Islands. She wanted to wait for me. I said, "No, I might come back. I might not. Enjoy your life." I came back on the island of Oahu. She was on the island of Hawaii. They wouldn't let us go to the other island. Some of my friends went back to the island of Hawaii later. She had moved to the island of Oahu. We kept in touch, the whole outfit—for a while. A lot passed away. Something happened.

We stayed there until there was transportation available to come back to the United States. I came back to the United States with much less points than other people because transportation was readily available from the Hawaiian Islands to the United States.

In December of 1945 we came up the Columbia River to Portland, Oregon. And they took us across the river to Vancouver, Washington. We didn't have anything but khakis on and it was freezing, snowing, and everything. So the first thing they did was to give us winter clothing.

What I remember most is that we crossed over in flat-bottomed boats from the Hawaiian Islands to the United States. They wouldn't let us shower with fresh water. We had to use seawater.

When we got to the United States I had $10. A friend was flat broke and asked me for a couple of dollars. I gave him half of what I had. I went to the barbershop. By the time I got out of there I had about $1 left. They told us to keep watch on the bulletin board and that our name would appear there and it will tell you where you are going for your discharge. I saw my name there. I wanted to let my folks know that I was coming home pretty soon. I didn't want them to be surprised.

I wrote a little note, and I had eighty-five cents. I went to Western Union on base there. They had a big line. I stood in line. When I got there they had this beautiful young lady about my age—twenty-one or twenty-two. I said, "Let's see if this message will go with eighty-five cents." She gave me a piece of paper and a pen. "Write all you want; I'll pay for it." That's one thing I will never forget.

From there we shipped out to Fort Bliss, El Paso, and got our discharge there. From there you are on your own. I rode the train home. The transportation was free. The train took me to Alice, Texas. I caught a ride from Alice to Benavides, Texas, by hitchhiking.

The first man to be killed in WWII was from Benavides, Texas. His name was Guadalupe Ramirez. He was a tail gunner; that's what I wanted to be. I was told that the life expectancy of a tail gunner is about thirty seconds. His sisters are still living. His brother was a geologist. His brother, Romeo Ramirez, was a pilot in WWII.

When I came back to Benavides, I was in the fifty-twenty Club. I was to get $20 a week for fifty-two weeks until I could find a job. I went to auto mechanic school after that. I graduated from it, but I didn't like it. At the same time I was studying radio/television, and I did that for fifteen-sixteen years.

I moved to Dallas and came to Hebronville to get married. We lived in Dallas. My wife's mother started getting sick, and we had to travel all the way from Dallas to Hebronville. So we moved to Corpus Christi. I got a job with the Civil Service. I retired from the base. My wife is Graciela Valdez Garza. We had three boys.

One son is in computer science. One son majored in languages and minored in math. He teaches Spanish, English, Italian, German in Bel Air High School in Houston. He takes a trip to Spain every year. Another son is a mechanic.

I went back in during the Korean conflict for one year. After San Antonio they sent me to Oklahoma City, and that was supposed to be a shipping point to send you over, but they never sent me. They called me in and asked me, "Do you want to go to Houston or San Antonio?" I said, "What do you mean? I just got here." I chose San Antonio. When I reported to North Kelly I was not taking my bag. Here comes a tough sergeant and he says, "I'm taking your bag. You're going to Houston." I got into an argument with him. "I just got here." I lost the argument. But close by was a second lieutenant and he listened to all the argument. After we broke off with the sergeant, he came back to me and talked to me and said, "Don't you want to go to Houston with him?" "I have no choice. I have to go."

It was early in the morning and he said, "Meet me over here by 2:00." So I was there about five or ten minutes early. He came through and said, "You don't get to go to Houston. I got somebody else to go over there. You can stay here." He'd been recalled same as I had. So I was assigned to North Kelly Airways and Air Communication Service. I did that one year, from October 1, 1950, to October 1, 1951. After I got out of this one, I got out of the Reserves. If I had stayed, they would have called me during Vietnam.

Anthony "Chico" Cubriel
25th Division, 27th Regiment, Company D
August 21, 2003
San Diego, Texas

Basketball Led the Way
Anthony "Chico" Cubriel was born in Moore, Texas, on May 15, 1913, to Mamie Duncan and Antonio Cubriel. His mother was half Hispanic and half Anglo. Chico joined the service twice. The first time he was recruited because of his skill in playing basketball. The second time it was because there was a war going on. Wherever Chico went, he made friends who appreciated him.

I went to school where they had those just for Spanish-speaking people. Just two rooms. My first teacher was Luz Saenz (male)—that school they have named here in Alice. Segregated badly.

When I was promoted to high school, I was the only one promoted. And they received me with rocks. They were very much against us. Very, very bitter. Moore had four hundred to five hundred people. I had two friends, Raymond Parks and Loyce Milan; they're the ones that defended me. They made the others stop throwing rocks at me. They were very close to me until they died. In fact their sons were honey men. They raised bees. Their grandsons raise bees, also.

I graduated from high school there in 1932. My brother was a grade behind me, and I had a cousin, Norberto Duncan, who also went there. We played basketball together.

We played basketball at Moore High School. My brother played basketball and my senior year, my brother's junior year, he was elected captain. After that they [the team] wouldn't play basketball because my brother was a "meskin." You may have 98 percent of the Anglos accept you very nice, the 2 percent ruin everything. So we did this. We went and talked with the coach. His name was Dave Brandt. What I am today, I owe it to him. We went to him and I said, "Coach we have a pretty good team. Let's do this. Let's alternate the captainship from game to game." At the end of the year I was elected captain by the boys. Like my brother who had all the votes, because he played in all the big games. So they voted, and he was elected captain. We alternated, one game after another game, and I was elected captain.

I was all-district man. I had a record there for a long time. I scored twenty-eight points, which was a lot of points in those years. District championship. I stayed out two years after I graduated from high school. Some schools [colleges] were interested in me in those days, but as soon as they found out I was a "meskin," they got cold. There were a lot of independent teams in those days. I played as an independent. After two years there was a boy who played basketball named Louis Monica. He went to Brooks Field. I had played basketball against . . . some of these . . . in those days after two years you had to go to the air corps to go to school there, Kelly Field. I had played against this team when I was in independent ball. So I was pretty good in those days.

So I played two years independent ball. This boy, Louis Monica. The cadets were there. They said, "Do you know Chico Cubriel?" He said, "Yes." They asked, "What's he doing?" "Nothing."

On a Monday morning four or five of these officers from Brook Field . . . I was six foot one. They came and talked to me. Louis Monica told them I was there. I was doing nothing. That was during the Depression. In the Army we got $21. So they talked to me. I said, "No, I don"t know." You're a country boy. They wanted me to go to the army and to go play basketball for them. The air corps—Brooks Field in San Antonio. I'm not about to go. A few days later I decided well—they told me you call us and we'll come pick you up and we'll take you. They came and I went with a man—I forgot his name—he had a store there—he took me over there. The first day they went and they got a man to fix my bed up and give me tea and all that stuff.

The first day we practiced they gave me a bag of shoes, gloves, bats, and a sack of balls, and back home we only had one ball [baseball] and if we lose it, we had to go look for it.

I liked it very much. I went back and told my mother and father. We didn't have nothing and I said, "I'll go join the army." Three years. So I went. My first baseball game—there was a first sergeant named Robert Duke. I hit two homeruns. I stayed there and I played ball. I played three years and was on first string, and in basketball I was pretty good there. So my last game I played at Breckenridge High School. We played against an all-star team. And I had a good night.

After the game—we'd get behind and they'd put me in to get ahead. So at the end of the game I was walking across the gym, two guys in black uniforms got by me. They said, "Chico, would you like to go to college?" It was my last year in the army. I said, "Yes, but I don't have the money." They said, "Report to St. Mary's in September." I did. I told them exactly. I didn't have any clothes at all. So I went and applied. St. Mary's first day: the coach assigned me to a room by myself. I went in there and two-three days later a boy name of Curtis Miller from Cleveland, Texas, came and asked me, "I would like to room with you, Chico." I said, "Well, you can ask the coach." He said yes. During the year—I was the only Meskin—they elected me captain for my sophomore year. I did not take it for this reason. There were too many upper classmen still playing basketball and I was afraid they might be a little envious, jealousy, so I did not take it. My junior year I took it. I played all four years and graduated from there.

At the end of the [first] year I went to the coach and said, "Coach, about next year?" "Oh, you got it." He said, "You can come back." He said, "Chico, remember when you first came here?" I said, "Yes sir." "Do you know why I put you in a room by yourself?" "Yes sir." "Why?" "Because I'm a Meskin." Coach said, "I was afraid that if I put you with someone, he might make a remark and it may hurt you and you might leave us. We need you here. But I'm going to tell you something. You became one of the most popular boys. I want to congratulate you."

Curtis Miller was my roommate my freshman year. The rest of the time, I didn't have any trouble. People asked me to room with them. During Lent—only one meal a day. So the well-to-do boys . . . packages come in. And they would say, "Chico, come to my room tonight. I have food." I was very well-liked and well-treated.

Well, I'm going to tell you something now. In basketball, in those days, so you went to West Texas. So you have here in Alice. You had it here in . . . We went to Abilene to play basketball. And the coach says, "Chico, you're going to room with me." The boys said, "Oh, no, Coach. He's going to room with us. We want him with us." We went to that place [restaurant], NO MEXICANS OR DOGS ALLOWED. The boys said, "Chico is going to eat here. If they don't serve you, we don't eat here." They were very, very supportive.

My father . . . in those days you got by with labor. He worked for the county. Back in those days it was a disgrace for a mother to work.

I started in 1937 and graduated in 1941. Even here in Kingsville, they would call us Mexicans "pepper-chili eater." All kinds of names. And I'm going to tell you something else. At A&I, they didn't allow Spanish-speaking girls to room in dormitories. When they would come to see me eat [means play basketball]—here's one of them [wife] they had a special room [place in the gym] for them. So they could attend [the games]. They had no freedom. They had a special place for them to sit to see me play.

His wife, Celia, was a student at A&I and attended games in which her future husband played. "We did not know each other at the time," Celia said. "I saw his picture in front in a poster. He was holding the ball. We Hispanic girls were eager to see him, because he was the only Hispanic playing. My dream was to study in Denton. My parents said to me, 'Go to Kingsville. Get a temporary teaching certificate.' My parents didn't want me to go to Denton. I graduated in '39. Go two-three years. Get your temporary teaching certificate. You'll get a job out in the country. So I did that. By then my parents will be used to my being away. So I did that. We were in apartments that were a mile from there (Texas A&I, Kingsville). I never met the guy—future husband. We would get together, because they had beautiful uniforms. Big announcement [posters]. He was right in the front holding the basketball. We would get together and we would walk, because it would be at night, to go watch him play. There was a place that had white cardboard. And we would just sit behind there. We had no choice. We had to sit in that special place because we were Hispanic. In the classrooms at A&I the Anglos sat on one side and the Hispanics sat on the other side. I graduated in 1939 from high school. I wanted so much to go to Denton. I got a temporary teaching certificate, and the superintendent gave me a job out in the country. I taught three years in Chilipitin. It is a ranch about ten miles from here [San Diego, Texas]. It was a one-room schoolhouse. I had from kindergarten through eighth grade. They would take me there on a Monday or Sunday night, and they would go after me on Friday night. I stayed at a house. I had some of the children. I graduated from Denton in 1946. We couldn't belong to any clubs. We wanted to move up and reach our goals. I forgave, but I can't forget."

After my first year I didn't have any troubles. They were very nice to me. All the boys were very nice to me. My team was very kind. Very nice to me.

They always had me in publicity that I was kin to Pancho Villa. I was a nephew somewhere back. We went to play in Toledo, Ohio. The girls said, "We want to see the Meskin," Pancho Villa's kin.

I went to Rochester University in St. Louis. I went there. I played basketball and I had a pretty good night. After the game the coach told me, "Go with that man." So I went with him. We went down to a bakery. So he gave me a big butcher knife, big knife, and he said, "Put it under your shirt. So I put it under my shirt. Coach said, "Sit down." After a while he said, "Chico, go in." I went in. I'm not comfortable with that knife by my side. After a while he called me, blew a whistle.

He said, "Raise your hands up." I raised my hands up, so he pulled that knife out of my side. I wasn't particularly being a Mexican kin with Pancho Villa. They had a big kick out of that. They wanted me to go the following year.

I came. I couldn't get a job in that part of the country, because I was a Mexican. I didn't apply in San Antonio but around Moore, Pearsall, and all those places. BA in History. I never taught history. I was going to Benavides, but I stopped here (San Diego, Texas) because of Ben Treviño, superintendent. He had a vacancy here. A guy named Montemayor had resigned. A vacancy in junior high. In those days we taught all classes. Like I taught eighth grade and taught every subject. I taught thirty-eight years and retired in '79. I graduated in 1941.

I will say this . . . When my country needs me to go defend it—if it is worth living in, it is worth defending. I was wounded twice. They drafted me on Nov 13, 1943. I went to Tyler, Texas, seventeen weeks. I went from there—Twenty-Fifth Division, Twenty-Seventh Regiment, Company D. Insignia was a bolt of lightning.

They sent me to California. From there they sent us to New Caledonia, training different men. Fighting in the mountains. From there they sent us to the Philippines on Jan 9, 1945, to invade Luzon. We went into the Lingayen Gulf. We were assigned to go North to Apery. That is mountains. The longer you live you get promoted. I was acting sergeant. I was wounded, knee mortar on Feb 26, 1945. I came back to the front lines after two weeks. Joined the same friends. April 19, 1945, I was wounded again. Lung and leg shrapnel They sent me back to an assembly point. They bring twenty-eight on an airplane. At Hawaii they take four off because it is such a long flight. Less weight and less gasoline. They brought me to California and sent me to Colorado, Fitzgerald General Hospital. I spent sixteen months in the hospital. I have 100 percent disability.

I was wounded at a summer resort, Bagio. People went there in the summer. I was wounded in that area. When we saw Japs coming, we shot them. Then, asked questions later. You couldn't trust them. A Jap can be dead and there are booby traps there.

I am a very proud person that I served my country. Murphy was the person in charge of us. We were together for a few months.

Division was activated in Hawaii. Our general was General "Vinegar Joe" Stillwell. I guarded MacArthur. He had a big place. We had dogs every few feet. He was a big, tall man, well-built. We guarded the CP, command post. He was a God to those people. It was out in the jungle. A square block and he was in the center. We never got near him.

Tokyo Rose flew in an airplane at night. They would play songs and they would tell us that the wives and girlfriends were back with men [here in the States]. And she was saying other things. They tried to get us homesick.

We married in 1947. Celia Benavides. We had a boy who works for the Department of Human Services. A daughter lives in Dallas. One granddaughter, three grandsons, one great-granddaughter.

I coached in San Diego, Texas. In 1964 we were [ranked] third in the state.

We went to Devine, my wife and I, and we had our two children. And people came in. A man, his name was Otis Jones, said to them [some folks], "You see that man sitting over there? He's the best basketball player we ever had in South Texas." And that was me.

John Castillo

487th Battalion, Company A
Antiaircraft

John Castillo was born on July 13, 1921, in Gregory, Texas, to José and Juan-ita Castillo. In 1930 John's family moved to Houston, Texas. Because of his training in the CCC, Civilian Conservation Corps, John had no trouble ad-justing to basic training. He would become acquainted with the Japanese method of fighting, including kamikaze suicide airplanes.

I had attended school in Victoria and continued in Houston. I finished junior high and went to the Civilian Conservation Corps [CCC], because at that time I was making $30 a month. Twenty-two dollars went to my mother, and I kept $8 to buy whatever we needed for the month. My fa-ther was alive, but steady jobs were hard to get. The Depression years. I was with the CCC for one year and worked at Zavala, Texas, near Lufkin. We planted trees, fought fires, built roads, and did just about any kind of work. We lived in an army-type camp. We had reveille in the morning, calisthenics, breakfast in the morning, and were assigned jobs and classes to learn different things.

It wasn't hard to get accustomed to the army because [CCC] had regu-lations. I got out of the CCC in December 1939. In 1940 in February I was married. I was eighteen. My wife was fifteen. We were not supposed to stay long together, and we stayed sixty years.

When I first tried to volunteer, I couldn't go because I was already mar-ried, even though we didn't have a child at that time. So I didn't think I was going to go. When I got drafted, I already had a five-month-old baby. They paid my wife $90 and $60 for the baby so she wouldn't have to worry.

My mother and my father gave me *la bendición* at home. They went with me and my wife to the train station and my mother was still praying. There was a couple there. We were *compadres* and we had baptized their baby. My compadre said, "Don't worry. The war is going to be over real quick, and you will be home before you know it." Eight or nine months later I found out that he had gone [into the service] and had already gotten killed. He was killed in Italy. And he was the one trying to give me courage.

I went to San Antonio. From there I went to Camp Haan in California. I was supposed to go to antiaircraft school, 487th Battalion, Company A. That's where I was first indoctrinated into the army. They told us all the rules and regulations. Basic training was in the Mojave Desert in Fort Irwin in California. Lots of space. We were with the 40mm gun, which we pulled on a trailer with trucks. Lateral gun pointer and lateral tracker on the M5 director attached to the 40mm gun. You fire with the director or you fire manually.

When you get the plane on the crosshairs, then you tell the director on target and they give the order to start firing the gun. I'm pointing. It takes four people to operate plus the ammunition carriers. The gunner presses something with his foot. If the plane gets out of range, we get an order to cease fire. We gave the information to the range setter and he was the one who commanded the gun.

In California we had to dig a hole, put the gun in a hole. Then you camouflaged it with terrain. We could fire from that. Then we'd get orders to move out. Then we went to dig a hole somewhere else.

Once you got overseas, you didn't do that. You'd get in one position and you would stay there. The sergeants were strict but they weren't all that mean. Many were not regular army. They were civilians just like us. Eleven months of training.

We embarked from Portland, Oregon, and went to San Pedro Harbor in California and waited for another ship. We started out in March 1944. We ended up in New Guinea with the army. Port Moresby was our first stop. From there we went to Finschhafen, Dutch New Guinea. That's where we got all our gear that we were going to use in battle.

From there we left for our first invasion. Namoor Island. After the island was taken, they built two airstrips, one for the fighter planes and one for the bombers. We were there to guard them. About fifteen people and four different guns, about sixty soldiers, but we were separated. We were spaced out. We were guarding the strips right near the ocean. We stayed there a good while because the bombers were going out and bombing Borneo. The fighters would escort them part of the way. The fighter pilots were from Australia. The bombers were Americans. The fighter planes could take a torpedo and drop it on a boat, but there was no need for it.

After we left that island, other units were taking other islands. After an island was taken we would go there. From there we would get ready to go to another island. We took our guns on the landing crafts to the next island to guard air strips. We knocked down some planes.

Then we went to the Philippine Islands. About that time President Roosevelt died. We heard it on the ship. We took a small island, Mindanao. That was in 1945. At that time they had already landed people in Leyte and some of the Northern Islands. We saw MacArthur in Hollandia. He had been in Leyte. I saw a bunch of people coming in and getting off landing crafts.

In New Guinea the natives were primitive. You would see them and you wouldn't get near them, because it was against our rules to get near them. We'd see them walking down the road, the women carrying things on their shoulders and the men would be carrying spears. They stayed to themselves. They were happy there weren't any Japanese but they weren't friendly to anybody.

The Philippines were different. A lot of the people had gone away from the city and had gone up into the mountains to live up there during the invasion. Some stayed and collaborated with the Japanese.

When we got to Mindanao, the people would tell us that so and so was a collaborator. We were stationary, getting ready to invade Japan. When the bomb was dropped and then the second bomb was dropped, I was asked if I wanted to go with the occupation forces. I had a child and was married, so I had enough points to come home. That was my choice, to come home.

I left the Philippines in November 1945. December 14 landed there in San Francisco. The Red Cross had doughnuts and coffee. We went down the channel to Pittsburgh to debrief.

Some of the Filipinos looked like Spanish people. Some were Oriental looking. Hard to understand [their] Spanish.

At the last I heard that General Wainwright was held prisoner for four years. When he came out he looked like a skeleton.

I was never wounded. Sometimes the Japanese would crash into landing crafts and battleships. I saw a kamikaze hit a landing craft. We were in a bigger landing craft. They were almost at the beach when they got hit.

Some of the Japanese would shoot at us from coconut trees. Snipers. Some of the Japanese would get shot and they would just hang from the tree because they had been tied up in the tree. They told us about banzai and to stay in our foxholes and to put bayonets on our guns. Don't fire. [This was at night.] You might hit someone you know. Nothing happened but the next morning we found out that a raiding party had gone into our kitchen trying to get food.

When things would get quiet you would go to sleep and you'd hear planes coming in at night. They'd wake us up.

There was a tribe in Mindanao called Moros, Muslims. Not Catholic like the other Filipinos. They weren't friendly at all; they were hostile. They used to have marketplaces. They would sell things and would overcharge. Mindanao is one of the biggest islands.

I had a friend, Mario Ramon. I met him in California. He was from Fort Worth. He was a range setter in my gun section. When we came back we were separated in the Philippines. He came to Houston one time. He was a good friend. He was in a meat-cutters' union. He used to work with Swift. He was a union representative. Every time he'd come, we'd eat together. Then he was a mediator.

Everyone was glad to see me back. Went to visit where I had worked before. I had worked for a buckle company. Went back and worked there for a while. I went to school and learned watch repairing, then electroplating. I did that nineteen years. I went to work with boilermakers, and I ended up working for a company that made railroad cars. Richmond Tank Car Company. I was the foreman there. We made them for train companies and for people who leased them.

We had four kids in all. All kids are here, but one child is in Austin.

I retired at sixty-five. I had lost a lot of time. It took civilians and service people to win the war.

Domingo Treviño
3rd Army Air Corps
66th Army Air Corps

Taking Aerial Shots
Domingo Treviño was born in Hempstead, Texas, on August 4, 1921, to Zacarías and Anastacia Gutierrez Treviño. His father worked on a farm

owned by Will Bennet, a judge, who eventually gave Mr. Treviño thirty acres. Out of twelve children born to the Treviños, only five survived. Their mother died in 1925. In 1927 the Treviños moved to Houston, where Zacarías wanted the children to attend a Catholic school. When he found out there was a charge, he said he couldn't afford to pay tuition. Domingo attended Elliot Elementary and Denver Harbor schools. Domingo began working at age fourteen. He turned out to be such a good worker that his employer did not want him to leave, even though Domingo had received his draft notice. That dedication transferred to his work as a soldier.

My sister got married, and we went to Mexico and stayed there. I was only fourteen. When my father remarried, that left us as orphans. I stayed there six months. Me and my brother decided to come back.

We came back to Houston and went to work. I started looking for a job and I was only fourteen years old. My daddy had a home here. That's where we stayed. I started working and worked for a hotel and at a motel and for a demolishing company. I was too light and couldn't handle the machinery. I was a washman.

A friend told me that they were hiring at a coat hanger company and he said to come on over. I went to work for Nagel Coat Hanger Company in 1937. I worked myself up until I was in a pretty good position. I was eighteen when I met my future wife. Since I was alone we were married in 1941 when I was twenty. My father had to sign for me because I wasn't old enough. We didn't have any children.

Here's what happened. I got married in August of 1941. The Japanese bombed Pearl Harbor in December 1941. At the [coat hanger] plant they had already taken the foreman, and they left me in that place. They took another fellow who was in charge of another department into the service, too. I became the foreman.

I finally got my draft notice in 1942. Mr. Nagel said, "Mingo, I can't afford to let you go. I have no foremen. I'm going to take it to Austin. You are already married." We went to Austin and saw a captain. He said, "I sure wish I could help but we don't need hangers; we need men who can fight."

I came back. John Castillo and I went in together and we both made it back. My sister gave me *la bendición,* and she gave me a *rezo,* a prayer card: *la sombra de San Pedro.* I still carry it all the time with me. I carry this rosary, which my wife gave me. It has been with me.

They sent me to San Antonio. It was real cold. It was December 5, 1943. It was cold and raining. They would put us in a room to check us and then we would go back out in the rain again. We come back into the warm room. On the second day I had a really bad cold. On the third day they took us out on a hike. I was really sick, coughing real bad. On the fourth or fifth day they lined us all up and a lieutenant came by. He said, "Okay you guys, you are going to be shipped out of here." I didn't want to lose my friends. I had already four friends who were going without me. The lieutenant said, "You look sick." I said, "I'm not sick."

He said, "I'll tell you what—go to the infirmary and get a slip saying you are all right because we are going to Ohio and the snow there is up to your moustache. By the way did anyone tell you to shave your moustache?" I said no. He said, "I'm a Lt. and they don't let me grow one."

I went into the infirmary and they told me I had pneumonia. They put me in a hospital. I stayed there ten days. That was miracle number one. I call it that way because I stayed behind and didn't go where the rest of them went.

They sent me with a bunch of fellows from A&M [Texas A&M]. They gave me an IQ test—it was about machinery, and I was familiar with all of that. My IQ was 115. They put me in the army air corps. They sent me to Wichita Falls, Texas, Sheppard Field. They gave me my basic training in about four weeks. Calisthenics training and all of that.

Then they put me through school to be an airplane mechanic. Code number 748.

My hours to go to school were from 11:00 at night to 7:00 in the morning. They were putting three crews through that. They put us in groups. Thirty-eight or forty men to a group.

When I first got to Sheppard Field with all those guys from A&M, one of those guys was named Thomas Pickett and the other was Ed Ducett. When we first got there they put Thomas Pickett, a graduate of A&M, in charge. He lined us all up and said, "Okay, I want all the Mexicans over on one side." I just stood there. He looked at me and said, "I'm talking to you."

I said, "Wait a minute. You're not talking to me. I'm just as American as you are." He said, "All right. All right. You can stay there."

From there on I stayed with this group. The other guys were out there marching by themselves. After I finished the airplane mechanic school I came up with real good grades. I still have records of my grades. I think I did well because I was a married man and I had nothing to distract me.

When we finished I went through gunnery school in Tyndall Field in Panama City, Florida. We trained there with shotguns and we were flying. Shooting in the air at targets. We took machine guns apart and put them back together again while blindfolded. I came in second in my class. In our shotgun training I also came up second in my class. So I did real good in gunnery school.

They sent us to Salt Lake City—the Eighteenth Replacement Wing. They would put you in a crew—pilot, copilot, navigator, bombardier, radio man, flight engineer (my qualification), and then the gunners.

On the third day they told us, "We want some volunteers to play football for our squadron," and I volunteered. They made me a halfback. The quarterback said, "We need a yard." I said, "Give me the ball and I'll go over the top."

I went over the top and when I hit the ground—this was in December and it was real cold—I knew something was wrong. A whole bunch fell on top. I knew something was wrong with my leg. They said, "Get up." I started sweating.

They took me to the infirmary and put me on a table. The doctor looked at me and said, "This bone here is way down there. You've got a completely dislocated shoulder."

So they wrapped me up and put me to sleep. When I woke up I was bandaged from here to here. I lost all my friends. They all took off. All those crews they had put together left. And I stayed behind. My wife followed me from post to post.

My wife started getting letters from the wives of the men who went to Europe. A lot of those men got killed. My friends. Some that were coming back used to tell me to go into town with them. I said that I was afraid to fall. They said, "We'll take you." They found out that whenever they took me all bandaged up, everything was free.

When I got well, I was put into a crew but not as a flight engineer, because there was already a group there. I became an assistant flight engineer. My job was to start the auxiliary power and take the generators off the power they were on and put them in auxiliary power. I had to check the tank. My job was to maintain the balance of the plane.

From there I went to Castle, Wyoming, to train for heavy bombardment. I became the photographer on the plane. I would get on my stomach. The guys would hold my feet. And I would stick my head out of the bottom of the plane. When the bombardier would say, "bombs away," I would count thirty seconds. Then I would start taking pictures. So they could see the targets they were hitting. We were training. For almost two months. One time I got my skin frozen because the temperature up there is thirty degrees below zero. It didn't hurt much.

We lost some planes. My wife used to stay in town and they used to wonder whose plane went down. They had malfunctions.

I was credited with saving the bombardier's life. He had a real bad cold. Once up in the air. I told him not to go up if he didn't feel good. He went up. Only ones who had contact with the mikes was me, the bombardier, and the pilot. I kept calling the bombardier, and he didn't answer. I called the pilot and told him something was wrong because he [the bombardier] is not answering.

He said, "Why don't you take your deals off and go up there and see what's wrong." When I went up there and since he had a cold, he had the oxygen mask on. He pulled it off to blow his nose and he didn't realize it. He forgot to put it back on. He passed out; his nails were purple. I put that thing back on him and he came to again.

From there we went to go overseas. We didn't know where we were going but all the crews that finished that training were ready to go overseas. We went home for a furlough for two weeks in Houston with my wife.

When I got back to Casper, Wyoming, they had four crews up in the morning. I was in crew two. They said these four crews are not going nowhere. We said, "What do you mean? We're not going overseas?" "No, you're not." "Why?" we asked. They said, "Something's happened and we are sending you to Will Rogers in Oklahoma City." They said, "Y'all are going to train for photo reconnaissance. Long-Range photo reconnaissance."

When we got to Oklahoma, they made me the photographer. I had a box with me that would fit on the plane. I was with the navigator. Every time he would say, "Go ahead," I would start taking pictures. What they call "mosaic pictures." I would take one every forty seconds. We were flying low. Then they would make another run and another run—up to four runs. When we got back I would go to the darkroom and develop those films. Then I put them altogether and they would make one big picture and that's how they would know what's down there. We were just about through with that training. This is in 1944, and we were still training. But the middle of 1944 that's when they sent us to Oklahoma City. When I got to Oklahoma City and we were just about to get into—they said hold everything. They had a big typhoon in the Pacific. It did a lot of damage to ships, boats, and they're having problems. The B-29s are going to start flying over Japan. Out of the Marianas. They are losing them. They go over there. They can't do anything. They get lost. The storm, the weather, and everything. We have to have long-range weather reconnaissance. That's my crew. Flight A, Crew Two.

Our missions were flying from the city. We were flying from New Orleans to Galveston and come back home. It would take us about twelve hours. We didn't carry bombs. We carried fuel tanks. So that we could go the distance. Training.

After we got through with that they sent us back to Will Rogers Field. From there we had to fly to Savannah, Georgia, to pick up our new B-24Js. Modern fighter planes that were completely for weather and combat.

When we took off from Oklahoma City, we had all our gear—everything in our possession, and we had fuel tanks to fly all the way to Savannah, Georgia, and we had at least sixty-two thousand pounds of weight on that plane. It was very heavy. Some colonel got the idea—since we were making history—we were going to be the first weather reconnaissance plane going up—he said, "We want the first plane to take off and the second to take off right behind it."

So that's how we took off from Oklahoma City. I don't see nothing when we are taking off [the second plane]. When we got up and I went to the back and I saw these guys. I said, "What the heck is going on?" I saw these guys in the back of the plane, and they were white as a sheet. They said, "We almost got killed. We almost hit the ground at takeoff."

What happened is the first plane—the slip string, the hair knocked us down. It went completely down and tipped it over to one side and hit. In the bottom of the plane is a little round thing and it only sticks out this much from the bottom. That hit the ground. The left engine bent that much. The wing barely touched the ground. The copilot was very smart;

he pulled the wheels or they would have cracked because there was no more runway. We got up and circled around and they asked the pilot if everything was OK and he said yes. We ran into a storm and had to land in Biloxi, Mississippi. We got out in Biloxi and looked at the plane and couldn't believe we had made it. That's how close we came to crashing.

We went to a Board of Inquiries and they questioned everyone on the plane except me, because I didn't see nothing. It was so cold in Mississippi. I pulled guard at night on New Year's Eve. From there we went off to Savannah, stayed three weeks and waited for a new plane. After we got a new B-24 plane with a ball turret and everything, we took off and landed in San Francisco and then took off again and landed in Clark Field in Hawaii.

January 1945, we flew up to Johnson Island and then to Kwajalein Island. And then we went to Guam. Our HQ. We became the Fifty-Fifth Weather Reconnaissance Squadron, attached to the Twentieth Air Force. We were a self-contained group. We had our own mess hall, doctor, priest, mechanics. We had our own personnel. We were on our own. We were the first four planes that started flying out of Guam. Every fourth day we would fly. At that time the marines were taking Iwo Jima.

You should have seen all the soldiers that were coming out of there. The wounded. They were taking them to a hospital near us. The last banzai attack—two hundred Japanese—on Iwo Jima—after they had been taken over. They stayed in caves in the back. We were supposed to fly over there because they were going to put fighter planes there. And they wanted us to fly over Japan for the fighters . . . [To look over the weather] so they could go bomb and strafe and all that.

They told us to go and we got our plane ready. I got up there and put the generators off and one engine wouldn't go. We tried and tried and tried. They "scratched" us and put another crew in our place. They said they had the scare of their lives when they went over there. They said the Japanese had taken their sabers and were just running through with them like this through the tents. They [the Japanese] all got killed.

The plane flew seven missions [to Japan] out of Iwo Jima, from 10:00 p.m. through 10:00 am. They checked the weather and turned in the information to the meteorologists, who would then send the information to Guam and to the armed forces.

I flew a day and a half before they dropped the first bomb [Hiroshima] and I flew a day and a half before they dropped the second bomb [Nagasaki]. We were flying for the fighter squadrons on Iwo Jima. They're the ones we were mainly flying [to find out about] the weather. They had B-47s and B-51s there on Iwo Jima. They would send them over to Japan if they could do any good. If the weather was not right they wouldn't go at all.

I'm not saying that we flew so they could drop the bomb; I'm just saying that they knew from our weather reports that there was no way they would drop it if the weather was bad.

We were told afterward that they were thinking of dropping it in Tokyo Bay. They would have killed less people. It would have killed a lot of military people. Navy, Army.

I have a child I baptized. She's graduated from St. Edwards and she won't even talk to me because I told her one day that we had dropped the bomb over there. She said we were murderers.

Discharged in Oct 1945. I was awarded the Distinguished Flying Cross and the air medal with two Oak leaf clusters. Asian Pacific Theater and three bronze service stars. I had enough points to be discharged.

I came back to work with Mr. Nagel. Wire and wood hangers. Chain link manufacturing. They got real, real big. Thirty-seven years with the company. They broke up the company. Sold the fence company. I came back and was in purchasing—they gave me all the books for purchasing and I learned all about it, and then I was personnel manager for seventeen years. I purchased from all over the world, even Japan.

I only had a sixth-grade education. I had one of the best men [bosses] in the world here. He taught me so much and he was so smart.

Retired eighteen years. They called me day before yesterday and want me to come have Thanksgiving Dinner with all the employees. Gerald Nagel was the boss. All his people are from Fredericksburg.

Married sixty-one years. Four daughters. Oldest is in Scottsdale. Second daughter here in Houston. Third daughter a research scientist—was with De-Bakey and Cooley. Now she is with a technology company. The other works in Austin—supervisor for the highway department. Graduated from St. Edwards. President of Highway Department Association. She goes out and makes speeches.

Last eight years I've been a chaplain for military honors [at funerals]. Granddaughter will go to college in Austin, Texas. Grandson is Chris Salmeron in Coast Guard in Corpus Christi.

Reynaldo Perez Gallardo
Squadron 201

Mexico Helps the USA

Reynaldo Perez Gallardo was born in San Luis Potosí on August 10, 1923. His father, General Reynaldo Perez Gallardo Sr., was a career man in the army [ejército]. During the revolution Gallardo Sr. fought with Obregón's army. Reynaldo, a Mexican citizen and a pilot, fought for the USA when Mexico joined the Allies. Although it was late in the war, the Mexican Airmen made an impact in the Pacific theater.

I had one brother and one sister. The family traveled with General Gallardo, our father, as he moved from one military assignment to another.

During WWII the Germans sank three Mexican oil tankers in the Gulf of Mexico. The tankers were on their way [to be sold] to the United States. As a result, Mexico reacted by declaring war on the Axis powers.

I had been a part of the cavalry since 1939. However, I had joined the cavalry with the assurance that this would lead me to the Mexican Air Force. After Mexico declared war on the Axis powers, airmen came to the United States to train.

My mother, a devoutly religious person, administered *la bendición* to me.

I trained in Corsicana, Texas, Waco, and finally Eagle Pass. Matagorda Bay, near Brownsville, Texas, was also training for gunnery and bombing ranges.

In Eagle Pass I received my wings. I then returned to Mexico to instruct in Mexican Air Flight School.

Three months later, *Escuadrón* 201 was formed. It consisted of 333 men, twenty-four airplanes, mechanics, communications men, ammunition, and twenty-eight pilots. The airplanes were fighter planes and accommodated only one pilot. During training two pilots died. In the war eight pilots died in combat. [Squadron 201 flew primarily in the Pacific theater and distinguished themselves as effective soldiers.]

After the war the soldiers returned to Mexico with great acclaim and much celebration. I remained in the service and retired twenty-five years ago. My wife Angelina and I live in Austin, Texas, where two sons and two grandsons also live.

PART III

Prisoners of War

Carlos Tomás McDermott
200 Coast Artillery

Philippine Field Artillery

This is the written account of Carlos McDermott, deceased, which was presented to the editor by his wife for publication in this book.

My name is Carlos Tomás McDermott. I was born in San Diego, Texas, on April 16, 1918, to Juan F. McDermott and Virginia S. McDermott. I attended schools in San Diego, Texas. I was drafted on April 16, 1941. My draft card number was 137, and my army serial number was 38031462. My first training was in Dodd Field, San Antonio, Texas; then I transferred to Camp Wallace. I completed my thirteen weeks of training there. From there I was sent to the 200 Coast Artillery, Regimental Headquarters in Fort Bliss, Texas. The 200 Coast Artillery was composed of the National Guard of New Mexico. After more training, we were sent to Fort Stotsenburg, Clark Field, Luzon Island in the Philippines before the war.

On December 7, 1941, Pearl Harbor was bombed. The next morning Fort Stotsenburg and Clark Field were bombed. All of our planes in Clark Field were destroyed. That same day I was transferred to the Philippine Field Artillery, which was composed of four half-tracks with 75 millimeter guns and one water-cooled .30-caliber machine gun. I was under the command of Lt. Crawford. The second day after joining the Philippine Field Artillery, we were sent to meet the enemy in Northern Luzon and fight a delay action war while our troops were moved to Bataan for a better position.

After days of fighting and retreating we fought our last stand in Lengayen. In the Bay of Lengayen the Japanese had twenty-two transports and about four cruisers, but the water was too rough for them to land. We fought them until daylight at which time we were all surrounded. We retreated to San Fernando and from there to Baguio. In Baguio we joined what was left of our outfit. With the few American soldiers that were stationed in Baguio and the few Philippine Army [soldiers] we retreated to Itogon, a small mining town south of Baguio. We spent the night there, but figuring it wasn't safe, we retreated to a saw mill on top of the mountains with all our equipment. From there we destroyed all of our equipment, except guns and ammunition. Trucks and half-tracks were dumped down the mountain. From there on we were infantry. We traveled the mountains of Baguio through trails for two nights and two days until we reached Cabanatuan.

From Cabanatuan we traveled to the southern part of Luzon where we were met by buses. Who sent them or how they were informed of our position, I do not know. They took us to Bataan and we were left in the little town of Mexico. That night the Japanese attacked our front lines. We had been in the front lines for a month and were sent further down to Mariveles to rest. We stayed there for about four days and were sent back to our 200 Coast Artillery, though what was left of it was nothing. We were bombed day and night. Our last stand was in Mariveles. We fought that night, and in the morning General King and his staff surrendered to the Japanese. He gave us orders to destroy our guns and ammunition by throwing them into the river. We were given the choice of surrendering or escaping into the mountains. In the mountains you were on your own. We were surrendered not for lack of men or ammunition but for hunger.

For about four weeks we had been eating one meal a day and sometimes not even that, just water. We were all very weak, and it was known that no help was on its way. We waited in the woods until a Japanese tank loaded with soldiers appeared on the road. I was ordered to stand in the middle of the road with a white towel above me and that the rest would emerge later. The tank approached pointing its barrel at my forehead, and all the Japanese soldiers surrounded me. The kept talking to me but no telling what they said. It seemed ages until the rest of the soldiers came out with their hands above their heads.

We were put in groups of one thousand men. Our group was put on top of a hill, and they put their field artillery right below us and opened fire to the island of Corregidor, which was on the other side of us. The American field artillery in Corregidor was very good, and they would fire above our heads and hit the Japanese directly. Their aiming was never wrong; there was not a single casualty in our group. From there they marched us down the road to prison. They were supposed to carry us in trucks because there were enough trucks and gas from the other troops that were not destroyed, but the Japs decided to eliminate some of us because we were too many. That's where the Bataan Death March began.

The Japanese infantry came to where we were being held. The guards would come to take us to prison and took all our pens, watches, blankets, and billfolds. In fact, some of our canteens, and the ones they didn't take, they threw the water out of them.

From April 9 to April 16 we marched day and night without food or water. After the first day of marching we stopped to change guard under some mango trees with a big shade and lots of fruit. One of our boys climbed the tree to get fruit for everybody. As soon as one of the Jap guards saw him, he raised his rifle and shot him. We traveled all night so we were very dirty, and when we passed a water well, some of the boys went to get a helmet full of water. One of the Jap guards opened fire and killed two of the boys. These wells were made by the government for the travelers to have water. They were right by the side of the road.

Most of the men were so weak they just fell on the road and were bayoneted. There was nothing we could do; just keep on going. All of us were so weak we were trying our best to survive. When we go to Oran, we were put on the school grounds that were fenced all around. While they changed guard one Japanese guard called me and a boy from the Thirty-First Infantry and gave us a shovel each. He then took us to where two Phillippinos (Filipinos) lay almost dead. They had been beaten by the Japs. There was a latrine trench close to them, and he told us to put them in the trench and cover them with dirt. I told him that they were still alive. Then he pointed the rifle with fixed bayonet at me, so we started covering them up. One Filipino tried to get out, and the Jap hit him with a pick handle on the head and he passed out. This was done in front of lots of civilians that were looking at us.

When we arrived at Camp O'Donnell, my first prison camp, we were given our first meal and plenty of water. We were assembled for our speech by the Japanese Camp Commander and his interpreter. In his speech there were some words that I never forget: "You all are not our prisoners; you are our captors [captives] and our slaves. You will work wherever we put you to work, and if you refuse to work, you will be shot by a firing squad for refusing to obey orders from the Imperial Japanese Army." And believe me, he meant every word he said. We were treated like slaves all the time we were there.

When General King surrendered, we were about 20,000 American soldiers and 50,000 Philippine soldiers. We lost very few of our men in battle, but when we surrendered, we lost more than half of our men in prison and in the Death March for lack of food, water, and medicine. Others were tortured to death or killed in firing squads. Some were killed by US submarines and airplanes when they were being taken by ships to Japan. These ships were not marked that they were carrying prisoners. Our submarines and airplanes sank quite a few loaded with prisoners of war.

When we were in Camp O'Donnell the Philippine soldiers were held prisoners across the road from us and we would see their burial detail. They were dying [at a rate of] about 500 a day. They died from lack of food and water.

We rested the first night and the next day they started us on a schedule. Three meals a day, but it was nothing else but rice, steamed rice with no salt or spices. We got used to it. We stayed about a month and were then transferred to the Cabanatuan POW camp. The hospital area was fenced outside of the prison camp. I had wet and dry beriberi, dysentery, scurvy, [and] malaria. You name it and I had it. We were made to sit all day in the hot sun waiting to be taken to the hospital area, which was only about three hundred feet away. There was no medicine, only nature to take its course. The only medication was water and very little food because the Japanese believed that anyone that was sick and not able to work should not eat. I was sent to the zero ward in the hospital. When you were sent there your chances of survival were less than ten percent. Every morning there were about forty or fifty dead prisoners. We would not report them dead until the afternoon so that their rations would be brought. We would then divide their rations among the living. After about three months in the hospital zero ward, I was sent back to work. I weighed 98 pounds. The work there was clearing land, about 700 acres, planting, and making dams. Everything was man-made. Dirt was hauled in baskets to build the dams and all land [was] worked with pick and shovel except the rice paddies. I worked with pick and shovel for about eight months. We planted corn, cucumbers, sweet potatoes, tomatoes, watermelons, and okra, but we never tasted any of that. We just planted; what the Japanese did with it, I do not know. Our menu was rice, sweet potato vine soup or whistle weed soup, which was a weed that grew by the roadside. Once in a while we would get a piece of horse meat; but their ration was about five pounds to a hundred men so it didn't even amount to a spoonful. After that I worked with a plow and caribous. They had about fifty plows and about a hundred caribous. Each man had two caribous and one plow. You used one caribou at a time. The other had to be soaking in water to cool off. You changed every thirty minutes. We plowed the soil with mud up to our knees day in and day out, but it was a little better than working with a pick and shovel.

While being in Cabanatuan, one of our fellow prisoners escaped. The next morning the Japanese made a roll call and picked nine men from the group. They were put in solitary for seventy-two hours, and if the escaped man did not appear at the end of the seventy-two hours, they took them across the fence, made them dig their own graves, and shot them into their own graves. The next day all prisoners were issued a number. Mine was "*yaco san u hashi*," which meant 138. It was for a buddy system. For example, any man that escaped from 131 to 140, the other nine would be shot in seventy-two hours. As far as I know, that was the only man that escaped from the Cabanatuan Prison Camp. Others were killed by firing squads but for other reasons.

After about two years in Cabanatuan I was transferred to *Las Piñas* to make airfields for trainers' airplanes. They were training pilots on airplanes something like a piper cub. We leveled hills and creeks with picks and shovels and mining cars. We had almost finished the airfield when the American Navy dive bombers came and bombed everything that was in that area except us. When they came we signaled them and they tipped their wings. I guess our message was received because they destroyed their airplanes in Clark Field and all the boats in the bay. The next day the Japanese got the boats that were left in the island. There were about twenty-eight small boats in all. They moved them to Manila Bay, loaded us prisoners into the boat hold and covered us. They told us that when the Americans came they would bomb and kill all of us. We sat there for two days and two nights during which time they stole all they could from the Philippines.

After they loaded the boats with all they could we sailed off. When we turned at the Island of Luzon towards Japan, American submarines came and started torpedoing the biggest boats. So they changed course and we went to Hong Kong, China. We stayed there about a week, and they again changed course because the American submarines were still following.

We then went to Taiwan. In all the time of sailing and staying in one place, we actually stayed forty-one days and nights in the boat. We were eating one meal a day, and our water was rationed to half a canteen cup a day per man. Men that had fever and malaria would go delirious. They would drink their own urine, but they wouldn't survive more than two days. So we tried to prevent anyone from doing that. Some got so thirsty they would swallow their own tongues. We would get a spoon and pull their tongues back and give them one or two spoons of water from our ration.

We were so crowded that we couldn't even stand up. At night since it was so dark, some would try to stand up to stretch their legs, but it was immediately felt since the heat from their bodies would block the little air circulating. The men that died were buried at sea. During that time at sea our boat came to some island. There the Japanese said that the very sick could get off and stay on that island and that the Americans would pick them up. There were many that got into the life-saving boats and taken to the island. When they got on the island all were machine-gunned.

In Taiwan we were loaded at some harbor. I do not remember its name. The Americans had just bombed the place and there were boats sunk in the harbor and smoke all over, nothing left but a sheet metal shed by the water. We were put in there, but it was so cold we couldn't go to sleep because if we did, we would freeze to death. We had no blankets and had to sit on damp concrete. As usual, very little food. We were kept a week there and then taken to a school house quite a few miles from there. That was a little better. It was a nice building with stone walls and not so cold. Here we were issued some clothing since all we were wearing was a G-string. From the time we surrendered we wore our army uniforms until they rotted. Then we were issued G-strings. The clothing we got were a pair of pants and a coat-like shirt made of something like burlap and a pair of tennis shoes. Our hair was always kept shaved because of lice.

Here again we cultivated the land and planted. We stayed here for about three months and then the Americans started coming. We were loaded on the boats again and took off towards Japan. I was lucky to be loaded in a small boat again. The big boats were sunk. In fact, the last boat to be sunk was before we got to the lighthouse in Tokyo Bay. The American submarines had followed all the way.

When we landed in Tokyo and were unloaded it was so cold that a number of our men caught pneumonia and died immediately. The boat hold was very hot and we came out to below-freezing temperatures. That night we were put on a train and taken to some town. From there we walked to the mining town of Odate. There we worked on open pit mines from which they mined zinc and ore. There was always snow to our stockade and on the outside had about six feet of snow all the time. Every day we removed the snow from the road with shovels since it would snow so much at night. As usual we were very poorly clothed, still wearing tennis shoes to work. By evening we were all muddy with melted snow, our toes frozen and very cold.

There were some Chinese prisoners that had been there for over twelve years. They were separated from us completely, and they worked in shaft mines. Once in a while some of our prisoners who could speak as many as seven languages would get in contact with them and they would tell us the score.

After being there about a year, the American marines landed in Aomori and the Japanese surrendered. The Japs never told us the war had ended, but we knew something was going on. The Japanese treatment of us was much better. And then on that wonderful day we saw an Air Force US Airplane over us. We signaled them and they dropped a message saying they would be back shortly with food and clothing. And they dropped plenty. We ate that day and night and each of us got two or three pairs of shoes and plenty of clothing.

The Japs took us in a train to Aomori and turned us over to the marines. The marines put us in LSD boats and took us to Tokyo. There, airplanes took us to Okinawa, fourteen to an airplane. We slept there that night and the next day were flown to the Philippines. When we landed in Clark Field the Red Cross was waiting, including doctors, which treated us splendidly. From there we had our choice of flying or sailing back to the United States. Since I decided to come back by boat, I had to wait fifteen days in the Philippines. Arrived in San Francisco and was taken to Letterman Hospital for a week. On October 19, 1945, we were put in a hospital train and brought to San Antonio, Texas. After check-ups and a short stay in Brooks General Hospital, I was sent home. I went back to the hospital for more check-ups until I got my discharge on June 23, 1946.

I was a prisoner of war from April 9, 1942 to September 10, 1945. The horrors of war and being a prisoner of the Japanese can never really be told. Maybe that is why I appreciate freedom so much and I will always fight for it.

(I am recording this tape in the presence of my wife Ninfa C. McDermott and my two sons Carlos T. McDermott, Jr. and David A. McDermott on this day of January, 1976. My home address is 812 E. Gravis Avenue, San Diego, Texas 78384. Carlos T. McDermott)

Vicente Molina
1st Armored Division
81st Company

Promise: Just One Year of Service
Vicente Molina was born in Laredo, Texas, on December 21, 1919, to Alberto and Enemencia Reyes Molina. He had two brothers and three sisters. Vicente quit school after the ninth grade and worked with the Civilian Conservation Corps from 1937 to 1938. After that he worked on a farm as a laborer. Vicente volunteered for the service with the comfort of knowing that it was a one-year commitment. There was no way anyone could predict that almost two of his total years in the army would be spent incarcerated on enemy land.

I volunteered on February 10, 1941, during peacetime. My obligation was for one year. My father said, "Wait until they call you." My mother said, "I don't want you to go," and she gave me *la bendición*.

I trained at Fort Knox, Kentucky, and one day during training we heard of a place called Pearl Harbor and that the Japanese had bombed this US territory. We busied ourselves with strict maneuvers in North Carolina, South Carolina, and near Memphis, Tennessee. Once, during training, the tanks kicked up so much dust that the driver of a tank couldn't see. He drove over an embankment and the men in the tank were killed. The news of Pearl Harbor caused all furloughs to be cancelled.

I shipped out on the *Queen Mary* on May 18, 1942. The ship docked in North Ireland. We spent three and a half months in Ireland. Then we spent two months in England, again in maneuvers.

From Liverpool we flew to Oran, North Africa. Out of about two hundred men in our company there were from fifty to sixty Mexican Americans. Gustavo Perez of Corpus Christi, Texas, was one of the men.

We passed over Spain and saw lots of lights. Some American boys bailed out over Spain and planned to spend their war years there, but they were caught later.

On January 1, 1943, in North Africa we fought Italians. The Germans placed some French men in front to fight for them.

On February 17, 1943, we were fighting the Germans. It was a hard battle. The German tanks were about to run over us. When they saw we were losing, some American soldiers tried to run away, and the Germans took their machine guns and mowed them down. Our Company A officers came out with a white flag. So then we all came out and surrendered.

We walked for two days with little food and not enough water until we reached Tunisia. From there we flew to *Stalag* 7A. A one-armed German officer interviewed me. I said, "Pvt. Vicente Molina, # 38027213." The German gave me a cigarette and was very nice to me. He kept asking me what I was doing. I just said, "I got lost. I tried to get away and got caught." Finally, he let me go. They were interrogating everyone to see what they could find out. We stayed one month.

They took us by cattle car to *Stalag* 3B. At the top of the cattle car, there was a window, which is where we got air. There were no benches to sit on, and it was very crowded. The officers stayed in quarters different from ours. Gabriel Cerda, one of the guys in our company, gave the officers haircuts.

At *Stalag* 3B, Spinelli [Angelo], an American, was a wheeler-dealer. He could deal with the Germans and get anything. We had a radio, which the Germans found and took. He took pictures and hid his camera in his clothes. Some Americans were friendly with the Germans and the other American soldiers got angry with them. They called them "Gerry Lovers." Then there would be a fight.

Every morning the Germans would have a roll count. One morning a German officer saw a soldier's bruises and asked, "Thompson, what happened to you?" and Thompson answered, "I fell off the bed." Thompson had been in a fight with other prisoners.

We had an electric fence all around us. The Polacks and the Russians lived away from us. I guess we were caged because they couldn't trust us. Beto Cano was a prisoner of war with me.

They had a young Jew assigned to be the cook, but he was always reading out of a book. So I volunteered to cook for the group. I cooked the cabbage, potatoes, and rice that were given to me and did the best I could.

One day the Germans came up to us and asked for volunteers to go work on farms. Well, I had worked on farms before and I knew that there was always food to eat on a farm. Here at the Stalag, there was never enough food. So I volunteered. Beto Cano said, "No, don't go, Vicente." I said, "Yes, Beto, there will be plenty of food for us to eat."

So Pete Carmona, a teacher from California, along with twenty-three other soldiers and I volunteered to go work on a farm. We worked on a farm in a community that experienced air raids. When the air raids occurred, the POWs were sent into a cellar where the milk cans were kept. We finally complained that if a bomb ever hit we would be buried alive. We wanted to go to the shelter where the civilians went.

The Germans, who didn't really treat us badly, decided to let us go to the shelter along with the civilians. Pete and I had talked about the possibility of escaping. Well when the air raid siren went off, Pete and I ran and climbed up into a silo which had the leaves from sugar beets in it. As we walked on the leaves, our weight made them sink down.

Now, how could we get out? We couldn't reach the rim of the silo. I told Pete to stand up on my shoulders and then I would climb up over him and reach the rim and we could get out that way. It worked.

We ran to a small farm where they knew us, and the owner hid us for two days and fed us eggs and bread. Finally, the owner said that the Germans were getting closer to us, that we had to leave "tonight."

After five days of running and hiding, the Germans found us. It was February 1945, and it was cold. We hadn't even gone far from *Stalag* 3A. The Germans asked us where we were going. Actually, we were hoping to run into the Russians, but we told the Germans that we were trying to hook up with the Americans, because we knew they didn't like the Russians.

They took us to Berlin by train and put us in solitary confinement for fifteen days with just bread and water at our place, *Stalag* 3A. A German would bring me a pitcher of water and a loaf of bread. Each morning he would tell me to take out my bucket. Then I saw no one for twenty-four hours. I had a blanket and hay on my bunk. There was a little window and if I stood on the bunk I could look out. I saw other POWs walking about on the compound. God makes miracles.

In the main compound of *Stalag* 3A, there were not enough blankets for Pete Carmona and me. So we put a blanket on the concrete and shared a blanket for cover at night. In the morning we could see that the concrete was wet from the body heat. Our food consisted of potato soup, fish soup, mustard greens and sauerkraut, all in small amounts. We knew they tried to keep us weak to keep us from escaping.

There was a Jew from New York who knew the German language and was our interpreter. We called him "Mac." Mac was very sick with hemorrhoids. I said, "Mac, go tell them you need to see the doctor." Mac answered, "I can't because if I go to them, they'll find out I'm a Jew and they'll kill me." So Mac suffered with his hemorrhoids until we were free.

On May 8, 1945, the Russians came in, and the Germans ran off. We wanted to leave as soon as possible, but they told us to stay because there might be a counterattack. We stayed three more weeks. We found out the Russians wanted to use us to trade for Russian POWs.

The Russians said, "Tonight we are going into Berlin." Pete said, "Look at that," as we saw Russian women climb out of tanks. They looked pretty strong.

We went walking around. There was a section of the compound that had been abandoned. There were bodies wrapped in blankets, some dead and others barely moving. Pete said, "Let's get out of here." And so we left. We had seen the Germans beating up these people [Jews] with whips. When the men saw us, they would ask for cigarettes by putting their index fingers in their mouths and puckering their lips.

The Russians made their exchanges and we were sent to France for processing. I weighed 108 pounds. They checked us all out. After three weeks of processing, Pete and I had a seven-day furlough to England. In the daytime we visited places, and at night we went dancing at the USO. We stayed twenty-eight days and missed two ships, the *Queen Mary* and *Queen Elizabeth*, two ships that were going back to the states.

Finally we reported to the Americans. In Southampton they put us and fifty other soldiers on a cargo ship loaded with sugar. Girls were at the docks kissing all the men while a band played.

I had volunteered to be in the service one year. I spent twenty-seven months as a POW out of fifty-two months in the US Army.

José Ángel Flores
28th Armored Division, The Bloody Bucket
112th Regiment
Machine Gunner

A Care Package for a Nazi Guard

José Ángel was born in Laredo, Texas, on October 2, 1917. After going to school through the sixth grade, José quit school so that he could help out his family financially. In time, he became a carpenter. José said, "I had to help my parents. They had a rough life." Although José was married and had two small daughters, he was nonetheless drafted because the war was getting more severe. When he was captured, however, he encountered a decent guard who did all he could for the POWs under him. The POWs rewarded him for his kindness.

In 1937, I joined the Civilian Conservation Corps, a job which earned me $30 a month. My boss suggested I keep $10 and send my parents back home $20. I opposed the suggestion and offered my own: I would keep only $5 for spending money and send my family $25 a month. I used the $5 to buy candy and toothpaste. I didn't drink or smoke. In 1939 I went to Corpus Christi, Texas.

After marrying, my wife and I had three girls. In 1944, when the country was deep into WWII, I was drafted on March 16 at age twenty-six. My mother and my wife gave me *la bendición*, both praying that I would return to my family and especially to my three young daughters.

For training I arrived at Camp Taylor near Taylor, Texas. The weather was hot and at the end of the training we had to walk fifteen miles into Taylor. We got up early in the morning and arrived at 11:30 a.m., and we walked in a parade.

All the sergeants were rough. When some of the men went in, they were rough and wouldn't mind anybody. The sergeants tried to break you down so you could respect and obey orders.

They tried to get single men first. There were some forty-year-old men.

After my training I went home on a ten-day furlough. I didn't know anything at that time. My wife asked me and I told her I didn't know anything.

From there I went to San Antonio. Then they sent me to a fort in Maryland. In August, I shipped out to England on the *Queen Mary*. We were there just twenty-four hours.

We went to France right after D-day. It was July or August. We landed at Omaha Beach. There were still a lot of boats, a bunch, stranded in the water. I saw trenches and foxholes.

They moved us a couple of miles in. The lieutenants told us what it was all about. They told us, "You're going to be fighting for your life. Each person has a gun. Never separate from your gun. If you sleep, you sleep with your gun. Go eat with your gun. Anywhere you go, you go with your gun. Never leave your gun." It was cold when the captain was talking to us. He was covered with a GI blanket. He said, "You can see that I'm over here, but you can see that I'm armed." He moved his blanket and showed us his pistol.

They moved us ahead to the front and then a little bit more. They moved us in trucks. They moved us about a mile behind the front lines. From there we had to walk. It was dangerous. The Germans had their positions already. They shot at us with cannons, 88s. We dug holes. I was a good digger and fast.

The first time I went into combat, I started walking on a dirt road and we saw lots of dead Germans in the ditches. It was cold and rainy. To one of my buddies I said, "Look at those dead men in the ditches." He said, "Maybe they are just dummies just to let us see what is going to happen." I said, "Dummies, nothing. They are Germans." They were dead Germans.

We were supposed to help each other as much as possible. We didn't see very many people in France. Once in a while we saw people in Belgium. They were happy to see us. They showed the victory sign, the V.

We were close to the front lines in Belgium in a wooded area. Lots of foxholes, empty but covered with branches and twigs. The Germans built them and ran off. We used them that night. The Germans had booby traps in some places but not there. We laid out our defense line. I set up my machine gun and there were two riflemen and another machine gun and another two riflemen and then another. There was a whole line like that. At night we took turns. I went in about 1:00 a.m. There was another man with me. His name was Dolores Flores, and he was from Laredo, Texas. We fought a little bit there. We moved on.

About two hundred yards, we had to dig holes. We had a big attack from the Germans in the Hürtgen Forest. They destroyed the Twenty-Eighth Division. The Lord was with me. I have been a very religious person. That night we had four-five tanks close to us, and the Germans hit them, direct hits. You could see the big fires, flames.

I was a machine gunner and I had a foxhole I was sharing with a buddy, Dolores Flores, in the Hürtgen Forest. Dolores decided that he was going to visit another guy in his foxhole. So he left. It was nighttime, and I couldn't sleep. So I got up and moved to another foxhole I had seen in the daytime. I fell asleep there.

The next morning, Dolores Flores went to look for me in the hole where he had left me. He found a pile of loose dirt. [Apparently a bomb had hit the hole.] So he thought I had been killed. At that time I woke up and walked in that direction. I saw them talking and looking at what had been my foxhole. Then they saw me and saw that I was alive. The Lord was with me at that time.

There was a big [farm] house. We were losing everybody so we went in there. It was 9 or 10 o'clock at night. Before going in, I broke my machine gun. We heard some guys hollering for help, close to the house. Me and another guy crawled up there not very far—maybe fifty yards—to get one of our buddies. We dragged him to the house and stayed there that night. The house had hay in it. The next morning was the seventh of November. Early in the morning we had a big battle there. We were in the house and when it was real hot [fighting]. I lay down against a wall in the house. Dolores Flores sat up close to me. Shrapnel from a big German gun took his chest out. After awhile another fellow who was sitting up by me was shot in the face. I was lying under them. Both men died right there. We had medics in the house. It was too late. Thirty minutes later, there were a bunch of Germans in the house. They pulled us out of the house.

I was caught on November 7, 1944, by the Germans. They took us to a pillbox. There were between fifteen or twenty of us. We had been a platoon but half were gone. When I had been in a foxhole, just before I went to the house, there were two of us in the foxhole, and there was a direct hit just about ten feet from where we were. Where there had been some buddies, there were just pieces of them [flesh]. Two guys.

The Germans took us out of the house. They motioned and said, "*Rout*." They marched us fifty yards to a pillbox and they had other Americans there. The Germans were young. We stayed there about an hour and they took us out of there. Thirty to forty American soldiers. They took us two-three miles walking. A little town. Took us to some buildings. Looked like motels. Big buildings. The Germans spoke English. We had a guy who spoke German. He translated for us.

They searched us. They found grenades. They walked us six to eight miles. We were walking on the road with guards, and German people, ladies offered us water. They felt sorry for us. The guards stopped us.

The Germans didn't hit or kick us. They took us to another place late in the evening, a two story building. Thought we were going to get something to eat, but we didn't get nothing. We didn't eat all day long.

The next day they gave us coffee but no flavor at all.

When first questioned José Ángel said, "No hablo Inglés." Then the German interrogator changed to Spanish.

They took us one at a time to interview. They wanted to know where we came from and who we were. Big German interviewed me. He asked me questions: "What were you doing? What kind of gun?"

He must have had some records, because he called me by my name. He said, "You didn't have a gun; you had a machine gun." They interviewed all these people. I got a little scared. I said, "I just had a gun." He asked a lot of questions.

To fire a machine gun you set a tripod. It took three to four guys. Ammunition, cartridges. One guy puts it in and another guy shoots it. When I went to the service I heard of guys who tried to get out of things. They would say, "I can't see real good, my knees are trouble." I never complained. I am five foot six. They asked me where do you want to go—Army? Navy? I said, "Whatever you want to give me."

My serial number is 3816732. They questioned everybody.

They put us in the same room. The next day they put us on a train in cattle cars. We traveled for two days. We stopped every now and then, because when the Germans saw the American airplanes, they ran away. They left us in there. The aviation, they knew where we were. They never hit us. They took us to a Prisoner of War Camp, close to Limburg [Stalag 12A]. After we got there, there were some American POWs. It was a big camp. They treated us good, but not enough food to eat. If you wanted more or to eat a little better, you had to go to work.

A few days after that a German sailor would ask for a detail: twenty volunteers to go to work. My buddy, Leopoldo Carranza, from Robstown, said, "Let's go." I said to myself, No, that's too many guys. I wanted to get on a small detail. The twenty men were picked up in the morning and brought back in the evening. The next day another German guard from the navy asked for twelve men. That's when I went. When I saw the guard, I thought he might be a better person. He was fifty-four years old—I found out later. We walked about two blocks from the camp. There was a bushy area and we went through there. He stopped us there and said, "I speak good English because I went to the US many years ago." He went to Mexico and the US when he was young.

He told us. I am a guard and I've got a gun. I have bullets. I have all the right to shoot you if you run away from me. Please don't do that. I'm not going to shoot anybody. I don't have the conscience to do that. You don't know where you are, and the way you are dressed they will know you are an American. They'll get you right away. And it's going to be real tough for you. So don't run away. I'm not going to shoot you." I said to myself, the Lord gave me this guard.

He said, "We're building some houses. Is anybody here who knows something about construction?" I waited a little while to see what anybody would say. So I told him, "I'm a carpenter." He said, "So you're a carpenter?" I said, "Yes." He said, "What do you do over there in the United States for a living?" I said, "That's what I do to support my family. I'm a carpenter." He said, "You're going to be the boss and we're going to work together." He was real nice.

His first name was Adolph. He preferred to talk to me before he talked to the rest of the guys. So we went. Someone else had done the foundations.

German notification to relatives of POW José Ángel Flores, front side. Mary and Jeff Bell Library at Texas A&M (Corpus Christi), Special Collections and Archives, Collection #151.

German notification to relatives of POW José Ángel Flores, back side. Mary and Jeff Bell Library at Texas A&M (Corpus Christi), Special Collections and Archives, Collection #151.

There was a naval base close by. And they had a carpenter shop. They had the blueprints in the shop. All the framing; they could send it like a puzzle. And they would send me the blueprints and we would frame them. They fed us better at the mess hall outside the naval base. A lot of the civilians who worked at the base ate at the mess hall. In the mornings Adolph came and picked us up at 8:00 a.m. and he took us to the mess hall. We ate toast, bread, coffee, and a little butter.

Lunch, we got vegetable soup. We ate enough. At night, 4:30 p.m. same thing. Different soups. Returned at 5:00 p.m. There was a Frenchman who used to work with us. He was a prisoner, but he was "loose." He had been in there many years. Maybe he wasn't a prisoner. We called him "Al." He wasn't in the camp. He helped us build it. Al measured. He was a real nice guy, too. He knew all the little towns.

They didn't have cigarettes up there. The German servicemen got three cigarettes a day. Some of them were chain-smokers, but they didn't have the cigarettes. So we received boxes from the Red Cross. We got boxes that were sealed, waterproofed, if they put them in the bay or in the ocean, nothing would happen to them. One box for two guys. Three or four packages of cigarettes, candies, bread, toothbrush, soap. It was cold up there. They gave me one of those Russian coats, but it was way too big for me. So I fixed me a bag and I put it under my coat and I went to the job and asked Al to give me three-four loaves of bread. I gave Al five cigarettes for each loaf of bread. And I put them in my bag. Adolph was a real nice guy. He went over there to talk to the guard at the gate. He's in charge of the whole platoon, and he's carrying the rations of bread.

I tried to help out Adolph. His wife looked pretty young, something like thirty. A beautiful lady. I said, "Tell your wife to come over here and we'll get something for her." The whole platoon got together and got a whole bag for her, cookies, candies, toothbrush, toothpaste, and chewing gum. He was so happy to get it. They had a little girl eight or ten years old. Another daughter in college. He was real nice to us. He took me to two or three different places; we went to get some bolts. He left this other guard to watch the workers while we went to town. We went to Limburg and I started walking ahead of him. He said, "Joe, don't walk ahead of me. Walk with me." I said, "I'm your prisoner." Adolph said, "Let's walk together." I appreciated that. He didn't treat me like a prisoner. He took me to the naval base to introduce me to the carpenter foreman. We couldn't talk to each other. Adolph was in between us and translated. He told me how they worked the construction there, and I told him how we work over here.

Two or three days before we were liberated, we could hear those big cannons from the ships. There was an old inspector who went to check the job every now and then. When we heard the thunder of the cannons, the old man said, "Russian, we don't want Russian. American, come, come." We would get news from the Red Cross. An American sergeant would give us the news. He would say, the battle is more on our side a little bit.

The last day of work, Adolph took us to the camp and he walked me inside of the barracks and said, "Joe, will you do something for me? Get me some clothes. American clothes. If I dress in American clothes and they liberate you, I can pass for an American, then later I can tell them I am a German." He didn't want to get killed. I didn't blame him. I said, "Adolph, I appreciate what you have done for me. I thank you. But this I cannot do." I started thinking about it. You never know what the next person is thinking. They might think I was collaborating with the Germans. I thought, *What are the rest of the guys going to think about me?* Adolph looked kind of sorry. He said, "Joe, I know. I just thought I would tell you." We didn't get to finish the structures. We started on three or four of them. The Russians came in and messed up everything.

About 1:00 in the morning we could hear the fighting; the day before we could see the airplanes and the dogfights, Germans with the Americans. We could hear the cannons. On April 28, 1945, the Russians arrived at 1:00 a.m. We could hear them a mile away. We knew they were Russians from the direction they were coming.

A Russian officer walked in and told us, "We've been after them for a week and couldn't catch up with them." Our translator told us what the Russian said. The next day, we were free. There were no guards or anything. The tanks went through the camp. I don't know what happened to Adolph. The Russians said, "Go. You're liberated."

The Germans ran off. I went to the office where they kept records and took my POW picture, which has a number and says St. XII A (Stalag 12A). I also took a picture of my friend from Robstown, Texas, Leopoldo Carranza, and walked out with them in my pocket.

Me and two more guys left the camp. We made a mistake because it

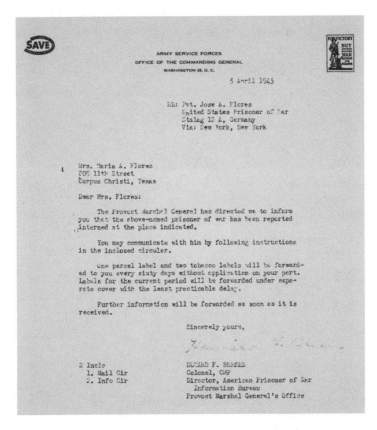

United States government informing the wife of José Ángel Flores of his captivity in POW camp. Mary and Jeff Bell Library at Texas A&M (Corpus Christi), Special Collections and Archives, Collection #151.

was late in the day. The first thing we did was to go to the little town and walked on the concrete a little ways and you could see things that nobody can think about. And on the roads you could find all sorts of things, women's underwear and clothes all messed up. The Russians had been through there. That day we stayed there.

The next day we walked away from there. We talked to a lady and she said that when the Russians came they were rough, messing up families. And she had family. And she begged them to do to her whatever they

Private José Ángel Flores, prisoner of war, held in Stalag 12A, 1944–45. After the Russians came in to the POW camp (and after the Germans ran off) and informed the American POWs that they were free, José Ángel Flores had the nerve to go into the German Warden's office to retrieve his picture, which is how we have this picture today. Mary and Jeff Bell Library at Texas A&M (Corpus Christi), Special Collections and Archives, Collection #151.

wanted and said, "But don't touch my daughters." She had some daughters. But they didn't pay any attention to her; they took them away from her. When the Germans went to Russia they made atrocities [early in the war]. So many with young girls and things. The Russians came to Germany and did the same things.

The next day late in the evening we were walking away from there and there was another little town about three miles away from there. It was getting dark. There were some Russians there. They had already taken that place. There were some Russian guards in there. We talked to them by signs. He took us to an office where a Russian colonel or a big shot was there. They told him, "These are Americans. They come from this camp over here." He ordered him, "Take them to this next house over here and tell them that I said to keep them in their house." So he took us up there and the Russian didn't knock on the door. He hit it with his gun. The lady came out there. The Russian soldier talked to her and said, "These are Americans. The colonel said to keep them for the night." A young lady eighteen or twenty years old. She was a German and she was in college studying English. She talked to us. She said that her father was not at home. He was a doctor and was checking on people in town. She took us to a back room and we cleaned up. They gave us a room with a big bed. Two hours later, her father came in. The young lady introduced us to her father. We ate supper with them. Real nice place. The next day we walked away from there.

We walked for three days. We asked questions, and we knew more or less where we were going. We stayed at a ranch. It was a big house. Nobody was there. We walked upstairs and there was a man hanging in there. I imagine the Russians hanged him or maybe he, himself did it. We didn't touch him; we got away from there. We slept in the barn.

The next day we went to another barn. A lady came out of the house. She motioned us to go to her house. Lots of potatoes in the barn. We were going to cook there, but she fed us in her house. It was a small house. She fed us canned food like corned beef. So we made potatoes and corned beef. We offered her some food but she said she didn't want anything. She wanted to take some to her daughter. She had a young daughter but she was sick. She was sick, something about her leg. We stayed in the barn.

The next day we walked away from there. It was close to a big city. We saw an American jeep. They came by and picked us up and took us to the Red Cross. It was a big place. A motel or something. Lots of American GIs. Girls working with the servicemen. We took a bath and put on nice, clean clothes. We stayed overnight and then they drove us to another place.

Another city. There they flew us to France, Camp Lucky Strike. We stayed there three weeks. From there we came to the states. Processing us and we were seeing doctors. I was never hurt.

After the war, I went to Arkansas. That's where I got my discharge. The 16th of November 1945.

Everyone is married. Back to carpentry work. I joined the union in 1947. Joined the International. Retired in 1982. I have a daughter in Dallas. I've got a real nice family. I try to be an honest person. I have built shelves for the church. I've saved them a lot of money. They wanted some recliners and the bill would be $10,000. I told the priest to get the materials and I would build them. Some other guys helped. I never charged the church a penny. I am a Eucharistic Minister and a Lector. My wife and I take Holy Communion to people who cannot come to church.

Below is a chronology of his experiences during the war as José Ángel Flores recorded it.

- Examen (test)   Feb. 17, 1944
- Entrenamiento (training)   March 25, 1944
- Terminado (finished) July 20, 1944   Furlough
- Returned to camp August 14, 1944
- Camp Fort Meade, Maryland eight days
- Camp Kilmer, New York 10 days
- Aug 28 on Ship Queen Mary to Scotland
- Arrived in Scotland Sept 4 at 2:00 pm
- Traveled by train all afternoon and night
- Camp in England spent 24 hours there
- 28th Div, Regiment 112 Company, 1st Army Sept. 14

- Action Sept 25, 1944

- Germans captured me on Nov 7, 1944 at 3:00 pm

- Siegfried Line in Germany

- Traveled ten miles on Nov 8

- Germans interrogated us for three days without eating or drinking

- Slept in a pasture

- Traveled 40 km and ate watery soup

- Went to Limberg Camp on Nov 14

- Nov 15 I mailed a letter back home through the Red Cross

- Nov 20 We were kept in box cars for seven or eight hours without moving the cars

- cold and hungry

- When American airplanes bombed us, the German guards ran away from the train

- Seven days and seven nights we arrived at Stalag 12A near Limberg, Germany

- Worked in construction for five months

- Liberated by Russian Army on April 28, 1945 at 1:00 a.m.

- Found my Army group on May 12, 1945

- May 14, took airplane to Belgium

- May 16, went to Camp Lucky Strike, France

- June 13 left Europe

- June 14 11:00 am arrived in Boston, Massachusetts on a Weds.

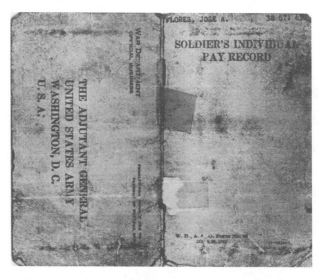

Typical pay for a private in WWII, p. 1. Mary and Jeff Bell
Library at Texas A&M (Corpus Christi), Special Collections
and Archives, Collection #151.

Typical pay for a private in WWII, p. 2. Mary and Jeff Bell
Library at Texas A&M (Corpus Christi), Special Collections
and Archives, Collection #151.

A. D. Azios
9th Armored Division
60th Infantry Battalion

With an Eagerness to Fight

A. D. Azios was born in the border town of Laredo, Texas, on February 5, 1921. He was born to José Maria and Petra Azios and was the youngest of six boys. His father was a customs broker and dealt with international trade. A. D. had three brothers in the service. He had a desire to join the army and defend his country. He relished the thought of fighting the enemy. Later, he admitted the foolishness of his wish. His knowledge of the German language assisted him in many ways during the war.

Thousands of guys in the United States were in the same situation. One morning before I even knew I was going into active duty, the bells in the University of Texas tower were playing "You're in the army now." They heard the news before we did. The *Daily Texan*, the university newspaper's headlines were ERC Emergency Reserve Called to Active Duty. Among those called were two football stars, another person, and me. I was active in student activities. April of 1943.

I didn't get the orders, so I went home to Laredo. Three weeks later I was working in the yard when here comes the mail including a torn letter addressed to me and opened by mistake. It had been mailed to the Laredo Air Force Base. I don't know how long it was there but I got it the afternoon before the morning I was due in Fort Sam Houston. Quickly I called my family and they all came to say goodbye to me. My brother, Henry, gave me a ride to San Antonio because the train had left. We spent the night in a railroad station waiting room. The next morning there were some MPs waiting for draftees. I told them what the situation was, and they gave me a ride to Fort Sam. I was in their hands.

My mother gave me *la bendición* before I left. She gave me *la bendición* every time I left to go out of town. My *abuelita* did, too, every time she came to visit us.

I had my basic training in Camp Maxey in Paris, Texas. It was May, June, July, August, and September in basic training in infantry. Summertime in Paris, Texas, is like being in Hell.

The sergeants were like—think of a word like the devil, but not quite because they are trying to train you to survive. If you disobeyed in the slightest degree, you caught hell. If you screwed up, you said, "No excuse, sir."

All college boys were sent to different universities, some to study engineering, some language, Japanese, Italian, or German, depending on where you went. Italian and Japanese were in California and German was at the University of Nebraska in Lincoln. That's where I was sent. All army guys went there. We were supposed to be there till we finished. After that we knew we were going to win the war in Germany. They were going to send occupation officers. We were supposed to be officers. I guess they would have one of us in each town as a boss man or something.

On December of 1943, they said the war is going real bad in Europe. "We need more fighting men so we are going to discontinue this program." It was terminated, and I went back into the infantry. Eventually all of us were dispersed to different outfits.

We were sent to Fort Leonard Wood near St. Louis, Missouri. There were lots of German prisoners there. It was two or three days after Christmas. I could see all the Christmas trees with Christmas lights in their mess hall. And they were eating beautifully like they deserve to eat, everything. And I was watching them. They were in heaven anyway, in warm beds.

We trained some more in ten-below-zero-degree weather. We were outside with the infantry. We were sleeping outside for ten days. They dropped me in with the Seventy-Fifth Infantry Division. From there we went to Camp Polk in Louisiana, where we spent about ninety days. We're still outside. Constantly drizzling. In maneuvers you don't have a tent. You literally live outside under a tree or whatever.

I was transferred in April of '44 to the Ninth Armored Division. We were in Kentucky. From there we shipped out to Europe in July 1944. When we were on the ship, *Queen Mary*, going overseas, dumb guys— us—we were getting the news that the Germans were retreating and that we were beating the hell out of them. We're pushing them back to Germany. We said, "I hope they're not finished fighting. We want to do some fighting."

We landed in Glasgow, Scotland. I thought, "What next?" When we were riding the train, it stopped at a little town. A bunch of GIs threw candy at the kids. We ran out of candy. We said, "No more candy." A little boy thought we were lying. He used a vulgar word on me. He told us he had an idea what we could do with our candy. We rode the train to England where we spent a few weeks training again. We crossed the channel in August '44. We landed in Cherbourg, France. Once you get in, the towns were demolished just everywhere, everywhere, everywhere beyond description. Because when the Americans landed the Germans began retreating. There was fight, fight, fighting. And if you see a soldier, you're going to bomb a building.

And we traveled through France in trucks and half-tracks, which carried men in the back. You sit back there six or so men facing each other. We went from Cherbourg to Luxemburg. We traveled in the daytime and stopped somewhere at night. We slept in tents. The natives waved at us and smiled.

We went to Beaufort, Luxemburg, two miles from Germany. We're on top of the hill in our foxholes and Germany is below the hill. In November we got a leave to go to Luxemburg City. I took a bath and that was the first bath I had taken since we left England, which had been a few days. I was so impressed with Luxemburg. I remember spending Thanksgiving in some little town. It was great. We had everything.

They took us back for R and R. We could take a bath and eat—real food—not the stuff in those little cans. We went back to our foxholes. After we left and came back, we found that our foxholes were flooded because of the snow. We had kept them warm by building little fires. So when we left nature betrayed us. So we had to dig new ones. An American plane had been returning to Germany but was shot down by the Germans right in our area. Luckily, we weren't there. [The plane] barely made it to Luxembourg. When we came back, the people in the airplane were gone. The plane crashed in this forested area where we had been. The foxholes are where you stay before you move forward or backward.

From there we went toward Germany walking. Action is always in front of you or beside you. Sometimes someone else is fighting. You hear the machine gun and everything, but you are not the target at that time. We were scouting, looking for the enemy.

December 12, we had been there about four days. We were fighting there in Beaufort, Luxembourg, with Company B, Sixtieth Infantry Battalion. We were getting artillery from both sides at that time. We were just caught in the middle.

When I got captured December 18, we didn't eat for the first three or four days. The experience of being captured—the curiosity of "what's going to happen next? When does POW life begin?" So I really wasn't hungry. I was just looking around. Can I escape? You're taught in the army: "It's your duty to escape." You always look around. Later on you look for something to eat. When we became desperate, I was the best "sniffer."

We were in transit. I thought that's all right. On Christmas Day, they'll feed us like we fed our prisoners (at Fort Leonard Wood). Well, Christmas came and went just like any other day.

When I was captured, I spoke German to the guys. Some people have told me that probably saved my life. I was in a house in the basement; I had been wounded. I had been left there by the captain. He told me and two other guys who had been slightly wounded, "Stay here and don't go anywhere." The two other guys looked at me and thought "We do what we want later on," because it got worse later on. I had a big patch here. I couldn't fight then. So he told me to get in the basement and stay there.

How could I go anywhere anyway? I lost my rifle. So he left on the 16th. And that was the command post. That's where the radios are in operation. You hear a lot of talking. They left on Dec 16, 1944. We waited in a house at #19 Grand Rue, in Beaufort, Luxembourg.

The front of the [basement] window is flush with the street. I heard, "click, click, click." I looked out through the side of my eyes and I saw two German soldiers walking right in front of me. And then they came into the house. They walked around and didn't see anybody. You have to check. So they started getting close to the stairs. I knew they were coming down. I try to think in advance. I had told the other two guys, "This is a two-story house; if we get hit, we're goners. We'll be safer in a bigger building," and there's only one bigger building in that little town. Shall we go there or stay here? We didn't decide. We just stayed there. They said, "We don't feel safe here." And they left. They had minor injuries.

On Dec. 18, when I heard the German come in, I said, "*Deutchen Soldaten, Ich bin ein American Soldat; Ich bin Verwundet; Ich bin alien; Ganz alien.*" [German soldiers, I am an American soldier. I am wounded. I am alone, all alone.] This happened quickly and it just rolled out. (We had spoken German all the time at the University of Nebraska.) They said, "Come on up."

I put out one hand and then the other (They must have thought "He thinks we're stupid.") I went like this [open hands] and they said, "Come on up." And I walked upstairs. I had a feeling they were going to shoot me; by that time you are so used to expecting death any minute. I thought, that's it. That's your destiny, Baby. I got up there and they searched me. They asked, "Are you German?" (They meant German-American, and they don't like them.) If I had said yes, they probably would have shot me. I said, "*Nein.*" "Are you sure?" "*Ya.*" "Is your mother German?" "*Nein.*" "Are you sure?" "*Ya.*" "Well, where did you learn German?" "At the University of Nebraska." I didn't know how to say "of" in that context. I used the word "von" which means from and it turned out to be right. They asked, "How long did you study?" I said, "Three months."

We crossed the river which separated Luxembourg from Germany on a two-tier raft. On the bottom they had German soldiers and on the top they had us—the POWs—with one guard. We crossed that river on the night of December 18th. It was a very narrow and shallow river. The snow melts continuously. (When my wife and I saw it in 1985, it was shallow.) When we crossed the river there was a long line of German soldiers waiting to advance further into Luxembourg. Their goal was to go to Paris. This was right after the Battle of the Bulge (December 16, 1944), and it was the new push. They're trying to get to Antwerp, but the German soldiers had more than one target. They wanted to capture all the goods [in Antwerp], Paris for political reasons, prestige, whatever. And here's what a kid told me in German, by the way, to two or three of us standing there. They thought they were going to win the war. I didn't argue with him. "We promised Hitler that we would deliver Paris to him for Christmas." I thought to myself, *y'all are crazy.*

Maybe because of my attitude or because I spoke a little German or because I was crazy or maybe that's the way to be, I felt free to talk to them. I wasn't arrogant or afraid of them. Hundreds of them lined up along the river bank. They had just arrived. They were youngish—from eighteen to twenty. Later I saw the old men.

We were about ten. They captured us separately. When I was captured, I was so mad at myself. As I walked out of that house where I was captured with my hands up, I thought, "Dadgummit, I betrayed my nation." We walked to the corner and turned left and walked about four blocks to a little so-called railroad station. They had a boxcar and there in the boxcar were my top sergeants—I was a PFC. They had corporals, sergeants, and top sergeants. One of the sergeant's legs had been shot—not off—but just shot. He just sat there. I realized then that I was not the only one [who had surrendered]. If top sergeants had been captured, why shouldn't I be captured.

From the railroad station we walked to the river. We had to carry that sergeant in a little wagon. We had to pull him. We walked to a little bitty village. We spent the night on the top floor of a two-story house. When we got to the house there was a German lieutenant who was to be in charge of us. I told him that my sergeant had been shot badly. Get us a doctor. I felt a little free. Then I told myself, they're not my equals. They're my captors. He said, "*Ya, ya, ya.*" An hour later the sergeant was really suffering. So I went to talk to the lieutenant sort of rough. (And I am telling myself—who do I think I am? I am just a Pfc. and a POW—what the hell...) I said, "Lt., that man is suffering. He hasn't had a doctor. You told us an hour and a half ago that he was going to have a doctor." He caught on that I was trying to . . . he said, "I told you I would bring a doctor. He will have a doctor. You go back to your place and you go join your group. Don't come here telling me what do to."

We didn't get a doctor. The next morning we left. The doctor never came. They put him in a little truck like an SUV in the back. There must have been ten guys [in our group]. I'm safe in saying he didn't go with us, because we didn't carry that guy. It took two days to get there. The first night after we left we spent in a schoolhouse. It wasn't being used probably because of the war.

The next morning they were going to feed us breakfast, which consisted of bread. That's all. The interesting thing is this: they had two guards and there were either eight or ten of us. It was an even number. The two guards are standing behind a table. The rest of us prisoners are about five yards in front of them. We are sitting there and they are standing there. We are looking at the bread, and nothing is happening. So I asked the guard, "What are we waiting for?"

"We don't know how to divide the bread because there are eight or ten of you and only two of us and we are afraid." They are afraid to get near us. It was an electrifying moment because I thought t*hey're waiting for us and we're waiting for them.*

I'm either getting brave or stupid or crazy. I said, "Let me come to you." I went and talked to them. "Why don't you divide us into twos and send one of the men from each group to this table where you give them their portion of the bread? You know how much bread each one is going to get." I'm glad we were an even number. It was easy. Send one representative to pick up the bread, and then the next group. One man at a time is no danger. Such a silly thing like that. So that's the way we handled it. Each man went to get the bread for his group, and that's how we got our bread.

That reminds me of what we were told in the army. The German soldiers are not trained to be leaders; they are trained to be followers. A simple problem like that and they couldn't figure it out. Here I am a POW, a dumb Pfc., and in a foreign language I told them how to do it.

The American soldiers are trained to follow orders but not to be stalled by not knowing what to do. If we were told to take Hill 28, we took Hill 28. You use your training to do something, but these guys are standing there, and we are unarmed. They have arms and they can't decide how to divide the bread. It's pretty weak mentally. And in a foreign language. They said, "*Vunderbar, vunderbar.*"

Then they put us in the little truck and took us to that building that looked like a penitentiary—Huntsville. It was about five stories high. Just like a penitentiary that you see in the movies. There we spent a night or two nights. We got bombed, not hit, but all around us. The Allies were hitting any big building that looked important.

That air raid made the headlines. From there we went to [Stalag] 12A in Limburg, Germany). In Limburg they made fun of us because of the bombing. One hundred sixty-seven prisoners were killed that time. The headlines said, "ALLIES KILL OWN SOLDIERS." One of these days I'm going to go to the German Consul here and ask him to communicate (connect) me with someone from that *Zeitung* newspaper and see if I can get a copy of that thing. I saw a picture but only from the inside. I didn't see the front page. That's what I want to see.

Right next door to us we had Indians from India. They were really subjects so they were fighting for England. On one side of us was a hospital, which got bombed on the same night we were bombed. They said they were Polish POWs. Poland had lost the war in 1939. The Poles went to England and were retrained. Some of the Polish soldiers were evacuated with the French and British soldiers at Dunkirk and then retrained. Then they were captured. Stalag 12A was huge. Thousands of prisoners were there. They'd bring you in at night, throw you in the barracks and you'd sleep on the floor on straw. The next morning they'd take you to interrogation. The next night you would sleep in a different place. That's when we took a bath. Everyday they'd move you for the next batch moving in or for interrogation.

The interrogation was very simple because they knew I was just a Pfc. I gave them the answer I was supposed to give them, which is name, rank, and serial number. I told them that that was all I could tell them. He [the German] raised his voice and asked me when did you come in . . . where did you land . . . whatever the question was, it was beyond my name, rank, and serial number. They got mad at me. And I refused to answer. The interrogator said, "Get him out of here." They figured I didn't know anything.

They want to know little things they can piece together and make something out of it. Like "When you left New York, where did you land?" If different groups come in and they all land in Glasgow, they'll say, "Aha, they all land in Glasgow." They make intelligence out of little details. An example: "How long did it take you to get from Cherbourg to here?" If I say ten days, it gives them another fact. We can cut them off or whatever.

We didn't eat. We spent that lonely Christmas Day. No eat, no nothing. They must have given us something one day but not every day. Your impressions are beginning to pile up. "Hey, what the hell is this? We are not getting fed. We are getting bombed. We're just floating here. This is not POW life. This is worse. You've abandoned me because they just throw you [in] and leave you there." They're not doing anything with us. We are just sitting there waiting.

You don't know what to expect the first few days. So you wait. Patiently, till you realize they are lying to you. 'Cause let me tell you something. I have to tell you this. Everywhere we went, every camp, they lied to us including in Limburg—Stalag 12A. "We did not know you were coming in, so we have nothing for you to eat." And Limburg wasn't so bad because there were just ten or twelve of us.

From 12A to Luckenwalde, there were several hundred of us guys, and when we got there they said, "We didn't know you were coming so we have nothing for you to eat." You don't send several men from one camp to another without clearing it with the recipient. You don't do that. This is the second time we hear this, "We didn't know you were coming; we don't have anything for you to eat."

I'll never forget. We got to Luckenwalde at 3:00 in the afternoon and we walked again. Dreary looking place. Then we were beginning to starve. "Didn't know you were coming, so we don't have anything for you to eat." The British heard it. They were next door to us. The British lined us up. It was tea time for them. They set up the tea—I don't know how they got it—Red Cross or something, and they gave us their tea. (It was a barbed wire fence between us and it was high.) Maybe they hadn't been there long enough because later on they wouldn't have done it. No way. Later we were starving. So how could you give anyone anything? We drank it and returned the cups. I'll never forget it. It was the best tea I ever drank in my life. It was good and I was suffering. That enhanced the taste.

Luckenwalde. We were there from the first of the year '45 to February 5. How do I know it was February 5th? It's my birthday. The Russians were coming and Luckenwalde is very close to the Oder River. And once they [Russians] cross the Oder River, they'll be there.

We were just counting. We were getting the news. The British next door had their own radio. They had made a radio. They were smart. They had been there a long time. So they get the news, write it down, and throw it over the fence with a rock. "The Russians are now thirty miles from the Oder River. Now twenty miles. Now ten miles."

The Germans did not want the POWs to be liberated, because they use the POWs as pawns. "You do this or we'll hurt your POWs." They take us away from the Russians. The Germans pulled us out of Luckenwalde and took us to Alten-Grabow on February 5, 1945. It was snowing and the wind was blowing. By that time, we are literally starving. We are going on a three-day trip walking. They gave each one of us a loaf of bread. "This is all you are going to get until we get to the next camp. Divide that into three parts, because it is going to take us three days to get there. You are starving to death, and you put your bread under your shirt. I said to myself, "A. D., this is it. I have willpower and you certainly have it when you are a POW." It didn't work. By the end of the day I had eaten half. The next day I couldn't stand it and ate the balance of the bread. I didn't dare look at anyone else's bread.

We get to Alten-Grabow. "We didn't know you were coming, so we have nothing for you to eat." Every camp. We were madder than hell. But what could we do? Nothing. We were there from February 8 until early March.

In Alten-Grabow I'm walking on a cold, horrible, morning, snow everywhere. To the assembly area, because every morning we had to assemble. Here comes this new guard, and he is checking the names of the POWs. He must have seen my name, and it attracted his attention. He spoke to me in perfect Spanish. I asked him, "How did you learn Spanish?" He had worked in Tampico at the oil refinery. There was an oil refinery owned by Shell Oil. It was a Dutch company. He worked there and naturally learned Spanish. To get a break he would go to San Antonio, and he would stop at the Hamilton Hotel in Laredo, which was four blocks from my house, and in which I helped install air-conditioning in 1939. In perfect Spanish he said to me, "I see you're from Laredo. I used to go to San Antonio on breaks and spend the night at the Hamilton Hotel." When he said that, I was excited. I said, "*Cuatro cuadras de mi casa.*" [Four blocks from my home.] I was so happy. He said, "I used to eat there." What he didn't know was that at Luckenwalde, where I had just left, there was a guy, a Mexican American, who had been a cook and a waiter at the Hamilton Hotel. When we moved out on my birthday, he stayed behind. His name was Rodriguez. I told him, "Do you know who the cook was or your waiter? He is now a POW at Luckenwalde." We talked two or three other times we met. Unfortunately for me we were transferred to Stendal. What I wanted to do with this guard was to get chummy with him so that when he went out on work details, he would take me with him. Away from camp, because once you are out of camp you can either escape or you can trade with people if they'll trade with you—bread for cigarettes or potatoes. I would do that.

Then we went to Stendal. It is a city, not a POW camp. We were going to be used as railroad workers there, replacing railroad tracks which had been bombed by our planes. We heard the same old story. There are two hundred of us. There were four groups of fifty. "We didn't know you were coming so we have nothing for you to eat." Mad as hell.

Luckily there were Dutch prisoners, POW civilian prisoners. They worked somewhere and they knew we had not eaten. One of them gave me an egg. These guys worked on a farm and came right through our building. We were coming in and they were walking by. One man called me over and gave me an egg. A raw egg. Here's the bad thing. I had a deal with two other guys. Everything we were going to get, we were going to split. And we were honest about it. So here I had this egg and how was I going to divide it? We put it on a flat surface and we ate one third each. I think we mixed it or something. It was my egg, but we had a word. So we split it.

And this building—twice as long as this [living room]—was right next to some railroad tracks. The reason I am telling you this is that one time when we were at work—it was close to Easter or right after Easter. I remember because at Easter I tried to get off for everybody. We were working. "*Nein, nein, nein.*" We finished very late that afternoon. Probably because it was raining, they decided to give us off. I asked the guard, "Please let me go to the church." There was a church nearby. It wasn't a Catholic Church. I didn't care. I just wanted an excuse to get out of there. If I told the people I could get bread, they'd say, "*Nein, nein.*" Now all of this is in German. My German was not perfect, but he understood me. He said, "You don't have to go to church to pray. God is everywhere." Confidentially, I was thinking asylum. Traditionally in Europe, you can go to a church and seek asylum. If Spain had had a consulate in Stendal where I was working, I could just walk in and ask for asylum, and they have to give it to me. And Germany couldn't say, "Give that man to me."

Every morning we two hundred men would go and work on the railroad lines that had been bombed the day before. We removed them because the rails are twisted. Sometimes they are twisted around a light pole. We couldn't touch that. So then the Germans would send welders to cut them down and then get out of our way. First we had to replace the dirt back in the craters. We had to remove the tracks, move them out of the way. They'd bring in new ones from somewhere, and we had to carry them not very far. They would come in pieces, and we had to be very careful because they were very heavy. We had to work absolutely together; if you don't, one of the guys will break his back. I was the group leader with one group. Why? Because I spoke a little bit of German. "All right guys, be very careful." We had to bend down at the same time, grab hold. "Everybody grab it?" "Yeah." "Now I'm going to count to three. One-two-three." And you lifted it. Not very high, about this high (coffee table). Move it. Before we did that, [we placed] the ties. Then we got there and put them down gently.

The American camp is divided from the Russian camp, which is right next door. There was a passage on which the guards could walk up and down. It was surrounded with a wire fence on each side. The Russians are on one side and we are on the other. Toward the end of the bitter winter—it is still cold but not as bad—some guys were so hungry they were willing to trade their jackets for bread. Well, you can't do it over the fence because the German guards won't let you. Sometimes you could if the guard was not alert.

This darn Joe, José Martinez, he would go to the Russian side—he would crawl from one side to the other. If they had seen him, they would have shot him. He would take jackets, say five jackets, and he would come back with five loaves of bread and he would get one third of each loaf. So he had more bread than anybody else. He was a hustler. He would take a package of cigarettes—now that he threw over the fence—and the Russians would throw bread over the fence. That he couldn't do with jackets. One time he would take a package very lightly and take out one or two cigarettes, reseal it, and throw it over. The next time he did it they said, "No, you are stealing cigarettes, and we are not getting a full package." I don't know how we understood. I said, "When that guy gets home, he is going to be a hustler. He'll be a good businessman." (I saw him in Houston later on.)

I'm working on the railroad tracks and here comes a choo choo train and it stops right in front of me. The engineer's up there and I said in German, "Do you want to trade bread for a cigarette? I have cigarettes." I used the wrong word for trade; I used switch. He understood me and (corrected me), and I appreciated it. From then on, I used the right word. He traded lots of pieces of bread—dry, hard—and it was the most bread I had had since I was a POW. For one cigarette. Oh my gosh!

There is another word I learned. During the day in an air raid we were working in the same railroad track area here come the Americans [airplanes]. The siren goes off. In the daytime it's the American airplanes. At night it's the British. They give you a twenty-minute warning. Enemy approaching. Twenty-minute warning—then a ten-minute warning. Then the bombs start falling. Somehow we delayed a little bit and we weren't assembling quickly enough, I guess, because the guys were spread out. The Germans said something; I thought he said, "Line up in columns of three." So I told the guys, "Line up in columns of three." So we lined up in columns of three and ran out of there because the bombs were beginning to fall. And guess who followed us? Some German soldiers who were traveling by train and they had stopped there and I was visiting with them. See how crazy it was? I got into the boxcar full of straw and was talking to them trying to get something to eat, which I didn't get. With the air raid warning I jumped out of the boxcar and went and lined up the guys. So we ran away from there. They ran, too, the same way we went. For a while we were in that forest in the ground. I found a little depression there and I lay there. Before long there were two Germans also in the depression because of the air raid. And that is when our building was bombed. You could hear the American planes fighting the Germans. They were fighting and dropping bombs. They bombed our little building where we were supposed to be. I had tried getting off work that day because if you get tired, you lie and say "I'm sick." The guard said, "No, you go to work." If I had been there [in the building] I would have been killed.

We saw the building when it got hit. This was in the daytime. We looked and no building. When we got back to camp, our little building was demolished. One guy got killed and one guy got hit in the leg; it was swollen this big [hands extended many inches apart]. Two other men were hurt but not too badly. There were three or four tiered steel beds. They jumped on the floor [from the beds]. The steel beds kept the other debris from killing them. They were under the beds. One was buried all the way to his neck, but he didn't get hurt. From there we moved to another building.

We would line up each morning in the very same place for head count, which meant that a certain soldier stood right before me every morning. He had painted on the back of his jacket a stack of pancakes with syrup dripping over the sides. So I got to see the back of his jacket every single day, and oh, I was starving. That was very hard.

When I was working on the railroad daily a guard would put a loaf of bread in a certain spot. I would give him one cigarette for the bread. The next day another soldier would benefit in the same manner and so on.

One day some German officers called in some of us soldiers to an area cordoned off with blankets. They told us that they were going to have to fight the Russians. They said, "If you will help us fight the Russians, we will feed you like we feed our German soldiers, and we will give you warm clothing to wear." Even though we were starving, no one accepted the offer.

We caught a guy stealing bread. We had a trial and he was found guilty. When you get sick in the head, you can't eat; so you hide your bread. But you had to go outside and assemble every morning. "Joe Blow" had been sick. Somebody would stay behind and steal. We didn't know who stole it. This time we are standing outside in the snow—whatever, talking, miserable, cold, hungry. Here comes a GI POW dragging another POW he had caught stealing. You just don't do that; you don't steal from another POW. We were all on the jury. Kangaroo Court. Well, there were only ten of us there standing and talking. Then the POW comes out, "I caught this guy stealing bread from Joe Blow." Two or three of us had been victimized; I was one of them. You don't forget that.

Our punishment was this: he ran a gauntlet as we beat him. Some tripped him. Some hit him with a belt buckle. We picked him up and swung him over the cesspool. Then we dropped him in. When he crawled out, we kicked him back in. The Germans would punish a thief by death.

We would get lunch, one bowl of soup. I think they were afraid we might escape while eating or going to get the soup from the railroad office. So they cut it out. Now this is inhumane. We didn't have breakfast. Lunch, they cancelled the lunch because they were afraid we would escape when we go get the soup or something. So now you go to work, no breakfast, no lunch. You go back in the afternoon for your bowl of soup and your slice of bread. The soup, turnip greens. They cut the greens and generally keep the turnips and they give us the greens but already made into a soup. That's the soup we got every day. They were feeding us just enough to keep us alive. Feed them enough so they don't charge you with murder.

There were four groups of fifty, and I'm the leader of one group. Remember we got bombed and they moved us to another place? That place got bombed, too. One morning we got up and there was a lot of noise outside. We had a high brick wall, and outside there was a lot of noise, people talking. Something was going on. So we looked out through the gate and we saw Germans going to some huge warehouses. They came back with little red wagons full of stuff. Those warehouses contained German army foodstuff. The Americans were approaching. They said rather than letting the Americans get all this stuff, give it to the locals. So they told the people, "Go get anything you want out of there." So we looked out the gate and could see them going and coming back with their little red wagons. There's something going on, we said. We went to work. There was a group of our boys coming back. They had gone to work and they had been sent back. "No work today. The Americans are coming." So we returned to our camp and there we stayed for a few hours.

The Germans told us, "We're going to deliver you to the Americans." And some of the guys didn't believe it. Why? Because they lied every time. Finally, I told the guys, "Gosh, you're right. We have no say-so. So we went. And we left Stendal. They're going to deliver us to the Americans; so we marched, four groups of fifty. We turned to a dirt road past a little bitty town and continued walking. And I noticed we were getting away from the artillery. You could hear the American artillery, but now we are getting further away from it. The artillery is over here, but we're going this way and we're over here now. I said, "Hey guys, they're not going to turn us over to the Americans." Remember I am just a Pfc. The only guy higher than me was a corporal. I said he's bound to know more than I do because he's a corporal. So we're marching. The idea as a group leader is to march up and down, up and down. I say, "Come on guys; don't fall. Don't fall. You know what happened to you. Come on guys. Come on." Keep them going. That's my duty.

I said, "Hey, Corporal, you want to escape?" As we are marching I asked him that. He said, "Yeah." The guy next to the corporal overheard me and he was a tattletale. He was always squealing on everybody. He overheard us and said, "Can I go too?" The corporal looked at me and I said, "We have no choice. Yeah, you can go with us."

So we marched a few more yards in four groups of fifty. When I decided it was time, I told the corporal, "This is it." We just left the group and sat on the side of the road. Remember I told you I was getting very macho? There we are sitting on the side of the road, two guys. The stoolie, that guy we hated, joined us with seven more guys. That's ten. Misery loves company. He (the stoolie) was afraid to escape. The more the merrier, but it was a mistake. The rear guard would say, "Let's go [in German]." I would tell him, "Nein, we're taking a ten-minute break." Macho man. I'm telling him what we're doing.

The next group comes and the lead guard says, "[something in German]" and I say, "*Nein*, we're taking a ten-minute break." They didn't care. They probably didn't believe us. They knew the Americans were coming. They probably thought *let's get out of here. To heck with those ten POWs.* They kept walking, two hundred men, and we stayed there very nonchalantly minding our own business.

I said, "Hey, let's get off this road." There was a little wooded area behind us about fifteen yards from where we were, a very small wooded area. Anybody could see us. I said, "If we stay here, we're going to be seen. A few yards away there is a huge forest. If we go there, nobody can see us." On the other hand, the American bombers are coming. If they see a lot of wooded area or factories, they are going to bomb because German tanks hide in wooded areas. They'll say, "Let's bomb that area. It's a good place for tanks." We didn't go to the wooded area. We stayed where we were, a little off to the side of the road. There was an irrigation ditch. It was April. It was still cool for us. We jumped in the ditch and faced each other, five and five. The guy facing me says, "Don't turn back, but there is a German officer coming." "It's all right. Don't panic. Don't panic." There is a curve in the ditch. He stands looking at five of us, then the other five. Coincidentally it was me. God or something gave me a lot of brains. All of this in German. He says, "What are you doing here?" I had to invent a lie very quickly. I told him in German, "We are wounded and just got out of the hospital in Stendal." I knew that he knew there was a hospital there, a German Army hospital. So he believed me. He said, "So what are you going to do?" I said, "We are going to rest a while and then catch up with the group."

He asked me, "Well, how will you know where to catch up with them?" Good question. Here comes A. D. with a perfect answer. I answered, "He said that they were going to walk ten kilometers and they were going to spend the night there, and when we get rested up, we are to walk over there and join them." I don't know if he believed us or not. He left.

We stayed there. There was a big farm a hundred yards from where we were. We went there trying to get something to eat. A big tough foreman told us to "get the hell out of here you ___ [dog, pig]. I'm not going to give you anything to eat." We left and got out the same way we got in. There were some Polish workers there, and they spoke perfect German because they had been there five years. They said, "Don't leave. Just hide in the haystack. When it gets dark, come back and we'll feed you." We did that. We went back. All they had was milk soup. That's all they had to eat. I think they boil it until it gets hard. They gave us milk soup. It was still soupy. That's all we got.

We spent the night in that barn under horrible circumstances because the Germans were retreating and the Americans were chasing them. They were fighting and we were getting all their artillery. And it was horrible. And I say that that was one of my worst times in the war was that afternoon and that evening with all of the artillery falling all over the place. It was horrible. Between a rock and a hard place. We were between both of them. It was hell. During the night two British guys who escaped joined us. The next morning one of the British guys said, "The Yahnks are heah." The next morning on Friday, April 13, 1945, an American jeep drove up with a lieutenant and a Tech 5. I saw them and I started to run toward them. I forgot I couldn't run because I was so darn weak. I fell and I got up and saluted the lieutenant. So everything was fine. He told me that President Roosevelt had died.

The other guys—the chicken guys, then they came out. Remember the big guy who wouldn't feed us the day before? I told the lieutenant that he wouldn't feed us and we hadn't eaten for a long time. The lieutenant ordered that guy to kill a pig. The guy said, "No." The lieutenant said, "You don't understand. I am ordering you to kill a pig." So I saw a German pig being killed. They tie the hind legs with a knot so they won't move. Pull them up and stick a dagger in its throat. The pig is upside down. All that blood comes out; they save the blood. They made blutwurst. Blood sausage. I still didn't get to eat.

Before we left the farm, one of the guys said, "Hey, one guy [German] out there wants to surrender. Everyone wanted to go see him. When we walked through a little village, they saw us. The German lieutenant who had spoken to us the day before asking, "What are you doing here?" They knew we were there. And they had seen the American lieutenant driving toward the farm. It was someone from his group [the German group]. So I wanted a German pistol and a German wristwatch. So I'm going out there to meet that German to search him. He had no wristwatch and no pistol. I took him in. The Germans were smart. They sent one man. They didn't hear any shots. So two more came [to surrender]. And all we have is a lieu-tenant and a Tech 5, but who's behind them? [Fifth Armored Division.] I search. No pistol, no wristwatch. I bring them in. That's three. To make a story short there were ten. No pistols and no wristwatches. I brought all ten of them in and left them there with the lieutenant. He probably got credit for capturing those guys.

The lieutenant said, "If you go out this gate and turn left, walk about two to three miles, you will find the Fifth Armored Division there." They're the ones who had done all that firing the night before. There they were, and then I was happy. I still didn't get to eat. They're fighting. They put me in a truck and took us to a little town nearby. The people are afraid of us because they have heard bad things about Americans and Russians. All we want is something to eat. So we ask for fried eggs. We don't want raw eggs. So we stayed several hours trying to find something to eat, but that's a different story. They made eggs for us and gave us bread, and we got sicker than hell. You don't eat. You were so hungry. Some of the guys kept on eating. I didn't. I said A. D, this is pointless. I had the will power to quit.

Later on a chow line opened up for the Fifth Armored Division. I ate very little. Only what I thought I needed. Just enough to sustain me.

A few days later we flew to France to a big camp, Lucky Strike. They warned us that some guys had died from eating too much oatmeal in the morning. We were there two to three days and then they shipped us to England. From England we sailed to the United States. The war was still on. Wouldn't that be ironic—after all the hell we've been through, we are go-ing to die in the high seas from a German submarine. We were on the high seas getting submarine threats and everything. They said to man the battle stations and they all ran, and then they dropped depth charges. They had detected something on the radar. Nothing came up. But the war was over as we were midway [to the US] on May 8, 1945.

They told us to go home and rest because we might have to go to Japan. I would have gone, of course, but we sure didn't want to. After I rested sixty days—remember Mousa Haver?

When I came back from the POW camp (much later), I was in Laredo on a sixty-day leave. My very best friend, a Jewish boy, who was in the air corps, was also on leave. I was leaving that afternoon to report for duty after my sixty-day leave and my mother gave me *la bendición* and "Mousa" Maurice Haver was standing next to me and my mother said, "Mousa, *hincate* (kneel)." I'm laughing today because he was Jewish. He did. She blessed him, too. He was a very good guy. And he came back.

I went to camp on the next day in the afternoon to Hotel Arlington in Warm Springs, Arkansas. A luxurious hotel where we spent ten days. Then we went to an Army Camp in Hot Springs, Arkansas. I went to town to eat dinner. As I was walking I crossed in front of the café and saw headlines in a newspaper that we had dropped a bomb on Japan. Five times as strong as some of our bombs. That's the first I had heard of the bomb.

We were getting on a train in August to go to Fort Bliss, Texas. Church bells started ringing. "The war is over. The war is over." I had no way of celebrating. I could have gotten drunk, raised hell. We were getting on the train to go to Fort Bliss. That's the way we celebrated VJ Day. Smoking train. Nothing to drink.

They trained me to be a counselor. We had to counsel all the people who were being discharged from the army. They don't know what's awaiting them. We read them their rights, the GI Bill. I did this for just a few weeks, probably two-three months. I was discharged in December. There they had German soldiers, POWs. We would eat at the same mess hall. They were eating the same as we were. I'm glad they were eating well. They were in no hurry to go home, I guess. They knew what was happening in Germany, that they were starving. If they were under guard, it was not conspicuous. In the army camp they had everything, food to eat, a shower, and a chance to get back home.

In December 1945, I went home. As soon as I could, the next few weeks I went to Austin, to UT (University of Texas). I didn't want to waste any time.

A. D. Azios returned to the University of Texas. He graduated from law school and became an attorney and eventually a district judge in Houston, Texas. In 2002 he is retired but substitutes wherever he is needed. He and his wife have three grown children and some grandchildren. In his spare time he likes to write.

PART IV

Also Affected

*There were folks who did not carry a gun and
didn't fight, but they were nonetheless directly
affected by the war. These folks, while not involved
in combat, were affected in a special way.*

Hector de Peña
Department of the Navy
Office of Censorship

Eavesdropping Assignment
Hector de Peña was born on October 22, 1914, in Hillsboro, Texas. It would be difficult to find a more honest person than Hector. He so wanted to be in the service and fight for his country. In spite of his being labeled "4F," he still made a contribution.

My brother Fernando was the first Hispanic to graduate from high school in Hillsboro. My father was a shoe cobbler. He also made chaps and saddles. The family moved to Itasca. In 1928 the family moved again to Alice and then to San Diego, Texas, on St. Valentine's Day in 1929. I graduated from San Diego High School.

As a student at Texas A&I in Kingsville, I ran for Student Council president in 1933. My opponent Cecil Burney ran using the slogan, "Remember the Alamo."

I attended the San Antonio School of Law, which is now St. Mary's Law School. I needed three letters of recommendation so that I could be accepted as an attorney. An older Anglo attorney wrote a letter. Two other Anglo attorneys told me that although they would like to write letters on my behalf, they couldn't for political reasons. A district judge advised me to go to Alice, Texas.

In July of 1937 I opened up an office in San Diego, Texas. In November I came to Corpus Christi, Texas, to practice. The conditions I found when I came to practice law in Corpus Christi were shocking. A Mexican American could not go into a restaurant. He could not get a haircut in a barbershop. If he decided to go to the movies, he sat upstairs with the Blacks who could not sit downstairs either. A Mexican American could not go swimming at Cole Park, a popular place on Ocean Drive in Corpus Christi Bay. The president of LULAC objected, and the city officials opened up Cole Park to the Hispanics.

The Corpus Christi Independent School District opened up Mirabeau Lamar on Morris Street for Mexican American children because it was located in a Hispanic neighborhood. From then on, the Corpus Christi

Independent School District became aware that LULAC was watching their every move in relation to how the Mexican American children were being assigned.

When WWII broke out I attempted to volunteer but was classified as 4F. The Office of the Navy, however, saw my bilingualism as an advantage and used me in the Office of Censorship. Part of my job involved listening in on conversations conducted in Spanish.

By early 1942 I was serving in San Antonio. Then I was moved to the Laredo office, which meant an increase in pay, a $30 bonus, actually. In 1942 I moved to McAllen to be the chief of Hearing and Recording.

Among my memories I recall were "steamy conversations" between the two famous Mexican stars, Agustín Lara and María Feliz. Also, I heard Mexican officials speak of President Roosevelt's forthcoming trip to Mexico, a secret in the United States, but common knowledge in Mexico.

I was on vacation when Japan surrendered.

After I married Elena, a registered nurse, and had three children, I ran for Justice of the Peace, for county attorney, and for the Court of Domestic Relations. I was defeated in all three races. But remember that I never give up. I ran for County Court at Law and was elected. [He became a well-known and highly respected judge.]

My sister-in-law Rosa Tamez Amos was an Army nurse during the war and served in the Philippines.

Sheila Maloney Mulligan

Experience As an Evacuee

Sheila Mulligan was born in England in Tidworth, Hampshire County, on Jan. 24, 1929. Her mother was Evelyn Doris Allsopp and her father was Owen Joseph Aloyuia Maloney (called Pat). He was born in 1900 and died in 1979. Sheila, a citizen of the United Kingdom, was evacuated during WWII from London to a rural area in England. It was difficult for all the children who were taken from their parents and placed in the homes of strangers. She tells an interesting story.

Both my father and my grandfather were army career men. My father was what they called "Black Irish" as he had dark skin and black curly hair.

Because his father was in the service he was born in India where his father was serving.

His father was also named Owen Joseph Aloyuia Maloney, and was in the Cheshire Regiment. He was born in Armath, North Ireland. His mother was named Kate Kelly. She had four children and died at childbirth with the fourth child. When my grandfather remarried, the new wife didn't want the four children. An Irish aunt raised them.

When Owen [Pat] was twelve he ran away from home and joined the army to escape his home life. In the 1930s they were living in Malta in the Mediterranean.

In 1938, when I was nine, they had air raid drills. Each child had a gas mask. When the bells went off, each child took the gas mask and marched with the teachers to the trenches. "Prefects" helped the teachers with the other students.

I remember living in Army Camps—Aldershot, south of London, for example. I attended the Infant School, Maider School. After that came middle school and then high school. I learned to knit at school. My mother always complimented my work. I went to bed with holes in my knitting [mistakes], but when I woke up, the holes had miraculously disappeared.

On September 3, 1939, I was living with my family in army housing. All British men were called into service, which meant that my mom and siblings must leave [vacate] the army housing for the new soldiers. My mother picked up our belongings and paid to have our things taken away. She moved in with her mother, my grandmother. Because it was too many folks for one home, my mom and baby sister stayed with our grandmother, and my little sister and I went to live with some aunts.

No children were left in Cheshire area. Whenever the evacuated children were lonely, they went back home. In 1940 the bombing was very bad. My mother had me and my two sisters there. My brother was in the service. I was ten and my little sister Evelyn was in the Infant School. We were evacuated. Evelyn went to North Wales and I went to Mid Wales to Llanidloes.

Although I was Catholic I attended a Welsh Methodist church with the new family. I didn't like the man in the first home to which I had been sent. He was a giant farmer type. I cried a lot and a man, sort of inspector, placed me in another home. He described me as a "Lovely girl, quiet. No accent like other children. Beautiful blue eyes." I was very happy there and stayed four years. I never saw my father and saw my mother only once. The new family had three older girls and then a young girl, Beryl, the same age as I. We became great friends and never quarreled. Auntie Maggie and Uncle Ted Ashton. He worked in a gas refinery. Ted the gas man is how people referred to him. In Wales, also, your profession was always attached to your name, e.g., James, the teacher, and David: Die (Welch), the milkman.

My sister Evelyn became a spoiled child. Her family was childless. Eventually, Evelyn became a teacher.

Some [evacuees] didn't want to return home. Some boys on farms were worked hard. In Wales, the Welch citizenry were against the "evacuees." There was a negative connotation to the term.

One day the evacuees were taken out of the school which the local children attended and were assigned to a cold room in another building. A teacher was hired to teach nineteen girl evacuees. The boys were also pulled out and taught in another place. Miss Jones, an excellent teacher, was hired to teach the evacuees.

The soldiers moved into the neighborhood and brought scabies with them. They lived in tents. Somehow or other the evacuees contracted scabies. I took treacle and sulfur. It was mixed and I took it. Also, Auntie Maggie made a salve and rubbed it on me.

My mother visited once but wrote me letters often. She never saw my father for four years.

We experienced no bombing but we did know nearby Liverpool was bombed. Occasionally, the Germans dropped a bomb on their way back to their airfield.

We visited Mr. Ashton's brother's farm. I was oblivious to what was happening in general.

Miss Jones worked six days a week so her students could pass the O test, which qualified them for high school. If one didn't pass the test, one couldn't go on. I even helped Beryl study for the O test. According to the school information, none of the nineteen evacuee girls passed the test.

The parents of two girls, Stella Evans and Iris Dodd, complained to the schoolboard and they declared the two girls had passed and therefore were allowed to attend high school.

Sheila's father was at Dunkirk when so many soldiers were evacuated.

Because my father was an excellent swimmer, he gave up his seat several times as men who couldn't swim were taken back to England from Dunkirk. Finally, my father Pat just swam back to England with only his underwear on, as his clothes tore off during the swimming.

My father, along with the Cheshire Regiment, landed on Normandy on D-day. My brother and father met again in Germany during the war. My brother worked on tanks—Royal Engineering. He broke down the chain at the gate of Bergen-Belsen Concentration Camp. My older sister, Dathleen Doreen, was in the Womens' Royal Army Corps and was stationed in Cairo for three years.

Neville Chamberlain sold Great Britain down the river. Winston Churchill of the Conservative Party pulled us out of the war. People thought he was a warmonger.

[After the war] I missed the countryside. I worked in an office with accounting machines. I took Civil Service Tests and worked in the post office at Liverpool. I also joined the Territorial Army in 1948. It was like a Reserve Unit.

I married an Irishman, Thomas Mulligan. We had two daughters, Colleen and Patricia. We immigrated to the US where Tom worked for a bank.

Thelma Conitz
Employee at a POW Camp

Camp Hearne (Texas)

Thelma Conitz lived in Calvert, Texas, a small town located eight miles from Hearne, Texas. She had a unique experience in WWII as an employee at a POW camp for Germans captured during the war. Camp Hearne had offices for a commanding officer and the adjunct, a headquarters, a personnel building with a personnel director, and a bookkeeper. The compound also had a hospital, a medical doctor, an Officers' Club, and an officers' building. Thelma chose to work with the personnel department.

After the camp was built in 1943 Thelma and other civilian employees were told to avoid staring or even looking at the POWs, and they would follow the rules established by the Geneva Convention. When the first soldiers captured during the North African Campaign were brought in and they walked past the personnel building, Thelma and others bent under the windows so that they would not be considered to be staring at the first inmates.

Some prisoners became trustees and were allowed to work on the grounds. Later on, some of the POWs worked outside the compound on nearby farms located on the Brazos Bottoms. You could see the prisoners on trucks as they passed in the neighborhood. They were well-behaved. One prisoner received a letter from Germany stating that a relative had been killed in the war. When that German POW went to work on a farm, he was so aggrieved that he threw himself in front of an approaching train.

When civilians wanted to get jobs at the compound, they went to the personnel office where Thelma worked. Thelma had to fingerprint all hired folks.

Thelma and her friends went out the back door of their building and walked to the PX when they wanted to take a break. One day as they left through the back door, her friend and she became separated with a German POW between them. The girls were reprimanded by the commanding officer, who warned them that the prisoner could easily have grabbed one of them and held her hostage.

When some of the POWs died, they were buried in a cemetery located on the grounds of the compound.

Cecelia Conitz, who was Thelma's niece, recalled attending movies at the POW camp with her friend Harriet Redwine, who happened to be the daughter of the camp doctor. "We were treated well and we sat among the prisoners," she said.

Acknowledgments

I became interested in World War II when my fifth-grade teacher, Mrs. Constance Pietsch, told our class not to ask the returning veterans any questions. She said they didn't want to talk about the war. To a child who was curious about everything, that comment only spurred me on to wonder and eventually to ask as many questions as I could, albeit many years later.

In the work I was doing—interviewing veterans—I discovered the story was not always in the fighting but rather in the quiet moments before and afterward.

The list of folks who helped me with my project is endless. My husband Nolan drove me to distant parts of Texas. Our four children encouraged me. My siblings William, Tony, and Ruben gave me names of veterans to interview. Tony and a friend Homer Garcia also read parts of my material. My friend Mary helped with the punctuation. Carolyn Westergren, a dear friend who is now deceased, gave me suggestions, which assisted me greatly. Clemente Garcia and Benny Martinez led me to some interesting veterans. Tom Kreneck of Texas A&M Corpus Christi also encouraged me.

My niece Catherine had ideas which I used and appreciated. My sister Mary Helen has always been in my corner, and has told others of my interest in WWII. My thanks to friends and even strangers who heard of the project and with their words helped me to carry on.

Finally, I extend my heartfelt gratitude to all of the veterans and their families who opened their homes to me. Their stories continue to amaze and inspire me, and I hope they do the same for others.

I also wish to thank my deceased fifth-grade teacher Mrs. Constance Pietsch, who always loved history and instilled that love of the past in me. You told us not to ask any questions of the returning veterans, but after many years, I couldn't help myself. I know you will understand, Mrs. Pietsch.

Lastly, I want to thank Dan Williams, the director of TCU Press, for giving me ideas thus improving my work. I thank you immensely! Kathy Walton, editor at TCU Press, helped me with the editing process and made helpful suggestions. Assistant Editor Molly Spain contributed her time and effort and answered my many questions. Thank you so much!

Special Collections and Archives at TAMU-CC holds the José A. Flores contributions. I thank them for their assistance. Lori Adkins works there and is helpful.

Thank you again to everyone. Thank you, thank you, thank you. And enjoy.

Questions I asked the veterans:

1. What is your name?

2. Birthdate?

3. Parents' names?

4. Where did you live?

5. What were you doing when you volunteered or when you were drafted?

6. What branch did you serve in, and what was your rank?

7. Your service experiences?

8. Where were you when you learned the war was over?

9. After the war?

10. Vets could elaborate as they wished.

Glossary

This list of terms is by no means a complete glossary of words relevant to WWII. I have included only the words that the veterans used, and pertinent words to facilitate understanding of the events recounted.

AMERICAN GI FORUM A national organization founded after WWII by Dr. Hector P. García and other veterans in Corpus Christi, Texas. The organization was created for the purpose of representing and obtaining due rights for Hispanic veterans.

AP Armor piercing capabilities found in Tank Destroyers.

ATABRINE Medicine administered to the soldiers to prevent malaria.

AXIS SALLY She was the German version of Tokyo Rose. Sally attempted to demoralize the American soldiers with her talks on the radio.

AWOL Absent without leave. A situation in which a soldier leaves his assignment without proper authorization.

BANZAI During WWII in the Pacific, the Japanese soldiers would rush toward American soldiers brandishing weapons while yelling "Banzai" in an effort to surprise and kill as many Americans as they could. A night banzai attack was quite unnerving.

BAR Browning Automatic Rifle, which is heavy and can be mounted on a bipod or fired from the hip or shoulder.

BATTLE OF THE BULGE As the Americans advanced in their drive to Germany, Hitler made one last push to try to reverse the situation and perhaps take the lead in the war. On December 16, 1944, he sent multiple divisions to the Ardennes forest. The Germans surprised the Americans, some of whom had been told they'd be home by Christmas. The "bulge" describes the curve in the front line where the Germans pushed back the Allied advance.

BATTLE STATIONS The sailors in the US Navy had assignments on the ships, manning guns, etc. Their assignments were known as battle stations.

CIVILIAN CONSERVATION CORPS (CCC) was started before WWII by President Franklin D. Roosevelt in an effort to provide jobs while protecting our natural resources.

CO Commanding Officer.

COXSWAIN The sailor who piloted the landing craft that took the soldiers to the shores or beaches to do battle.

C-RATIONS Two small cans comprised the C-rations. One can had some sort of meat, and the second can had crackers, a cookie, chocolate candy, toilet paper, and a small packet of coffee.

D BARS These were enriched candy bars which, when cut into three parts, were to serve as three meals.

D-DAY June 6, 1945, was one of the largest amphibious assaults in history, when some 156,000 Allied troops landed on the beaches of Normandy. The invasion is regarded as the "beginning of the end" of the war in Europe.

DUKW (colloquially referred to as a "duck") A two-and-a-half ton military truck modified to operate both on land and in water.

FORWARD OBSERVERS were soldiers who were assigned to precede the infantry and establish observation posts. From these posts the observers radioed the artillery to give firing directions.

GENEVA CONVENTIONS Meetings of world leaders that among other things established guidelines pertaining to the treatment of prisoners of war.

GIs Government Issue; American soldiers.

G2 Intelligence Officer.

HALAZONE PURIFICTION TABLETS used to sterilize water to make it drinkable.

HEDGEHOGS Heavy metal rail obstacles welded together so that they appeared to be giant "jacks" located on the French beaches; their purpose was to damage Allied landing craft.

HIGGINS BOATS Landing crafts designed by Andrew Jackson Higgins specifically for landing on beaches in WWII.

HMAS His Majesty's Australian Ship preceded the name of the ship on Australian vessels during the war (HMS, His Majesty's Ship, denoted British vessels; USS denoted American).

HQ Headquarters.

HUMP, THE A flight path in which airmen flew over Burma, including the steep Himalayan Mountains, from India to China to deliver needed supplies, thereby assisting China in their war with Japan.

HÜRTGEN FOREST A locale in which a deadly battle occurred involving the Twenty-Eighth Division fighting the entrenched Germans.

IFF Identification Friend or Foe, used by Army Air Corps to identify airplanes.

KAMIKAZE Japanese pilots executing a suicide mission by crashing into American. Navy ships, which resulted in many American deaths.

KP Kitchen Patrol. Soldiers had to cook for many GIs and then clean and wash many, many pots and pans.

K RATIONS Breakfast, dinner, and supper units. Variations of the following were included in small cans: biscuits; meat (eggs for breakfast); fruit; chewing gum; four cigarettes and matches; one packet of either coffee, lemon powder, or bullion; toilet tissue.

LCM landing craft, mechanized.

LCP landing craft, personnel.

LCPL landing craft, personnel, large.

LCT Landing craft, tank.

LCVP landing craft, vehicle, personnel.

LST Landing ship, tank.

LULAC League of United Latin American Citizens. Founded in 1929 in Corpus Christi, Texas, LULAC is the nation's oldest Hispanic advocacy organization, which strives to improve the quality of life for Hispanics by stressing job development, civil rights enforcement, and educational advancement.

M1 Standard rifle for infantrymen in WWII. A bayonet could be attached to the rifle, and a grenade could be launched from this weapon.

MP Military Police.

NAZI National Socialist German Workers Party.

ODs Olive Drabs. Soldiers' wool dress attire as distinguished from their regular uniforms.

OP Observation Post. A location chosen by the forward observer so that he can observe the enemy and report to artillery resulting in action.

PATHFINDERS British airmen known for their talents and skills. They preceded the Allied invasion forces at Normandy.

PILLBOXES Fortified, entrenched, strategically located, and secure places, i. e., built with thick concrete walls from which the Germans fired at the Allies.

POD Point of debarkation. The locale from which the soldiers were shipped out.

POE Point of embarkation. The locale from which the soldiers were shipped back home.

PONTOON BRIDGE A temporary bridge American engineers built of empty barrels, for example, so that vehicles and personnel could cross over the water.

PX Post Exchange. A store for soldiers.

QUARTERMASTERS Soldiers assigned to supply soldiers with clothing and subsistence.

R and R Rest and rehabilitation.

SAKE Japanese alcoholic drink made of fermented rice.

SCHNAPPS Strong alcoholic drink made in Germany.

SLIT TRENCHES Foxholes dug in long rectangular shapes.

SS *Schutzstaffel* was composed of men who initially worked as Hitler's personal guards. Eventually they became a powerful, dreaded group of ruthless men.

STRAFE To rake with gunfire, often from low-flying aircraft, directed toward soldiers on the ground.

TETRAHEDRA Large concrete, triangular-shaped obstacles created to damage Allied landing vehicles and placed on the beaches of Normandy prior to the Allied landings.

TOKYO ROSE A Japanese American woman who spoke English on Japanese radio so that American soldiers could hear negative comments about the USA, their families, their wives, etc.

TOMMY GUN Thompson Machine Gun used as a field weapon. Also known as a "grease gun."

V-E DAY Victory in Europe Day. May 8, 1945.

V-J DAY Victory over Japan Day. August 15, 1945.

VIRGIN DE GUADALUPE The Patron Saint of Mexico. According to legend she appeared in 1531 to an Indian boy named Juan Diego. Her image was miraculously imprinted on his tilma [cloak], and is on display in Mexico even today. Millions in Mexico and many Hispanics in the Americas believe in her miraculous power.

About the Author

Esther Bonilla Read graduated with a bachelor of arts degree from Baylor University. Later, she earned a master's from Corpus Christi State University. She worked in public and private schools teaching at the elementary, middle school, and college level, while writing in her spare time.

Her publishing credits include the following: a story in *Chicken Soup for the Latino Soul*; coauthor of *Kindergarden Kapers*; and in magazines *Games, Vista, Texas Highways, International Reading Association*, and LULAC *News*. Newspapers that have carried her columns include *Caller-Times, San Antonio Express, Dallas Morning News, Amarillo Globe*, and *Pecos Enterprise*. Hispanic Link Syndicate also published some columns. Anthologies that published her work include *Puentes* (Texas A&M: Corpus Christi, Texas, 2006) and *Corpus Christi Writers* (2018, 2019, 2020, and 2021). Esther Read lives in Corpus Christi. Her husband of fifty-seven years is now deceased. She has four grown children and five grandchildren.